Maverick

Maverick

A DIRECTOR'S PERSONAL EXPERIENCE

IN OPERA AND THEATER

BY

Frank Corsaro

WITH A PREFACE BY

JULIUS RUDEL

AND A FOREWORD BY

LEE STRASBERG

NEW YORK

THE VANGUARD PRESS, INC.

Library of Congress Catalogue Card Number: 77-77036
ISBN: 0-8149-0790-3

Designer: Ernst Reichl

Manufactured in the United States of America.

Dedicated to my wife Bonnie,
who read it all
and had the nerve to
criticize

ACKNOWLEDGMENTS I should like to thank Polydor International GmbH for its kind permission to reprint the article "The Stage Production" that appeared originally in the booklet accompanying the Original Cast Recording of *Treemonisha* (Deutsche Grammaphon, 2707 083 (LP) 3370 #012 (MC), and Angel/EMI Records for its permission to use my liner notes from its recording of *Koanga*.

Special thanks to my charming editors *à deux*—Evelyn Shrifte and Bernice Woll—in stature petite but the reverse in all the other callings of their art. Without their canny ministrations these pages would have never seen a bound cover.

F.C.

Contents

Illustrations

La Traviata: The fête galante in Moorish style at Flora's estate

Madama Butterfly: The love duet, Act I

Faust: Marguerite encounters Faust at the Kermesse

The Makropoulos Affair: Emilia Marty becomes the Eugenia Montez of the past

The Makropoulos Affair: Emilia Marty reveals herself as the ancient 342-year-old woman

Pelléas and Mélisande: The fountain in the park

Lulu: Returning from prison, Lulu makes love to the son of the husband she murdered

Die Tote Stadt: Marietta torments the obsessed Paul with his dead wife's tresses

Poppea: Poppea pleads with Nero to remain with her after a night of love

A Village Romeo and Juliet: Sali's and Vreli's dream of their wedding day in the village church

Treemonisha: The voodoo conjuremen torment Treemonisha

Korngold, the "*Wunderkind*"

Preface
by
Julius Rudel

I flew down to Buenos Aires in 1967 engaged to conduct the
first performance there of *Bomarzo* by the Argentinian composer, Alberto Ginastera, and looked forward to a successful debut at the great Teatro Colon as a sure thing. The work had
already had its world premiere in Washington and received
wonderful reviews by the American as well as some Argentine
critics. Same cast, same director; it was going to be a shoo-in. At
the airport, I was met, grandiosely, I thought, by the always
rather somber composer, his agent, television cameras and re-
porters with their ready "mikes." After the kissing amenities
were over, Ginastera grimly told me that while I was en route to
Buenos Aires, the opera had been banned by the government as
"being obsessed with sex and violence." My spontaneous response, recorded for posterity by the Argentine television crew,
was: "but all opera is obsessed with sex and violence." I preface my Preface with this story to shake the conviction of those
who believe that sex and violence in opera were invented by
Frank Corsaro. A patron once complained that Corsaro even
managed to get a bed into so "pure" an opera as *Pelléas and
Mélisande.* When it was pointed out that the bed was needed
for the wounded Golaud and the dying Mélisande, the patron
responded that in Corsaro's hands the bed had turned into a
"symbol of sexuality." Evil, like beauty, is in the eye of the
beholder.

Frank Corsaro, my dear friend and frequent collaborator, is
very inventive but did not need to invent sex and violence for
opera; they have always been there, at least from the time of
Monteverdi's *Coronation of Poppea*, probably the most amoral
opera ever written. In it lust triumphs, wisdom is a suicide, and
virtue is exiled. The fact that a couple of goddesses push things
around a bit doesn't mitigate the amorality; it just gives it divine
sanction. *Poppea* may indeed have been the operatic mother of
them all, establishing over three hundred years ago that sex and
violence provided the broad range of human emotion that music
so profoundly expresses, however unconvincing the story being
told.

It is in the telling of the story that every stage director will
insist that he alone approaches the work with a fresh view, as if it
had never been done before and is uncontaminated by tradition.
When you get down to details, the "fresh view" often consists
of moving the church or cigarette factory from stage left to stage
right. One director came to the conclusion, after rethinking *Rigoletto,* that the key to the opera lay in establishing the tragedy
of Borsa. Some of you will rightly ask "who is Borsa?" (Others
will ask who was that director?) But Frank really has the "fresh
view," not because he doesn't know the traditions but because
he knows them too terribly well. There was always opera in
Frank's life, and while his early encounter with it was so different from my own, we were both ultimately led to the same
crazy devotion. We were both opera "claqueurs," paid to applaud in exchange for the privilege of standing room. While
Frank led the cheering at the Met, I did my bit in the hallowed
halls of the Vienna Staatsoper. The experience obviously left us
both with a deep sense of skepticism about whatever it is that
gets the most applause.

One has to be something of an iconoclast to persist in the
"fresh view," and Frank is certainly that, shattering prejudice
and pretentions with a vengeance but also with facts. He writes
the way he talks, tough, opinionated and full of subjective insights that may be wrong but never dull. It fascinates me to
watch him evolve a sense of a character. He will give the singer
some object to hold or some small unimportant thing to do and
his own personal way with that object becomes a Pirandelloan

extension of the operatic character. At the very least, it prevents him from waving his arms around. Frank's point of departure in directing is that while customs and costumes may change, the human heart remains the same. If an audience is to respond to the symbolism of Faust, his inner humaneness, his capacity for love, pain, terror, and guilt must all be there. The surrender of Marguerite is all the more touching when it springs from some inner sensuousness than from a projected backstage red glow. Corsaro's "fresh view" has also forever advanced the technology of opera staging with his innovative use of projections and films. This alone should assure him a most uncontroversial claim to opera history's hall of fame.

I have a theory about fame that applies particularly well to Frank. When a man (or woman) has a single great success (let's say *The Makropoulos Affair*), he is forever remembered for it. Should he have a string of successes, he may simply lose his identity in a wave of the future and be taken for granted. Should he have a single failure among those successes, he will forever be remembered for that failure. A single striking instance is always more easily remembered than a string of instances. Thus, when we come to the end of that catalogue of Corsaro successes, *Faust, Traviata, Makropoulos, Pelléas,* to mention but a few of my favorites, someone inevitably brings up *Don Giovanni*. (Yes, Frank, it was a failure.)

There is nothing easier than to fail with *Don Giovanni*, the story of the world's original sex symbol, the "macho" superman, the hero whose bravado literally turns to ashes. Undoubtedly the situation surrounding the production was as difficult as Frank says it was. The set turned out to be nothing like what had been conceived, the costumes were ludicrous eyesores, and it all arrived too late for anything to be done. But these are everyday catastrophes in an opera house and productions have been known to triumph over them. Our *Don Giovanni* failed, I believe, because Frank heavily underlined a sexuality that easily becomes caricature but which Mozart, in the very first scene, turns to terror. The somberness that runs through *Don Giovanni* has nothing to do with morality, Victorian or any other, but with reality, the reality that total freedom is impossible and even incompatible with life. Giovanni chooses death much as Carmen does or as Ariadne seeks *"das Reich wo alles rein ist, Toten-reich"* (that realm where all is pure, the realm of death). In life, nothing is pure: one man's freedom is another's ruin, a thousand and three seductions (in Spain alone) have left behind torment, broken hearts, shattered lives, at least one murdered father, and, possibly the most deadly of all, boredom.

One of the many aspects of Mozart's genius is that he imparts to comedy a sense of the tragic imperfection of life. No staging of *Cosi Fan Tutte,* the most comic of all his operas, is worth a damn unless it leaves you at its so-called happy end with a sense of personal betrayal at Don Alfonso's winning his bet on the frailty of feminine fidelity. This feeling is not nineteenth-century Romanticism but simply Mozart's music; he put the most sublime avowals of love into the mouth of Fiordiligi and he must have wanted her, at least, to mean it.

But this is Frank's book and some day perhaps I will write my own version of what happened in all those productions. Then the singers will write their versions and there will be a rash of Rashomons. That's the beauty of running a lively house, of doing controversial productions, of luring the Frank Corsaros of the theater to opera.

Foreword
by
Lee Strasberg

Opera is drama in music, not drama with music. The origin of opera lies in the efforts of Renaissance artists to reconstruct their idea of what the Greek theater was like. The intention behind Monteverdi's and his colleagues' achievements consists in their effort to make music more dramatically expressive, not simply more melodically enjoyable, and to capture in musical drama the intonation of heightened expression of human speech.

The great performers in the opera that I have been privileged to observe, Chaliapin, Lotte Lehmann, Pinza, Callas, were not singers who also acted. There was in their endeavor no separation between the two. The music was not simply added to the character, but the characters they created acted and expressed themselves in musical terms. Chaliapin, when he sang what might seem to be the same part, Mephistopheles in *Faust*, and also in *Mefistofele*, created two totally different characters, not only behaving differently, but the tonal values were completely dissimilar. One was a French cavalier with the insinuation, the manners, and behavior of a Frenchman and the nasality of French sound; and the other was the Miltonic devil, the adversary and the equal of God, with completely different tonal values, color, and emphasis — full, domineering, and authoritative. Lotte Lehmann's achievement was to some extent even more extraordinary because, by the very expressiveness of the music, we would ordinarily assume the impossibility of creating subtle psychological inner characterizations. This she superbly accomplished in her famous Marschallin in *Rosenkavalier*. Her performance, alone in her room, examining the ravages of age in the mirror, was completely achieved without benefit of the music, and the music, like words, only helped her to make clear what she was thinking. Callas, by her magnificent portrayals, actually brought back into the repertoire operas that had seemed concerned only with musical rather than dramatic values and helped them to become a part of the modern repertoire. These artists succeeded completely in creating a total character that would have remained equally splendid without the benefit of the musical addition. They help to demonstrate that there could be a total unity achieved by the singing-actor.

Frank Corsaro's contribution lies precisely in the effort to stress the prime nature of opera. Even his excesses that have sometimes been observed are an effort to explore and investigate the possibilities that are inherent in the medium. Many opera productions consist in nothing more than staging, arranging the proper tableaus, providing attitudes and the "business" of the role within the basic shape provided by the conductor. Corsaro's special and individual contributions lie in his emphasis on the character the singer is portraying, on the effort to help the singer create a character, and the situations and experiences that motivate the natural flow of the melody. In doing this he broadens the possibility of operatic production. In this respect he serves as a great educational stimulus in the field of opera that provides a basis for its future growth and promise.

Maverick

1

A
March of Time Featurette

Astrologically speaking, I am a bane to all chartmakers—for while I can attest to the year and day of my birth, I cannot fix time or place accurately enough to satisfy their metaphysical cravings. Since my surname translates as "pirate," it seems appropriate I should claim the sea as my birthplace. In actual fact, I first saw the light of day on a liner approaching New York harbor from South America. The liner's name is lost to memory, but certain it was nigh onto Christmas day, a coincidence I have rued ever since. Systematically forgotten as a birthday boy, I have been denied the parceling out of goodies twice a year, and my Christmas gifts must, like the fare of a pregnant woman, suffice for two. My mother had been visiting a cousin embroiled in some fascist machinations that periodically rock the land of the samba. The cousin was never heard from again but the detour from Naples to New York provided the operatic setting for my own setting forth.

My parents' whirlwind romance (my father had literally swiped my mother off her feet from the arms of another Lothario) had been capped by a hasty marriage, followed by a performance of *La Bohème* at the San Carlo Opera House. Childhood lullabies were mixed with Mimi's and Rudolpho's airs, and so my musical heritage had already taken wing. Thus succored, I navigated past MacDowell's "Wild Rose" and Nevin's "Narcissus"—the Scylla and Charybdis of early music-appreciation courses—and in my first knickers found ravishment in the magic of radio.

Little Orphan Annie buttons and Omar the Mystic badges in exchange for Ovaltine garnished with Black Crows licorice—the late thirties and the revelation one Saturday afternoon that *La Bohème* was not a figment of my parents' imagination but an actuality. Switching my allegiance from Ovaltine to Buck Rogers's cocomalt, I would have gladly added a dollop of Texaco gasoline if, in the process, I could insure the continuance of the Metropolitan Opera broadcasts. In our household the daytime serials were petty annoyances; perfect syntony came only on Saturdays. It was enough to see my parents' misty-eyed smiles during these broadcasts to confirm I was listening to the stuff of life.

The inevitable step was to make the spirit flesh, and, prodded by those merry bedmates, love and chutzpah, I descended to Thirty-ninth Street. I was a thin, gangling fourteen at the time, graduated into long trousers that my father, a tailor by trade, had personally fashioned. I could not afford a seat at the opera, but my allowance permitted standing room. It was there I was approached and persuaded to lease my youthful energies to the underground organization known as The Claque.

The Master Claquer was a smallish gentleman with an Albert Einstein hairdo. Avuncular, dressed in Barney's best, he took up his station in the Met lobby at exactly ten minutes before the house opened its doors, where he gave us our specific instructions for the evening. About ten of us were then deployed like troops throughout the auditorium. Our task was to provide instant—nay, maniacal—applause for the divas and divos who had payed for this special service. The reward was free standing room of choice location. One obviously needed to have working knowledge of the operas to participate in these rites. My Saturdays by the tube had been my boot camp. There was no short-changing our general—for while I never once saw him put palm to palm, he was an absolute dervish as he whipped from pillar to post checking the intensity of our cacophony and the heavenly lengths of that enthusiasm. I reveled in this exercise of my power for more than a season. When it became increasingly apparent that the opposition (a term applied to singers not soliciting our aid) deserved the greater applause, I wearied of bolstering the sagging notes of our clientele and, at the age of fifteen, found myself this side of banishment. The spirit had indeed been made flesh (in many instances, alas, too much so) but I cried basta to all this diva-itis, not to mention the execrable quality of the stage spectacle that my precocity permitted me to see in clear perspective. I retired to my growing collection of records and the invisible pleasure of the Saturday broadcasts.

When the Met reinstated its Wagnerian repertoire a year later, I made another sortie down to Thirty-ninth Street ready to do penance. The grand brotherhood had vanished—our commander was nowhere in evidence—and his replacement difficult to spot (claquers thrive on anonymity). To add insult to injury, matters had grossly deteriorated onstage. The acting obeyed Ernest Newman's dictum completely; roughly: "If an opera singer raises her arm during a performance, it is an indication that something's afoot. If she raises both arms, it is a sign of disaster."

Except for the Metropolitan, opera at that time hardly existed in our great metropolis, unlike its remarkable proliferation today in unlikely places. One not unlikely place in the early forties was the Brooklyn Academy of Music. I had up to then avoided the blandishments of Alfredo Salmaggi's company, but, enticed by the infrequently performed *Andrea Chénier*, by Giordano, I yelled *coraggio* and put my nickel in the subway slot (oh, innocent $ days). The house was packed and noisy, and it was a half hour past the advertised curtain time before the conductor made his appearance. A hound-dog creature with a multispotted vest (read "tomato sauce"), he proceeded to slouch toward the podium like Yeats's rough beast, while a slightly curled lip exposed an acknowledging fang. His downbeat, when it came, was minuscule, more an indication of lethargy than a signal. Each section of the orchestra tooted in—one half beat or so behind the other. The singers, caparisoned in costumes out of Robin Hood, were their perfect allies. Clutching at each other, the two "stars" held onto top notes with agonizing fervor. Their lung power seemed incredible, until one realized they were vainly listening for the next leading tone. The pit obliged by redoubling its efforts to catch up. Poised over this abyss of their mutual contriving, their climaxes were pure Arnold Schön- berg. It was an evening at the Hoffnungs, starring Anna Russell.

This clinched it for me regarding opera! From then on, as far as I was concerned, Orpheus had hocked his lyre and Bel Canto was the name of a stripper.

There is an old Zen aphorism that can be paraphrased as:

A man who is on the path of repression will suppress his desire. He will close his eyes toward the object and run away. Closing the eyes won't help—you can see in the imagination. Be alert!

It took all my years at the Yale Drama School and later at the Actors Studio to understand I had merely declared an armistice with opera.

In the days of MacDowell's "Wild Rose," I had made my unofficial acting debut as a brownie in the class play about the Pilgrim fathers. Eight Thanksgivings later I upped the ante by impersonating Noel Coward. The bug to mug and strut led me to the Yale Drama School in my teens and I acted in everything from *Box and Cox* to *The Glass Menagerie* (my graduating exer- cise). Allowed to roam the deserted halls of Old Eli (these were the World War II years), I dabbled in everything from playwrit- ing to costume design. When possible, I ran across the plaza to the Music Department, where I wolfed through scores and rec- ords while hoping to ogle Paul Hindemith, then composer-in- residence. Occasionally I caught glimpses of his bald pate re- flecting the autumn sunlight as he berated students on the mall. I never got close enough to do homage.

Much to my surprise, in the second semester I found my interests turning toward directing. Somehow I seemed able to arouse emotional states in other actors and to display a certain dexterity in creating dramatic moods and conflicts. Some Napo- leonic instinct also craved larger canvasses, armies of actors to drill instead of my single self. At that time the directing classes at the Drama School were based on *The Fundamentals of Play Directing* by an ex-Yalie, Alexander Dean. It was a green- covered textbook that instructed, among other precious insights, that ghosts in classical plays should always make their initial appearance upstage left and then approach the proscenium on the diagonal. So much for your average classical ghost.

My nights were spent at various odd jobs to help foot the New Haven bills. Favorite occupations included ushering at local movie houses and, along with my roommate, writing one-act plays on commission for other members of the playwriting class. Such undertakings, at black-market prices, had their antic sides. Subjects were chosen in direct contradiction to a given customer's persona. The pure and demure young thing from Somewhere, New Jersey, found herself the author of a playlet about a whore, and the beer-swilling "white-shoe" Yalie became the creator of metaphysical puzzlers. Delivery was guaranteed by the deadline set by the instructor. Payment: in advance. Refunds: none.

In my third and final year at Yale I directed Sartre's *No Exit* and acted in Camus's *Caligula* in its American première. Riding the crest of the craze for alienation *à la française,* my production of Sartre's three-character purgative was snapped up by two enterprising young producers and brought to New York. It opened at the Cherry Lane Theater in the early fall of 1948—exactly a year after the play's demise on Broadway—and literally paved the way for Off Broadway as a way of life. *No Exit* ran for over a year. I earned exactly $30 for adapting my Yale staging to the miniature theater off Barrow Street, and maintained a royalty of $15 per week for the extent of its run. Two distinct memories of that happy time were the glowing notice (my first) given the production by George Jean Nathan on the eve of his retirement, and the odd paranoid fantasy haunting my leading man—a sort of sawed-off Charles Boyer from Greece. Whenever I was in the theater he felt enormous relief, for he could be reassured I would run backstage to tell him if his trousers had fallen down round his ankles unexpectedly. He could not confide his phobic fear to anyone but me, his director.

I next staged my own adaptation of Strindberg's *The Creditors*—another three-character set-to that had an even longer run than *No Exit*. The new bedeviled trio included Beatrice Arthur (of recent "Maude" fame) and George Roy Hill (the latter-day film director). This time I earned $75 and was guaranteed a $30-per-week royalty. The actors in those days (1949) were raking in

$60 a week, tax free. On opening night we picked up the re-
views (raves) on Sheridan Square, and shared them with the
company of The Circle in the Square, which was just beginning
its operations across the street.

The next assignment was T.S. Eliot's abstruse and preten-
tious closet-drama, *The Family Reunion* (my homage to Drama-
Lit. courses). It played at the Cherry Lane for more than three
months and represented the first and only encounter I've had in
the theater with a customer, seated in the front row, reading the
text of the play as it was being enacted onstage—much as one
follows the score of an opera.

Eliot's incantation was followed by G.B. Shaw's rueful
Heartbreak House and then Pirandello's *Naked*, in which, one
night, I was forced to go onstage in its last act in the role of
landlady. The actress playing the part had not shown up. There
was no understudy (who could afford such luxuries?) and nobody else had the nerve to substitute. The usual discreet an-
nouncement was made, and when the curtain parted the audience saw one determined director wearing a tatty apron while
simulating some cleaning-up business on his hands and knees.
Simultaneously I shoved a script around the stage along with
my bucket and brush, in order to read his/her lines. There was
nary a snicker.

Those were also the years of the Theatre Guild of the Air,
where I earned extras for bit roles, and my outings directing in
summer stock, with its endless procession of would-be, could-
be, but mostly has-been stars of film, stage, and opera. It was
there I encountered Lawrence Tibbett, the erstwhile great star
of the Metropolitan Opera. During my training period with the
Met's claque, I had been witness to the vocal decline of this
once brilliant American artist. I recall dramatically gripping
Boccanegras, Iagos, and Khovantchinas overriding his shredded
patch of a voice. Tibbett had made a sudden exit from the Met's
ranks during my time at Yale, and just as suddenly he was back
in my life—only now he was front and center. We were involved in a double package: a summer tour of *Rain*, Guy Bol-
ton's version of Somerset Maugham's story, and, at a later date,
a national tour of *Peter Pan*. As the Reverend Davidson in
Rain—the missionary who discovers his baser instincts in tropi-

cal climes—Tibbett sang a hymn or two during the evening as a sop to his former career. This was interpolated into the acting text like a vaudevillian's turn. He managed such nonsense with good humor, considering his problem. Before taking off to the summer hills I had been called to a private meeting by several people near and dear to Tibbett. I was asked to keep a sharp eye on our star and, at the first sight that he might be tippling, was to report the incident to those concerned. Tibbett was an alcoholic. He withstood the rigors of the stock tour splendidly, but *Peter Pan* was another matter. *Peter Pan* was my Broadway directing debut and it costarred that touching waif, Veronica Lake, as Peter, sans hairdo. Early in the run Tibbett found he was unable to negotiate Lennie Bernstein's music; within weeks he was back on the bottle. My last sight of him was in a hotel room blubbering like an abandoned child, unable to make it onstage for the evening's performance. It was a heartbreaking conclusion to an illustrious career. *Peter Pan* foundered in Chicago before it could reach its destination and closed during a severe snowstorm that was its coup de grâce. The producer filed bankruptcy papers thereafter, and I was never to realize a dime for all my labors. Better to have remained in the sure, if penny-pinching, arms of Off Broadway, I argued, than risk the fool's gold of Broadway itself.

I went back to acting for a while and replaced the comic Irwin Corey in Mary Chase's success, *Mrs. McThing*. The star was Helen Hayes—a reigning great lady of the theater at the time. The cast was zippy: Jules Munshin, Fred Gwynne, the late Brandon de Wilde, and Ernest Borgnine, among others. I played a comic tough who was more brownie than gangster.

A sort of quiet climax took place at the time and all unbeknownst to me. My parents had always been in opposing camps regarding my early acting ambitions. A confirmed ham himself, my father had often donned cap and bells in the old country. Some memory of that distant bliss still lingered, and when I solemnly announced my intention to study at the Drama School, his acquiescence was both unexpected and touching. Overcoming my mother's scruples, he paid my tuition and supplied half my daily subsistence all during the first semester. *Mrs. McThing* was my first Broadway job. I was to discover via a relative, several years after my father's death, that he had quietly attended a Saturday matinee performance. He never told me he had. We had grown apart somewhere along the line and found communication difficult. He confided to this relative the satisfaction and pleasure he felt that Saturday afternoon. The money and hopes had not gone to waste. . . .

The play closed. Lacking work, I had begun performing in nightclubs in and around New York City, doing various routines, pantomimes, and imitations to popular and classical music. I had an engagement at an Atlantic City resort the day after my father died. In the tradition of *"ridi pagliaccio,"* I fulfilled it. In the hotel room in which I spent the night the full force of our estrangement hit me forcibly. It was an exercise in loneliness and loss I will never forget.

2
The
Actors
Studio

The Actors Studio became an active part of my life in 1952. At Yale, the name Stanislavski had been a burnished statistic in the annals of theater history. At the Studio he was chapter and verse, and Lee Strasberg his American counterpart. Besides being the grand vizier of the Method (American style), Lee was an incurable opera buff. In fact, he seemed happiest when the subject turned to music.

The Studio was an extraordinary phenomenon in those days (1950–1965). Suspect, yet respected in the trade, it deserved to be represented, along with other artistic guilds, in some imaginary *Die Meistersinger* of the mind. Lee was our Hans Sachs, and every aspirant at the Studio's doors a potential Walther or Eva—even if these acolytes came from such places as Fairmount, Indiana, or Spear Fish, Arkansas, and had only a vague suspicion of what a Wagner was. In the Studio rite the actor was the holy of holies, and the development of individual talent its clearest function. Lee's work had picked up where the Group Theatre* had left off, and at the time of my involvement he (and the Studio) were accredited as the originator and exponent of

*The American counterpart of the Moscow Art Theater, which flourished here from 1931 to 1941 under the aegis of Cheryl Crawford, Harold Clurman, and Lee Strasberg. Personalities who matriculated there include Elia Kazan, John Garfield, Franchot Tone, Morris Carnovsky, Luther and Stella Adler, and Robert Lewis, among others.

the preferred acting style of the fifties and sixties (that of Marlon Brando, James Dean, Montgomery Clift, et al).

On Tuesday and Friday mornings we gathered at the Studio—wherever it happened to be lodged at the time—to watch actors, both known and unknown, working on scenes and exercises of the most personal nature. Our ultimate goal was to coalesce the Studio's experiments into a functioning theater that would be a development of the ideals that had permeated the Group Theatre. These sessions were free of charge; admission to the Studio was through audition or invitation, and the members read like pages from *Who's Who in the Theatre*. I divided my time between acting scenes with Anne Bancroft, Gene Saks, and Herbert Berghof while directing projects with James Dean, Shelley Winters, Steve McQueen, and Ben Gazzara. On occasion I experimented as director with a musical scene, but first-rate singers were not readily available to us then as they were to be later on.

My own professional career took a significant leap forward one afternoon when I wandered through the seemingly empty Studio offices to recover some books or records I had left behind that morning. The Studio then was located in a series of rooms above the ANTA Theater on Fifty-second Street. Passing one of those rehearsal spaces, I noticed three men slumped around the darkened area in various degrees of apathy.

I watched them from the doorway, fascinated by their immobility. Finally they stirred, and three puzzled faces met my curious look. The young actors were Anthony Franciosa, Paul Richards, and Henry Silva. They were trying to figure out a scene about drug addiction written by another Studio member, Michael Gazzo. Intrigued by the problem, I asked if I could help them toward a working solution.

The scene was written mostly in the hyped-up lingo of junkies. But behind the addiction lay the human being in torment. The actual life histories of the characters and the location of the scene were purposely left ambiguous. I started a series of questions and answers, probing into the personal lives of the actors. Our work sessions were private one-to-one affairs. The actors spoke freely and longingly about their frustrations and desires, both real and imagined. This private material was gathered in the manner of a priest or a therapist—and entrusted to me in strictest confidence. Eventually I processed this information into a set of improvisations, wherein the actor's personal conflicts were projected into hypothetical situations. It was not too astonishing to discover that none of the actors, despite their early tenement environs, had ever had a brush with drugs. Stanislavski's mighty "as if" came to the rescue. Relying on the actor's personal set of references in any given situation, the "as if" allows him an opportunity to re-create any and all emotional or physical states required by a given text. If the actor lacks within him experiences parallel to the needs of the play, he can find a surrogate substitution in Stanislavski's deductive method.

Clinical research into the symptomatology of addiction yielded further pertinent information. The effects of drugs on the body could be likened to certain states of drunkenness, or the fever, chills, and aches of pulmonary disorders. Such symptoms were obviously within the range of each actor's experience, and we set about re-creating them per se. At the point where the actor had accomplished this task, his imagination could impel the results toward resembling a drug "high." He had a working, believable foundation—his "as if" had been tapped. I then added the personal devil of his emotional difficulties. These emotional realities, exacerbated by the physical evidence, created the singular world of the junkie.

The attenuated dialogue took on the overtones of personal suffering, and the scene became the seismograph of collective "as ifs." We presented it at one of the morning sessions moderated by Strasberg. The effect was electrifying, and we were encouraged to go further and dig deeper. That night I sat down with the author Mike Gazzo and began developing extensions in the lives of his three protagonists. Seated in the back room of our favorite local restaurant—the Capri on Fifty-second Street (one of the last strongholds of mother's spaghetti sauce went with its closing)—we devised an outline for a three-act play. Gazzo promised he would have a completed script in six weeks. Not to lose ground in the interim, I gathered a group of actors at the Studio who would be perfect for their roles when Gazzo had accomplished his task. Besides the three actors mentioned earlier, we added Ben Gazzara, Eve Marie Saint, the late Frank

Silvera, and Peggy Feury. Based on my knowledge of Gazzo's play in process, I invented and strung together a long line of improvisations that would explore the interrelationships of the various characters leading to Gazzo's opening scene. In other words, a complete play was improvised by us that, it was hoped, would fit Gazzo's written play like a glove. We worked mostly at night—usually ending our sessions at two or three in the morning. Much the same method was employed as in the original scene—that is, private biographies and sensory exercises. Franciosa would be required to play three distinct phases of drunkenness. Gazzara had to run the gamut from a drug high to a gradual state of withdrawal leading to violent convulsions. These "clinical" states were developed separately and then used as triggers for the emotional material.

At night the Studio often resembled a ward in some local hospital. Actors were assigned to various small, and purposefully claustrophobic, rehearsal spaces where they could work on the required sensory problems unimpeded and uninterrupted. I would act as an ambulant intern in reverse—sitting with each actor, helping him create the needed symptoms rather than alleviating them. I would spend many an evening hopping from cubicle to cubicle, checking each patient's acting temperature. When any of them was in doubt, he was encouraged to talk aloud and in so doing he placed himself back on the assigned track.

Gazzo would often walk the ward with me, and while the cubicles simmered and stewed we would go over some of the written material. The actual play was growing apace with the one we were improvising. I made sure these improvisations would not get out of hand or go down corridors contrary to Gazzo's intent. Such a deviation would have made our work useless.

When the script finally arrived, five weeks later, none of the actors had read a single word of it. The merging of their improvised world and Gazzo's written play was a unique and thrilling experience.

Along the line we lost Eve Marie Saint (who would benefit from her participation later in the movie version of the play); Carol Baker took her place. The fruits of all our nocturnal gnashings were presented a month and a half later, in a series of special showings to invited audiences. This was the first orthodox major-scaled amalgam of Studio methods put together on the premises for the premises that would achieve commercial success. Eventually the completed play, *A Hatful of Rain*, reached Broadway (with Shelley Winters replacing Carol Baker), and would represent the Actors Studio in full glory. Unfortunately not yet geared to be a producing company, the Studio did not take the responsibility for producing the play commercially (the Actors Studio Theatre would be almost ten more years in the making). The play had a two-year run on Broadway and on the road. Many of its players went on to rich careers—but not necessarily to a richer development of their talents. For most of the players, this would be their shining hour.

Steve McQueen took over Gazzara's role during the play's New York run, but "Cornflakes," as we all affectionately called him, lacked the inner techniques to make the role his own. He was a special actor, however, who under less pressured circumstances had done some unusually sensitive and even bold work at the Studio. I directed him in another exploratory scene by Gazzo, which became part of the author's second play, *Night Circus*. I have not yet seen a young male actor explore areas of sensuality with as much feeling and tact as McQueen displayed. But, unable to deal with *Rain*'s drug aspects, Steve eventually had to be replaced. The young hopeful moaned all the way to Beverly Hills.

The usual problems of greed and power attendant on success blighted the aftermath of *Rain*. *Night Circus* was stillborn in conception and execution. Success had assuaged too many hungers, and the preparatory work at the Studio was bypassed. The result was a one-week failure on Broadway. The play was full of interesting scenes (it predated the hippie invasion by five years) signifying . . . not much.

Classes at the Studio continued unabated during these periods of *rouge et noir*. James Dean made his appearance and, later, his female counterpart, Marilyn Monroe. Dean and I had met during the run of *Mrs. McThing*. He was acting across the street in a play by Richard Nash called *See the Jaguar*. In it he played an illiterate country boy locked up in a cage like an ani-

mal. In many ways, combing the word illiterate down several
hairs, the role was a quick-sketch portrait of Dean himself. Dean
has become such a cult figure that, knowing him as I did, I still
marvel how such things come to be. Not that he didn't work his
mysterious ends. He saw himself as Saint-Exupéry's Little
Prince—a self-appointed aristocrat condemned to wander the
earth forever homeless. His talent was instinctual; his technique: zero. He admired Montgomery Clift and adored Brando
inordinately. Once, cornered with the then already legendary
Brando at a party, Dean had to be pried off the famous man's
back. In all the years at the Studio he performed once or twice
for the aggregate and retired thereafter in abject terror of the
Studio's sophisticated and high-standard judgments. He would
never submit to Lee's supremacy as a guide. Verging on thirty,
he was still twelve years old emotionally. He could be a warm
and cuddly beast of the field, but he demanded the world protect him in return. For all the supernal light he radiated on
screen, he had a perverse cruel streak in him which negated
that image in life. Rebellious, secretive, and calculating, he
opted for acceptance via the route of stardom. He was practically a male Judy Garland—without a song. Sensitive and violent by turns, both the boy and the girl next door, he projected
the ambivalent sexuality and chastity of the classic ideal—if in
spirit he was perhaps more Icarus than Apollo.

Brando and Clift, before Dean, had at one time or another
been members of the Studio, and while the Studio was not directly responsible for the growth of their talents, it grooved on
their prototype. Its insistence on the actor's individuality and
freedom of expression jived with the needs of the time—and
inadvertently the Studio became eponymous in the public eye
with the Brando-Clift acting style. These stars were not just actors, they were Actors Studio actors—a special distinction, and
"The Method" their special cross. It is still difficult for the man
with the girl's eyes to find happiness in male chauvinist America. Yet for a time (and who knows? perhaps forever) America
doted on them—entered into a secret confraternity with their
ambivalence, and accorded them riches and fame. Dean's ascendancy to the holy grail of stardom left him more of a self-
conscious wreck than ever. Given dangerous toys to play with,
and more powerful expensive racing cars, his downhill ride

went alarmingly out of control. He was basically a young and highly gifted adolescent in desperate need of help, yet distrustful of almost everyone who could help him. I learned of his death one morning on arrival at rehearsals for the Broadway-bound *Hatful of Rain*. Gazzara was sitting just inside the stage entrance when I came in. "Guess who died last night," he said. "Your pal, Dean." My immediate response was, "How did he do it?"

Marilyn Monroe found her way to the Studio just about then. Her presence there signaled the dizzy tobboganing down the slope of the raggedy chic—the only mountain terrain in Manhattan. "Stars fell on Alabama," as the old song goes. I believe it—but in those days they all decamped to New York, where the first stop was the Actors Studio. They gathered like humming bees—all innocence and some talent, brandishing the weapon of reputation and fame. The Studio became a spiritual sanatorium of sorts for these refugees from Burbank. It was both inevitable and touching, since essentially the Studio had more to do with art than money. Contrary to Dean, Monroe appointed Strasberg her special Method father and guru, working with him privately when she was not attending Studio sessions. She took a liking to me as a sympathetic and knowledgable Studio member. She would invariably arrive late at our biweekly classes and snuggle up next to me before removing her pitch-black sunshades—a semidishabille goddess. She would listen with half-closed lids to Lee's discourse, then whisper in my ear, "What does he mean?"—and I would begin my literal translation of the master's discourse. After class we would end up at a nearby coffee shop where we shared coffee & in its oleagenous splendor. Turning in my seat at the counter one day, I could see through the window the heads of construction workers across the street dangling upside down on their girders to cop a snook at the adored one. One day she surprised everyone by doing a scene from *Anna Christie* with Maureen Stapleton. I was out of town at the time, but the reports of her performance were promising. And why not?

While I was weighing offers to direct other Broadway plays, I received a most unexpected call from Julius Rudel, the head of The New York City Opera Company, who was looking for

new faces to direct opera. The vehicle would be *Susannah* by
Carlisle Floyd: *mirabile dictu,* it was to be part of a season devoted entirely to American opera. Not a *maledizione* or *mamma
mia* in the batch—home-grown all the way. *Susannah* and the
season were a rousing success, and while my operatic appetite
had been whetted and my debut feted, I concluded that first
musical affair on the side other than the one I am accustomed to
in bed—sated, curious, yet disoriented.

So it was back to the backroom of Downey's restaurant on
Forty-fourth Street and the all-night coffee klatches. Everyone
came to Downey's in the late fifties and early sixties; it was the
informal man's Sardi's—complete with the midnight delivery of
the all-important theater reviews. Its jammed booths (always
room for one more, dearie) jumped with hope and talent. One
shared foaming Irish coffee with a merry-toothed Brendan Be-
han while arguing the pros and cons of Stanislavski with Strasberg and visiting Habimah players (in translation). The Old Vic
also pitched its heraldic tents there, reminiscent as the place
was of a good old English pub.

Weekends with my mother were fewer and farther between.
I had my own apartment, my own mysteries. Our only *umbili-
cus extendus* were the Saturday-afternoon broadcasts, when I
left the world behind me or occasionally drew a recalcitrant
rosebud to my lair, where seduction was accompanied before
the second intermission feature. Mimi's artificial flowers and
Carmen's coffee grinding were marvellous stimulants for conquest. I remember a *Tristan and Isolde* heard on a small porta-
ble radio in an empty apartment—except for a pallet and a live
Hungarian. The image replaces the Lanvin ad in my recollection.

A call from Gian Carlo Menotti was to pull me back to the
operatic fold, while again encouraging my work at the Actors
Studio in professional circumstances. Gian Carlo asked me to
prepare a program of one-act plays for the second season of his
festival at Spoleto. Impressed by my work in *Susannah,* he further asked me to tackle Prokofiev's occult jamboree, *The Flaming Angel.* Menotti was particularly interested in utilizing the
talents of Studio actors in the bill of one-acters. I inveigled Tennessee Williams and William Inge to write something for this

very special occasion. Both playwrights had admired *Hatful* and seemed respectful of the Studio's aims in general. Williams sent me a ten-page play called *The Night of the Iguana,* and Inge another, called *The Tiny Closet. Iguana* was so clearly a sketch for a longer play that when I approached Williams with the idea of developing it, he seemed receptive and willing.

In Spoleto (Lucrezia Borgia's secret hideout loomed over the piazza) I went about wearing two hats. Mornings and evenings I spent uphill rehearsing with the Studio actors. As they cooked away on their inner burners during the long Italian siestas, I trudged downhill to rehearse with my Italian singers. While working on *Iguana,* we received daily packets of new materials from Tennessee in America. Evidently, by the looks of things, the full-length play we had discussed was about to come into being. The original ten pages stretched to a hundred and ten by the time we raised the curtain at the charming Teatro Caio Melissa uphill.

On our return to the States, the Studio presented the two plays as they had been performed in Italy. Williams, unable to attend at Spoleto, saw all three of the showings in New York and profited considerably by our "work in progress" methods. Similar to that applied to *Hatful,* my approach was about to reap another harvest. Again the Studio failed to pick up the gauntlet of commercial presentation. The full-length play was finally unveiled at the Coconut Grove Theater in Florida with the original Studio cast intact. Then started the *via misericordia* to Broadway. Before the plunge north, I spent two weeks with Williams at his home in Key West, where we attacked the problems of rewrites.

Tennessee proved an indefatigable and prodigious worker, often producing three or four versions of the same scene for me to wrestle with. On especially warm nights we toyed around with ideas for operatic adaptations of his plays. Tennessee never stopped chuckling during these profitable hiatuses. Later, on Broadway, surrounded with sycophants and hangers-on, Williams visibly changed his stripes. Forever his own best drummer and hustler, he found himself dancing desperately to the tunes of Bette Davis—our "difficult" star and the play's single assurance of box-office success. The out-of-town tryout was a

nightmare of incompatabilities, but the quality of the actors'
work that had been established in the earlier one-act version
prevailed. On opening night in New York *Iguana* still resembled the play done in the name of the Studio. Tennessee and I
remained friendly throughout the melee. But ultimately he was
forced to jump through the hoop and was pushed into making
several ill-advised decisions regarding personnel and, most especially, yours truly. By mandate of Miss Davis, I was ordered
out of the theater. Don't ask for the reasons—They would "last
out a night in Russia, when nights are longest. . . ." I left Chicago during the last two weeks of its run there, and was only
reinstated as director when Miss Davis had left the cast, three
months after its opening in New York. Williams was in his own
personal doghouse during this fracas and lamented that *Iguana*
would be his last play. Events have proved this a prophecy,
although such a subjective judgment on his genius will, it is
hoped, be altered by his own "enemy time."

Broadway was becoming a more and more forbidding place
in which to work. The season in which *Iguana* was to win the
Drama Critics' Circle award (1962) was also the last major season of serious drama for some time to come. Thereafter saw the
rise of musical comedy and the two-character one-set syndrome.
The Actors Studio Theatre made a brave but abortive effort to
restore some balance to the theatrical scene, but its efforts were
short-lived. It was during this chaotic period of upheaval that I
first became acquainted with Stanislavski's essays on opera. I
thought I had managed to read everything of his available in
print, but here were these inconclusive but touching notes on
operatic production that put that grizzled art form in a new perspective. One essay dealt specifically with the mounting of
Verdi's *Otello,* one of my great loves. Stanislavski spoke tenderly of the problems of opera, for they constituted part of his
holy work in the theater. The full extent of his involvement was
not to be made clear until the appearance of *Stanislavski on
Opera* in 1976. By that time I was already in up to my neck.

Susannah and the Italian production of *The Flaming Angel*
had been two distinct but disconnected ventures. In their separate ways they had left me more frustrated than fulfilled. I had
been used to working with the best kind of actor, trained to the

gills and capable of infinite variety. Opera people (with few exceptions) seemed a breed apart . . . creatures from another world, almost. Then an event took place that really opened my eyes. Maria Callas was making her debut at the old stand on Thirty-ninth Street. This time, sitting in the orchestra, I came to see and hear her perform.

The Claque was very much in evidence that night. Like the snake alluded to in *Macbeth,* it had re-formed and was itself again—this time showing its poisonous fangs. Obviously in the pay of the "opposition" that evening, it greeted Callas at the final curtain with catcalls and a shower of carrot bouquets. Looking sharply in the direction of old haunts, I swore I discerned the Einstein hairdo disappearing through a door. The aging general had not died, he had merely faded away in the service. Callas herself was a revelation. Like Eleanora Duse, who had often appeared in second-rate vehicles she transformed by her genius, Callas was accomplishing a similar feat with the venerable chestnut, *Lucia di Lammermoor.* One moment particularly impressed me. It occurred during the famous sextet in Act II. As the introduction to the familiar music sounded, one could see her colleagues onstage jockeying into their traditional positions front and center. Callas remained as she had been, singing quietly to herself. While the others shouted at the audience, Callas closed her eyes and meditated. I suddenly realized what I was watching. This sextet was not mere musical horseplay. It was a series of inner monologues, the projection of six voices in private thought—something the theater could not do! My imagination was never more alert than at that moment. What I had secretly conceived in opera had been made flesh. It turned my head around completely. For certain, the stand-off I had declared with opera was about to be officially over.

3

On the Way to Directing Opera

No gongs reverberated in my head, no whistles blew! I didn't rush home and swear fidelity on Kobbé's *Complete Opera Book*—I called Julius Rudel instead. It had been more than six years since I had last spoken to him. Was there anything cooking on his burners, I asked, that might be of interest to me? It was as if we had talked only the day before. Yes, believe it or not, there was, and would I come up and discuss it with him? The something turned out to be Shostakovich's *Katerina Ismailova*. It was to be given its New York première in the upcoming spring season, 1965. No director had as yet been assigned to it.

The Actors Studio Theatre had just come to a sudden and unexpected end. For complicated reasons that prevailed in the arts, its life span was cut off literally at the source. The reverberations are being felt even today. We are still pursuing the Studio's ideals in all sorts of unlikely places. I, among others, had devoted three years in helping shape its policies and establish it in the public eye. It had been my first experience with a theater devoted to the idea of the ensemble, and while its failure is not the concern of this book, its working concepts are. Callas was the personification of such ideals—for all her superstardom, she was a walking ensemble in one!

Much to my surprise, I discovered on my visit to Fifty-fifth Street that my 1958 production of *Susannah* was still in repertory—a little worse for wear but hanging in there. She had weathered all my recent storms, and, seeing her again, I couldn't help feeling a tinge of pride. The company of singers was as plucky, yet as woebegone, as ever. The rapid-fire change of regime at City Center (four managements in less than ten years) and the unrelenting pressures and demoralizing effect of penny-saving operations had left the talented company gasping for its life. My own musical snobbery had prevented a continued contact with its efforts: its tacky if well-intentioned endeavors could not possibly vie with the more splendid pretenses of the old Met. The Metropolitan had occasionally sought out new directors to enliven their productions. Men like Peter Brook, Garson Kanin, Alfred Lunt, Cyril Ritchard, and Joseph Mankiewicz were chosen from the top of the heap to rub a little of their magic into the old formula. The City Opera had reached out for fresher bloods instead, and while that was a welcome change of venue, nothing much came of their operatic participation after the American season of '58.* Curiously, my own success with *Susannah* did not make me eligible for Carlisle Floyd's next première, *Wuthering Heights*, in 1959.

Had I not called Rudel, I was on the verge of pulling up stakes and following the sun out West, where I supposed I might have made my pile entrenched in television and film (I certainly had enough credits to open up a few doors there). Obviously I was not destined to go the route taken by most of my contemporaries in the theater. Instead of the real Far West, I struck out for the figurative one—that pioneering country called Opera. I decided to look for gold in them thar hills—literally, figuratively, and any other ively.

Taking a hard gander at my new-gained territory, I found the landscape parched. I had come from the legitimate theater whose history was crowded with the names of great directors and the companies they had created. Opera could boast no such perennials. Men like Max Reinhardt, David Belasco, Sergei Eisenstein, and Vsevolod Meyerhold had staggered in and out of its embrace but had not lingered to cultivate its desiccated

*The new bloods were José Quintero (Dello Joio's *Triumph of St. Joan*); William Ball (Weisgall's *Six Characters in Search of an Author*); and Carmen Capalbo (Kurka's *Good Soldier Schweik*). Only Ball was to continue on any major level of involvement.

charms. Stanislavski remained an exception—to what an extent
I was to discover only years later. The name of Walter Felsen-
stein and his Komische Oper surfaced in the news now and
again through the red tape of East Berlin propaganda, suggesting that somewhere there was an operatic outpost involved with
solving the problems of style, actors' reality, and the ensemble.
Mostly, opera houses were great import-export emporiums,
dominated by singers and conductors with little theatrical
knowledge and practice, where convention and sacred-cowism
maintained an iron grip. There were perhaps two or three
American theatrical directors who persisted in mounting opera
in this country at the time. With the exception of William Ball,
their work lacked originality and profile.

My productions of *Katerina Ismailova* and Prokofiev's *The
Flaming Angel* in an English version in 1966 did not raise the
barometric pressure one centigrade. (*Katerina* was effective;
Angel hardly even that.) It was with the move to Lincoln Center
in 1966 that a new burst of energy shot through the creative
ranks and matters directorial began to pop. Coincidentally the
European scene began to brighten equally with the revolution-
ary work of Wieland Wagner at Bayreuth and the emergence of
such distinctive talents as Jean Pierre Ponnelle in France and
Giorgio Strehler in Italy. At the same time, here in America,
Sarah Caldwell and her Boston company broke onto the scene,
while the rejuvenated City Opera was again inviting new directing talents into its midst. The dawning age of Aquarius was
about to witness the ascendancy of the stage director in the operatic firmament. I joined the incipient elevation in one
stroke—with my production of Verdi's *La Traviata* at the new
home for the City Opera at the State Theater. It was greeted as
innovative and pathbreaking. Critics and public did handstands
of delight. I was stopped in the State Theater lobby by parents
with children who wanted to meet and partake of my new-
found radiance. As "innovative" productions followed on one
another's heels, however, the climate began to alter. People still
stopped me—but the villifications now balanced the praise.

To date I have directed over seventy opera productions,
twenty-five or more for the New York City Opera—my home
away from home. At present I have become the opera critics'
favorite whipping boy—"intelligent," if I don't get in the way of

the music; at worst, the opera I've directed is recommended despite the havoc I have wrought. I now appear in reviews of other directors as a cautionary example of egotism in matters theatrical; I have been labeled "scandalous," "controversial," and just plain "bad boy." Only recently it was proposed that a movement be initiated to "prevent" my "tampering with the classics."

The igniting cause of pique and resentment from the various critical bodies lies in the personal quality of vision (subjectivity) brought to my interpretation of operatic literature. This subjectivity the critics consider anarchic and, more often than not, it is dismissed as pure gimmickry. But gimmickry in opera replaces vision and feeling with trendiness and fancy footwork— the triumph of props over life. I would like to believe that the ideas I invent in my stagework help define life, not dominate it. Opera is not a junkyard of fads for me but a place of very special grace. I approach each work, old or new, as if regarding a clear, clean space. The most thumbnailed musical chestnut becomes virgin territory; no matter how rouged or battered by time, each time is the first time—for both of us!

In fact, most opera projects I have undertaken come into my life like blind dates. Only about twenty-five percent of the time have I been able to exercise any influence in the selection of a work. This was the case with the Delius operas, Korngold's *Tote Stadt*, Handel's *Rinaldo*, and Joplin's *Treemonisha*, among a handful. Either way, the prime task in bringing a work to life is the search for its psychologic and spiritual reality. With the help of all and any source materials, I try to get inside the composer's head, so to speak. The personal conception that follows is my own intuitive and imaginary re-creation of what I think was the composer's subconscious experience. I then try to find very real and practical terms for implementing that journey. Initial emphasis is placed on fleshing out the lives of the characters in the work—paying particular regard to their ambivalences and contradictions. The mise en scène that follows develops from this point of departure. Stage design as decoration is a secondary function—primarily it must help serve the characters live out their experiences in all their special ramifications. This is such an idiosyncratic approach that most opera companies find it difficult to deal with my sets if put to use in any but

productions under my direction. The singing-actor (a term invented by Stanislavski) is the most important cog in the wheel
of my conception. In awakening and guiding his or her response, I employ a variety of acting techniques, both self-cre-
ated and derived from the Stanislavski method.

The resulting stage production becomes a natural extension
of the original work itself—a projection of its values toward
modern psychologic perspectives, and it is this "extension" that
is considered blasphemous. Supposedly its paradoxes are irrec-
oncilable with historic intent. My argument is that extension in
no way excludes historical intent (authenticity)—rather, it ab-
sorbs such elements for a fresh look. Authenticity per se rather
reminds me of the psychiatric patient's lifelong search for the
mother/father ideal—a fruitless and self-defeating mania from
which one emerges second best *in aeternum*.

What is the authentic overview in dealing, say, with the
stage works of Monteverdi, or with the proper scoring for Bach's
B Minor Mass? In such pursuits we often confuse temporal exi-
gencies with a composer's ultimate purpose: Monteverdi gathered his theatrical and musical forces as best he could—what
was available to him at any given instant dictated quantity and
quality. Nothing in these areas was "fixed" and, accordingly, repeated ad infinitum. Bach's Mass with string quartet and a modest brace of winds and brass may tickle one's fancy for the ar-
chaic, but it may also suggest penury masquerading as
authenticity. Often overlooked in such scholarly pursuits are
the desperate letters pleading for more and better that the Oracle of Venice and the Cantor of St. Thomas dispatched to their
various lords and masters. I believe a performance of any given
work reflects the limitations of its time and the circumstances of
performance. Such factors must not encroach upon the fresh
prerogatives and insights of future generations, for there is a
greater freedom in musical life, a larger sense of possibility than
we allow for in artistic endeavor. Call this folly, gimmickry, or
what you will; I find jousting with windmill authorities a Christian duty. Ultimately, the changing fads of taste and fashion will
defang my detractors—and in that instant I will have begun my
own journey toward being old hat in the next cultural turnover.

Yet how really "new" is this idea of "extension"? I recall an exchange between the composer Gluck and a pupil-friend who complained to the master of the discrepancy existing between the agitated orchestral figurations accompanying the words "Calm is returning to my breast," sung by Orestes in *Iphigenia in Aulis*. Orestes, pursued by the Furies for having committed matricide, is pausing momentarily in the forest. The friend could not breach the contradiction between the words and music. Gluck's answer was simple: "Orestes is lying!" he said.

4

The
Opera Director's
Functions

Recently a young aspiring director called and asked me to
check his artistic pulse. How did I think he was doing in this
department and that—and suddenly I was faced with the whole
picture of what it means to be a stage director in opera.

As in the theater of the purely spoken word, an opera director must be able to conceptualize a work and have the tools to
implement it. This means the ability to deal with actors in
translating emotional states into stage behavior, and creating
the essential patterns of stage movement to elucidate such behavior. He must be able to see the total stage picture in the
mind's eye—both as a dramatic and a decorative entity—and be
prepared to achieve it. In my own case, a lifetime study of
painting and film images has been of great importance in sharp-
ening my receptivity and focus. Such influence impinges ultimately in evolving the stage setting, costumes, hand props, and
final lighting scheme. Within the created stage environment,
the director must be prepared to deal with one or one hundred
people concurrently. He must apply his ingenuity toward solving the problem of the solo aria (read "monologue") and coping
with that formidable beast, the chorus—deploying them en
masse or as individualized beings. Today most theater directors
find little opportunity to exercise their muscles in this area . . .
unless they are dealing with classical drama or involved, outside the theater, in grand-scale film-making. About one play in

hundreds may require a chorus; not so in opera. There the chorus is one of the director's most specialized and taxing areas of concern. Because of cost, its rehearsal time is severely restricted and a director can ill afford to improvise with *la grande bête*. He must face it with clear-cut solutions and plans of execution. The unstimulated chorus has an uncanny way of slipping into conventional patterns—a convenient, time-saving device that I call purposeless ambling, an innocuous and lifeless shuffling about appropriate to any and all village greens or royal enclosures.

An opera director who speaks only his own native tongue is both an anomoly and working at a disadvantage. He is often faced with multilingual casts where film dubbing is impossible. Besides ye basic English, primitive Italian is mandatory; a smattering of French and a steinful of German help. If the director can play the piano, all the better. In the final analysis, whether he can play the piano or the contra bassoon, it is his innate musicality that will be the unerring arbiter in all matters concerning the stage.

While I am far from being a professional pianist, I am capable of toying with a score at the keyboard. I would say about two out of ten directors can do the same. I studied piano late in life (in my early thirties) with the recently deceased Israel Citkowitz. He encouraged me to read everything in sight, leaving the Czerny stuff for such time, as Israel put it, "my head was ahead of my fingers." I never got to Czerny. I save the piano for my "close-up" work on a score—when I need to zero in on a scene or examine various thematic materials. But I am a very professional record flipper, and therein lies an important source of information. I prefer to work with as many taped or recorded performances of a work as are available, commercially or otherwise. Ideas are sparked by different interpretations, and I am not unduly influenced by any single one. I work with a piano vocal score in hand all the time, and can accordingly evaluate the individual interpretations against the printed notes. When working on a newly composed opera, I ask the composer to prepare a piano-vocal tape for my private use. These tapes I savor *cum grano salis*. Most composers are notorious for their interpretative fluctuations, and you must adjust accordingly.

Once the conception of an opera has been sufficiently established, I write it down in outline and then literally put it away somewhere. I will let it lie sometimes for months at a time, purposefully avoiding it until some inner signal prompts me to return to it. Such moments are quite unnerving. Does it hold up on re-examination or was it a whim of the moment—full of holes, with no backbone to it? If such is the lamentable case (and one must not be lulled by a brilliant stroke or two), I start over from scratch. My only guide in such decisions is my own conscience and sense of theatrical rightness. If, indeed, the concept holds, the inner details suggest themselves naturally.

Thus far it has been a one-man operation. Next comes the business of exposing and testing the vision to the necessary collaborators. This process terminates only on opening night, and sometimes not even then.

A scenic designer is chosen to give the concept a face. The estimation of his suitability is mostly my affair. I discuss the concept with him and encourage him to improvise on my secret. His initial sketches will indicate whether the secret is shared or not. If not, the collaboration course must be set straight, or you must move on to another designer. My failure to make such decisions in the past has invariably spelled disaster. As the characters develop in my imagination, I suggest physical set details. Overall, the gestation period of arriving at a working design is usually six months. Most new productions take a year to realize, from the initial preparatory stages to actual rehearsal time.

Somewhere in midstream (it varies from production to production) a meeting is arranged with the conductor. He is the most important and, potentially, the trickiest member of the collaboration team. It is the conductor who fuses all the ingredients in the last stages of production. He supersedes the stage director in that instant, and takes sole responsibility for the interpretation.

Less than half the time I have some say as to who this is to be. With a traditionalist stick-wielder I am in trouble. With a man of the theater one can mutually pursue the questions of musical atmosphere, tempi, the use and timing of pauses, vocal balances . . . all the countless details that make up the extraordinary sung play called opera. One out of ten conductors is able to participate and share in this adventure. Three out of five are willing to do "anything you want"—out of boredom or convenience. Two out of ten conduct with their heads buried in the score, rarely ever checking the stage. Without a conductor's implicit collaboration, the final mixture will not jell properly. It remains a theoretic cake, with the yeast missing.

When the stage design is complete, I usually ask the designer to make a miniature model, which helps with the problems of costuming and lighting. These elements have been under discussion all along, but a well-scaled model adds a finishing insight into all areas. The artists involved at this end of the work join the team and the final stages of "Show and Tell" take place. Naturally, once we are onstage during dress rehearsals all manner of new changes can occur as befit the needs of the production. A pox on all of us if the scene fails to register. As in a show breaking in out of town, you can change a scene or an emphasis if the foundation is secure. If there is no foundation, all the clever manipulation will afford you nought. Every set looks ghastly until the lighting designer has completed his end of the job. Then and then alone is the story complete—as far as the physical side of the production goes.

During rehearsals, the director's assistant prepares the stage guide—the blueprint of movement, distribution of furniture and props that will serve to re-create this particular production in one opera house or another, season after season. If the director is available during an opera's revival, these guides are supportive. Without his presence (and this is more often the rule than the exception), the guide represents his concept by proxy. In this situation an assistant can either be a stick-wielder himself or a sensitive collaborator. It takes a good deal of prescience, horse sense, and talent on his part to reproduce another artist's work from a copybook. While following closely the patterns of stage movement created by the original director, he must be prepared to accommodate the production to the changing needs of a rotating cast—willing and able to alter details without changing the overall concept. If another director stages the work afresh, a similar stage guide is created relevant to the new conception.

The all-important matter of casting an opera entails special difficulties. On his own, in a nonrepertory setup, the director has the full panoply of available talent at his disposal. In a repertory setup, singers are chosen and contracted for years in advance of a given production—even before a director is assigned. This permits the producer to maintain his liaison with valuable artists over an extended period of time. The choice of any individual for a role is thus at his discretion. Sometimes a director may be involved in long-distance planning; more often he is not. Faced with a fait accompli (this can include designer, conductor, and others), he can either take it or leave it! Contretemps naturally occur, and it depends on the efficacy and excitement of the director's vision, not to mention his general clout, to affect rearrangement or even alteration in these affairs.

Rehearsals for a new production vary from two to three weeks. Anything more is rare, but not unheard of. If the acting problems offer unusual difficulties, private work can be accomplished before the official rehearsal time. Such accommodations are much influenced by the demands of time placed on a singer, who must fulfill several assignments in a repertory house, frequently in rapid succession. The initial stages of rehearsal are usually accomplished without benefit of a conductor. With only a piano accompanist at our disposal, the singers and I explore the characters' behavior and life styles. Musical tempi at such rehearsals are flexible in order to accommodate our work. I am usually quite precise as to what my specific demands are in any given instance. It is the performer's process of arriving at the desired results that requires trial and patience. I am always open to new possibilities other than my own. But if a response does not come, I am then forced to create matters directorally (that is: by particular movements or gestures, by a piece of business, even by the long-range lighting plan). When I was in Spoleto in 1959, I witnessed a production of Donizetti's *Il Duca d'Alba,* directed by Luchino Visconti. It did not say very much for his actors. They sang and performed mostly in stygian darkness—only the sets were in light. I have sometimes wished I could duplicate that feat on several occasions myself.

A week or ten days into rehearsal the conductor makes his appearance. If he is one of the team, he is also able to assess the level of the work and proceed toward his designated tempi organically. Oh, rarity of rarities! Mostly his introduction in our midst creates panic and disillusion. An unsympathetic conductor strikes out to protect his own interests at all costs—negating our own. I have often been put in the position of protecting the singers and myself against such assaults. These moments are blood-curdling, and if personally expressed convictions, cajolery, diplomatic footwork of all varieties fail to persuade, an artistic intermediary (usually the impresario) is brought in to arbitrate. The felony often can be compounded at the time the chorus and soloists are first brought together. Having worked separately, these divisions usually fuse in the midst of angry shouts, imprecations in three languages, and flying scores. Invariably at such times conductors invoke the shades of the dead composer being maligned. This often represents the best performance he will give, in or out of the pit. There is nothing worse than the international conductor who deposits his rigid musical baggage in one opera house after another—crucifying the best efforts of young artists on the cross of his own "correctness."

In 1965, when I began devoting my full energy toward directing opera, the field was crowded with sorcerers' apprentices but few sorcerers. When one did emerge, he was usually a bird of foreign stripe, whose unpronounceable name added a note of dubious authenticity to the trying business of selling the lost cause of opera to a surfeited public. Today the picture has altered a little—there are many more sorcerers who have apprentices. Some of the apprentices have graduated rapidly into the maven class, and their small number replaced by similar hopefuls.

Public interest in matters operatic is now at its zenith. It is therefore possible to include an emissary from its ranks on popular television talk shows without embarrassment to the sponsors or their public. The soprano Beverly Sills, for instance, is, at this writing, almost as well known as Barbra Streisand. She has managed to make opera a household word, and although I fear her facsimile will pop out of my breakfast cereal box any morning now, one cannot underestimate her accomplishment in popularizing and even glamorizing the medium.

With all the upgrading and wider dissemination of opera in America today, it is still a tough area in which to make a living. This is particularly true of the American director. Even at the top of the heap, he is the least well paid among the performing artists in the field.

Consider that there are singers who now command as much as $13,000 a performance—and get it! Other fees for singers in high demand rarely go below the $5,000-per-performance level here and abroad—where, in fact, they tend to go higher. This affords an almost Pasha-like outlook on life for the singer. Once a role is learned, the escalating benefits can be dizzying. Having in one's repertory Lucia (*di Lammermoor*), Rosina (*Barber of Seville*), or Turandot alone, among others, can make a small fortune for a singer in the world's market. For such personalities, rehearsals are usually minimal, since the demand on their services and time is so great. One role can be repeated in as many as four different cities within a given month, and in sets of two or three performances in each single instance. The stage director hardly ever comes within bargaining distance of such demands. If he can manage $3,000 as a total fee for a single production, he is doing well.

A director is responsible for every detail of any given production he undertakes. Months of preparation go into a single new production, where his value is at its highest. If he is capable of mounting five new productions annually, he is really going some. However, in order to accomplish this at the top-fee level ($5,000 to $7,000), one must either work for a large international house, of which there are three in this country (the Metropolitan, San Francisco, and Chicago Opera Companies), or work in Europe, where the American director often seems *persona non grata*. A singing star will get his or her $13,000 in the boondocks of the world. The director in similar circumstances can be asked to cut his fee in half. Some directors become artistic heads of hinterland opera companies and can average as high as $30,000 to $35,000 a year. Others are forced to supplement their directing with sundry moonlighting activities to help make ends meet.

Wrapped up in this phenomenon is one even more incredible. A month doesn't go by when I don't receive a call from some singer or impresario asking my sanction to use either a concept, a bit of business, or a total characterization dreamed up by me elsewhere. Sometimes I am not even asked, and nary a royalty accrues my way from such borrowings. How do you copyright a production?

Film, television, and the Broadway stage are, of course, rich sources of revenue. However, unless one has established roots in these professions, the opera director is strictly an *auslander* here. Men like the late Luchino Visconti and Franco Zeffirelli, who started in film before gravitating to opera, have never given up their relationship with home base. My own background outside the theater has been minimal. Film and television credits make up less than half a paragraph. Out of necessity and much painful pleasure (masochism is not an unknown savor to me) I have thrice detoured my life in the past ten years in favor of Broadway and its Klondike prospects. The load has been heavy in each instance. The lode: mostly fool's gold.

Jesus Christ Superstar was one such trial. *Treemonisha* proved another; while it achieved a success of sorts in the big time, it was sadly mismanaged by its New York producers and its potentially long career cut off in mid-bloom. There is only the happy memory of the production itself to warm me. *1600 Pennsylvania Ave* was the most recent shot at the moon . . . "she comes more nearer earth than she was wont / and makes men mad."

Directing opera is basically no different than directing on Broadway. It prepares you for all the curious entanglements and suspicious undergrowths to be found in the jungle of the Broadway musical. What the operatic world does not prepare you for is the debasing emotional and aesthetic climate that often surrounds the making of a Broadway show. Each return to this nether region only reminds me of Dante's dictum before the entrance to Hell: ABANDON HOPE, ALL YE WHO ENTER HERE!

5

La

Traviata

A RE-EXAMINATION

It is uncanny how my initial foray into the pleasures of standard opera was in the arms of two gorgon ladies—La Traviata and Madama Butterfly. Earlier encounters with Shostakovich's Katerina Ismailova and Prokofiev's Renata * were off the beaten track; while in practice more deserving of the "gorgon" appellation, their misdeeds were new-minted as compared to the half-century of shopworn martyrdoms Violetta and Butterfly had inflicted on a sinking public. Rather than being put out to a well-deserved pasture, they suddenly entered my life one May day in 1966, when Julius Rudel entrusted them to my care. I approached the task of dealing with these ladies as one marooned on a desert island must: i.e.: change dragon ladies into acceptable sleeping companions out of sheer necessity in bedding down.

La Traviata was to be revived in the fall of 1966—practically the last "new" production in a series including Handel's *Julius Caesar*, Mozart's *Magic Flute*, and Puccini's *La Bohème* and *Tosca*. I had five months from the assignment date to accomplish transformation Number One. Armed with the score, records, and historical data, I started on my courtship of the Lady of the Camellias.

Dumas's novel, based on the well-known career of Marie Duplessis, courtesan *exemplaire*, had created a scandal on pub-

*In *The Flaming Angel*

lication. The play Dumas adapted from his novel a year later was regarded by the Establishment as a manifesto for free love, if not a philippic aimed against the institution of marriage itself. Both the play and, later, Verdi's opera were to become symbols of revolt against the sexual mores of their day. In our own time a similar revolution is taking place: nudity rampant and total sexual license have become the latest solutions to the Puritan problem as envisioned by the younger generation. The new theater that reflects the change, while throbbing with life, is immensely cynical and pugnacious in its march forward. The older generations, half-heartedly joining the bandwagon, have had a difficult time finding cultural oases to slake their more ancient thirsts.

Such sentiments are still to be found in opera, which I think partly explains the phenomenal popularity of opera in America over the past ten years. But we have all been bitten by the flea of progress, and while the more traditionally minded seek out the old verities, they have begun to regard them with jaundiced eyes, reflecting the unease and distrust of the younger groups.

Dumas's original Camille was a fireball. Her operatic counterpart in performance has come to resemble her duchess mother instead. How to reconcile the Lady of the Camellias with Miss Sempre Libera? Dumas's lady leaves actual threads of blood in her silver sputum cup in the midst of revelry; the other neither spits nor really revels. She languishes, stylishly upholstered, flicking an occasional champagned *"Olé,"* but essentially remains a center-stage fixture, expressive and mobile as a tank. Indeed, she has died long before the final act—not of tuberculosis, but of a slower, more disfiguring malady: convention. And her sepulcher is glorified by the name of tradition. Instinctively I felt that the first step in transformation *Numero Uno* was to be a reversal—not a building up but a breaking down—from dowager to doxy. It would also represent for me my first assay in opera as a living experience.

Before plunging into the opera itself, I sought perspective by examining the libretti of Verdi's total operatic output. An interesting and instructive picture emerged: a typical plot outline of a Verdi opera runs something like this:

Oberto (bass) discovers that his daughter Leonora (soprano) has been seduced by Riccardo (tenor). Unable to bear the stigma of shame, Oberto casts out his daughter and disowns her. Although still professing her love for Riccardo, Leonora promises to publicly expose him. Thus joining her father in a mutual drive for revenge, Leonora is reconciled with him.

Familiar? Of course! Change the names of the contestants and you have the preamble to the vicissitudes of *Rigoletto* (Verdi's fifteenth opera, composed in 1851). This brief precis, however, also describes the background of *Oberto,* Verdi's very first opera (1839).

There is a truism that suggests that first works usually foreshadow the entire course of a composer's output. *Oberto,* then, is an encyclopedic bit of Verdiana. Even musical themes to be developed in *Rigoletto* and *Traviata* pepper its overture. Its subject materials, prime stock for many an operatic broth, were to exercise an inordinate fascination for the Italian master, and in one variation or another constitute the basis for over half of his twenty-seven operas.

The holy (or unholy) trinity of this majority consists of a father figure, a madonna-like wife or daughter fallen into disgrace, and a young man, inevitably cast in the role of transgressor. In this tightly run ship, the patriarch rules supreme. The matriarchy was to have a single field day in *Trovatore,* whose action revolves around the mother-witch Azucena. With this single exception, the formula remains the same: the father figure guards his daughter's virtue and honor with an almost obsessive love, and to brook his judgment or authority is to incur dire punishment. The good old domineering father *con amore.* Invariably there is no wife or mother present in such circumstances. Her absence has forced the father to assume her duties, as well as his own, in guiding the daughter's destiny. She, in turn, assimilates her missing mother's role and must bear the extra burden of that relationship. This precarious combination is fraught with anxiety, but it is held under wraps by the father's iron hand and inflexible will. The daughter is jealously supervised, and almost all the young suitors are or become unworthy of her love for one reason or another. Often in the sociopolitical extensions of the problem, the young swain is a member of an enemy faction.

Verdi (1813–1901) was himself an only child who adored his

mother. Raised in poverty, he early in life came to *"conosce il sacrifizio"* (know about sacrifice), as Violetta so touchingly repeats in *Traviata*. He married at twenty-five, and two years later lost both his wife and two children. This blow was to solidify an already pronounced tendency toward melancholy, taciturnity, and hypochondria. Thenceforth his life was devoted to musical composition, which in part celebrated his other passion—the freedom and unification of Italy. In her behalf, Verdi served as surely as did Garibaldi or any of the champions in that great struggle. After living with singer Giuseppina Strepponi for more than ten years (still a surprising move to contemplate for a man of his rectitude), he overcame his misgivings and made her his legal wife. This marriage was childless but happy. Strepponi was to insure the lion's privacy at St. Agate, to which Verdi retired as a country squire and where he lived until his death in 1901. To the very end, for all his amiability, he remained a man of peasant stock, superstitious and withdrawn in the glamourous world that idolized his genius.

But in his operas passion certainly burns in abundance, the pure flame of a seemingly uncomplicated citizen, full of a fastidious love of family and country. Within this context, the patriarchal syndrome can take on Greek-like dimensions. The patriarch father (in part the fatherland) becomes synonymous with God the Father, who invariably is a God of wrath. This vindictive force (viz: *la maladizione* or the curse in *Rigoletto*, *La Forza del Destino*, and, by implication, between Germont and Violetta in *La Traviata*) reappears constantly like a plague in his works. Its manifestations are often strange and even dreamlike.

In *I Lombardi* (The Lombards), Verdi's fourth opera (1843), two brothers, Pagano and Arvino—both sons of Folco—are in love with Viclinda. The latter chooses to marry Arvino. Unable to accept her decision, Pagano decides to take revenge and one night descends on his brother's house, intending to kill him and abduct the maid, now Arvino's wife. In the darkness it is not Arvino who is killed by Pagano, but Folco, his father. Unable to bear the guilt for this primal crime, Pagano, after being banished amid the execrations of his townspeople, expiates his sin by withdrawing as a hermit to a mountain retreat. Switch penitential cassocks and we have Leonora and *Forza del Destino*, with equal blood guilt laid on fairer hands.

Both lover and beloved are culpable in the land of patriarchal authority. Thus it follows that love and sexual desire amount to a taboo, being the instruments of patriarchal disapproval.

With *Rigoletto*, a new light is shed on this subject. The patriarch himself is questioned. Still inwardly guided by the old verities of love, duty, and honor, he forces decisions that will wreck the lives of others—and is thus made responsible for the tragic denouement. Ultimately it is Rigoletto's intemperate love for his daughter Gilda that is the string of his undoing. Love, at least sexual love, appears as a debasing force in Verdi's operas, particularly in *Traviata* and *Rigoletto*.

This sexual pressure takes a new tack in *Don Carlos* (1867, revised in 1884). King Philip of Spain, often both secretive and indecisive, finally becomes villainous in authorizing his son's death sentence. Verdi, however, cannot quite break the patriarch's back. He cannot allow Philip to hand his son Carlos over to the Inquisition, as Schiller's play indicates. If he did, it would be in part the troublesome but final solution of the father-son rivalry for the wife-mother Elisabeth. Verdi cannot manage the coldhearted gesture—the punishment would be too close to home. How else explain the mysterious figure who fortuitously abducts Don Carlos at the final moment? It is a dilemma that possibly sheds light on Verdi's difficulties in managing a workable scheme for *King Lear*. Consider the hazards facing him with this greatest of all patriarchal dramas, and its crisscross currents of familial punishments.

This psychosexual fever chart of Verdi, while rather truncated, was of immense help in my gaining the courage of my own convictions. It clearly emphasized that not everything necessary for a given production is to be found in the music alone—certainly as it pertains to *Traviata*.

"My music is never fortuitous," Verdi wrote to the management of the Fenice opera house. "I always try to give it a definite character." But his reticent setting of the erotic portions of Dumas's play still seems a tepid affair. Intention or intimidation? In Verdi's case, I think they played into each other's hands.

Was Verdi's inhibition in erotic matters only to be explained as a sign of the times? Who else was writing sexual music? Well, among others, we have Meyerbeer. His lascivious nuns of *Robert le Diable* (1831) had made their vivid impression; Wagner's *Tannhäuser*, premièred in 1844, had introduced the court of Venus (to be amplified in the more erotically geared Paris edition of 1861); Rossini had written his transvestite fun fest, *Le Comte d'Ory* in 1828, and Marschner's *Hans Heiling* (1833) and *Der Vampyr* (1828) had musicalized almost Krafft-Ebbing relationships. Sticking to his last, Verdi remained a puritan, locked in his own private closet with the thrashings of his family group—his *croce e delizia.*

In production, the director must either shut off the promptings of his imagination regarding the bawdy elements of *Traviata* or totally accept the opera's limitations. I decided in this case that to maintain strict allegiance to the promptings of its music would be adding a slimming diet to undernourishment.

It may very well have been Verdi who instituted the whore with a heart of gold as an operatic cliché. His spiritualized concept of Dumas's Camille therefore plays down the wanton and lifts her out of the specificity of her trade. The model for Dumas's romance, the beautiful and fragile Marie Duplessis, was still alive and kicking at the time of the novel's publication. Unfortunately, when Verdi finally visited Paris, she had been dead over five months. It is more than possible that Verdi's mistress, Giuseppina Strepponi, had been wined and dined at the Duplessis establishment and had entertained her guests in return. Strepponi was a reigning diva and much sought after for such *soirée musicales.* The singer was a bit of a *traviata* (lost one) herself—being the unwed mother of two bastard children by a wayfaring tenor. She had upgraded her lot by capturing Verdi's fancy, and at the time of their stay in Paris they were living together ex cathedra in a local suburb near Passy, much in the manner of Violetta and Alfredo in Act II of *Traviata.* Verdi must have been acutely sensitive to all the implications of his arrangement with "Peppina," especially of his father-in-law's disapproval, à la Germont. The opera *Stiffelio*, composed in 1850, and revolving around an errant woman, concludes with that adjuration from the New Testament: "He that is without sin among you, let him first cast a stone at her." It is little wonder that Camille was to be transmuted from whore into madonna. In addition, Francesco Maria Piave, *Traviata*'s librettist, was a commonplace versifier and totally out of sync with Dumas's realistic conversational approach. While more willing to trip the Dumas light fantastic of sex, Piave seemed ultimately acquiescent to Verdi's strictures toward *la chose débauchée*, and at least in their version of Camille, such things hardly exist. This bit of catholic uplift from a pair of nonbelievers deserves a more detailed study than these pages can allow.

Piave's idea of postprandial dalliance and sin goes like this:
Enjoy each moment of today, what is done you can't undo.
Forget all else, only today is true.

This is only one of several bland apostrophes to the goddess Aphrodite that besprinkle Acts I and III of the opera. Piave, in all fairness, did make some effort at creating a less buttoned-down atmosphere. He directs Violetta's guests to make a rowdy exit at the end of Act I—possibly to stir up Verdi's juices. The composer's concession to the idea is to repeat the opening well-mannered music, only louder and faster, with a tacked-on coda. The cat and mouse game between these collaborators in such matters of decadence must have had its moments of unintentional hilarity. Imagine the following hypothetical scene: *Piave arrives at Verdi's lodgings with his latest verses. Act I, scene 2, Violetta and Alfredo's duet.*

PIAVE (*reading aloud, after much throat-clearing*):
  Violetta hands Alfredo a red camellia. "Take this—"
  Alfredo: When shall I see you again?
  Violetta: When this camellia changes color.
  Alfredo: And when will it change its color?
  *Violetta:*Oh, between eleven and twelve tomorrow night.
VERDI (*moaning*):   Piave . . . Piave . . .
PIAVE: But Maestro, it's directly from the novel. Marguerite changed from white to red camellias at certain periods of the month. Don't you see how important it is? Why else does she say *"Qual pallor!"* [How pale I am!]? It is not just her lungs, you see. . . .
VERDI: We are not composing music to a medical report. I'm interested in this unfortunate's soul, not her menstrual cycle. Cut it, cut it!

PIAVE: But Maestro, think of the effect! It's a *coup de théâtre*.
Not even Dumas dared repeat it in his play. Just think . . .
VERDI: I *am* thinking, and I say cut it—cut it!
PIAVE (*pleading*): Maestro, *caro* . . .
VERDI: Are you deaf, Piave, or am I losing my mind?

Piave had been equally dunned in shaping Victor Hugo's *Le Roi S'amuse* into *Rigoletto* a year prior to *Traviata*. In both instances, Verdi, while ultimately triumphant, had failed Piave in only one respect—the erotic. *Traviata* is a cut above *Rigoletto* in this regard—but only a cut. Eroticism was simply not part of the Verdi lexicon. His blindness or, better, rectitude in such matters reached its apogee with the première of *La Traviata* at the Teatro la Fenice in Venice (1853), where he permitted an extremely outsized soprano, Fanny Salvini-Donatelli, to create Violetta. The first performance did not so much herald a new masterpiece as represent a cautionary chapter in the weight-watcher's manual. There were other reasons besides the presence of the fat lady militating against initial success. The action of the opera was contemporary and realistic. Nothing like it had been seen in an opera house before. Yet, through the years, productions of the work, by not seeking to re-create spontaneously an equally contemporary frame of reference, would seem to belie this startling fact. These productions, foundering in shopworn tradition, support the theory of those who regard opera as basically unreal—and any approximation of life-like behavior antithetical to its esthetic.

In order to shatter the grip of my own antipathy, I composed a *Traviata* hate list based partly on past productions I had witnessed:

1. Act I: The party has never been a real party. It usually comes off as a polite soiree given by a lady of means; it never helps define the lady or tell how she acquired those means. The opening music, while bristling with the sounds of gaiety, still seems a "fiesta in the piazza" sort of affair. Chalk one down to Verdi.

2. The Baron Douphol is a mere adumbration as compared to his counterpart de Varville in Dumas's play. Completely submerged in the opening ensemble, he hangs around only to support the bass line, for he contributes nothing to the

action. Yet in Act II Violetta returns to him. Since he has
hardly made any impression, his later reappearance seems
fortuitous and a little mechanical, thereby lessening the effectiveness of his role in the drama. Alas, this is also true of
Gastone, and most lamentably of Flora, who nowhere approaches Dumas's parasitic Prudence. Chalk three down to
Piave.

3. The Alfredo-Violetta duet usually seems vintage Nelson
   Eddy & Jeanette MacDonald (hand-and-shoulder mutual-
   clutch time). Everybody just rests, smiles for the camera, and
   sings—the story be damned.

4. What about Violetta's final monologue in Act I—*Sempre libera!* (Always free!)? A show stopper, no doubt! Bravo Verdi!
   But as managed by most sopranos, it seems like a guest appearance in a variety show. Convention, convention, here is
   thy sting!

5. In Act II we find the lovers gamboling about Violetta's country place. There has been no preparation for this turn of
   events. We have left Violetta in a *sempre libera* mood, yet
   here they are, seemingly ensconced for months in their idyl-
   lic paradise. A veritable operatic jump cut!

6. Violetta hastily descends the pit of self-pity and bathos when
   confronted by Germont. Except for the designated outbursts,
   she wallows in self-abuse. Convention, which mistakes such
   goings-on as a means of achieving and sustaining audience
   sympathy, is directly responsible. In most productions Violetta's final scene with Alfredo in this act so maintains this
   stock Victorian mood that everyone but Alfredo sees right
   through Violetta's shining tears. Of course, we can just give
   up on such matters of credibility and logic—it's only opera.

7. The chorus in Act III defies description. They seem to run
   on and off stage at whim. They must obviously listen at
   doors. And, forsaking good wine and supper in mid-act, they
   trample one another to make their breathless musical cue to
   support Piave's dubious poetic license.

8. Alfredo discovers that Violetta's servant, Annina, has just returned from Paris, where she has sold all Violetta's horses,
   carriages, and other possessions to foot the bills of dalliance.
   Alfredo vows to rectify matters—just how, no one exactly

knows. He has obviously been sponging off Violetta all this time and is about to take off for Paris himself. How? On foot? There are no horses left. The vociferous aria and cabaletta that follow suggest direct and positive action will be taken. But it is a ruse. He returns fifteen minutes later with all his resolve and good intentions left offstage. This hardly helps shape up an already wishy-washy leading tenor.

9. There must have been quite an active taxi service out Passy way—for within minutes Annina is again dispatched to Paris with Violetta's compromising note to Douphol. And a duet later, a servant courier gives Alfredo a note from a lady who stopped outside in a coach. These matters of transits and Krazy Kat letter-writing are logically explained by Dumas in his play, but Piave and Verdi would not pause for such niceties (as in 8). Their hysterically telescoped action in this act is pure absurdity.

10. The Baron Douphol had warned Violetta not to speak one word to Alfredo. Yet within seconds she leaves his side and disobeys him. How does the Baron rationalize her absence? Why does he reappear only on schedule?

11. The gypsy-matador sequences are tiresome stuff indeed! The final ensemble in Act III is another major problem. It adheres to an earlier musical style of Verdi's, and its musical convention is difficult to combat dramatically.

The first order of the day in diagraming a production of *Traviata* was to create a believable and continuous inner reality derived from a psychologic restudy of the characters and their motivations. Each moment in the stage action would find its meaning and logic from the resulting interpretation. The goal in terms of the actors' behavior was to trigger spontaneous reactions from the characters—reactions perhaps unforeseen by the text, but illuminating it above and beyond any literal meaning of the words. The orchestra was to have its own independence in supporting and elucidating the action.

For me, all dramatic action is rooted in discovering the extraordinary (the crisis of the stage events) as it occurs within the ordinary (the norm or typical background of the events). Without an active and participating definition of the ordinary (the

day-by-day realities), one cannot measure the impact of the extraordinary. The four acts of *Traviata* were analyzed in this context.

What is the real character of the opening Act I party? Violetta has given hundreds of them, both formal and informal,
but this is to be her last. She herself is at a crisis point. Both
physically and emotionally she is exhausted. The more feverish
she becomes, the greater the need to blunt her sensibilities
through license and frivolity. In that context a formal affair
seems an unlikely prospect and a bore for a lady lighting her
candle at both ends. A party of intimates allows Violetta to let
down her hair and even encourages her worst tendencies. Dumas's novel tells us that the four-letter word was the rule rather
than the exception at these suppers, and Marguerite (Violetta)
topped the off-color merriment with a verbal resilience worthy
of a bargeman. Her guests are accustomed to her seizures and
would be prone to disregard their seriousness. Elements of cal-
lousness and even spite enter the picture, and in that light the
marauding quality of the chorus in Act I is explicable. Alfredo is
a stranger in Violetta's house. In a house full of strangers (that
is, in a more formal setting) his entrance would lose its singular
meaning and impact. Gastone has brought him as to a special
event. Unless the party has thrust and abandon, it does not explain why people wanted to be there in the first place—particularly the footloose men who yearn to make fresh contacts and
break away from the dullness of routine. Another elegant stand-
up party would only emphasize that routine. Any Parisian matron could manage that—and at this stage of her crisis, Violetta
is hard pressed to simulate an earlier social pretense. In Dumas's view she *is* Establishment. No—the party must swing.
This is the ordinary of her life. It must allow Violetta a chance
to rampage, to exercise the brittle, cynical, and even vulgar
charms only great ladies can toss off with impunity. She is courtesan, grande dame, and a child of the provinces all at once. She
relates to each character in the drama accordingly.

Alfredo, when he arrives, is just another man brought pan-
derlike by Gastone to titilate m'lady's fancy. He appears out of
his depth but is sustained by his fascination with Violetta. This
fact does not rub off on the lady—at first. His ardor brooking no

delay, Alfredo will return at the final curtain in Act I to explode her *sempre libera* to bits. This is the accent on the extraordinary event in the first act. It will also lead logically into the second act.*

Act II is the one and only "happy" act of the four. The ordinary is the contentment Alfredo and Violetta have found together in their country retreat. Strangely, the libretto does not ever allow us to see the lovers together in their blissful state. Alfredo reports it in his *"De miei bollenti spiriti,"* (my ebullient spirits) and Violetta only echoes it, *"era felice troppo,"* (we were too happy) but it is a dying fall. Germont's appearance quickly dashes all spirits—*bollenti* or otherwise—and in no time a barely established love affair is over. Therefore every opportunity must be found to create the norm and to sustain it even as the shadows lengthen. Violetta must battle with Germont for her happiness. And even if she must finally simulate it with Alfredo, it is based on an established truth and thus doubly poignant. Alfredo would accept Violetta's protestations and vagaries as part of their badinage, on this particular summer day, and accordingly view her *"Addio"* with some equanimity. How much greater the shock of her actual desertion then! The second act will therefore be called game: joy and fulfillment is its ordinary; the extraordinary, Violetta relinquishing this fulfillment. Her death begins at this point. Therefore time is of the essence. The curtain will rise immediately and the lovers will be discovered together in play. The mood will be extended into the ensuing action as vividly and logically as possible.

The dominating problem of Act III is how to make the action of the chorus convincing or even believable, and in the concluding ensemble how to define what is happening within it in order to achieve some sort of climax. This, the most old-fashioned of the four acts, is without doubt the most difficult to stage properly. The new setting must allow the chorus to "live" continuously during all the events of the scene, in order to add verisimilitude to the lovers' confrontation and prevent its almost whimsical rushing in and out. Tradition leaves Violetta

---

* Piave seemed reluctant to follow Dumas here, perhaps afraid of an anticlimax after such a brilliant aria.

and Alfredo alone on a bare stage for their encounter. Alfredo's
"Or tutti a me" (Attention everyone) is a signal for the chorus to
drop their hors d'oeuvre, wipe their chins, and be in position
five bars after Alfredo's call. What *follie*! Some attention must
also be paid to the Baron's admonition of a few pages earlier.
"You are not to say one word to him," he warns Violetta. It
implies that he now holds the reins. We must make credible the
means Violetta employs to dupe the Baron and manage her assignation with Alfredo. It seems both natural and logical that
the supper be served onstage, and that the quarrel take place for
all to see. In fact, an extra measure of tension is thereby created,
for there is nothing more terrible than washing one's linen in
public. The area for dining should even extend offstage, where
Flora (the hostess) may have placed the Baron and Violetta at
her table. The setting will be outdoors, and Flora will accompany Violetta on her secret rendezvous with Alfredo. Two ladies leaving the table together would hardly arouse the Baron's
suspicions. Flora, now placed in an embarrassing position between the lovers, will try both to calm them and keep the rest of
the party going. The ordinary, therefore, will be a masked *"fete
gâlant"*—it will contrast nicely with Violetta's bash. The guests
in the background will gradually become aware of the quarrel
taking place in their midst, and only the few who had retired
offstage (notably the Baron) need make a rush for that five-bar
cue—and then with some special effect. The extraordinary
event is Alfredo's denunciation of Violetta, merging the private
and public events.

Act IV should find Violetta's bedroom stripped of all valu-
ables. The pictures have been sold; only the outlines of their
frames remain. Illness should permeate every top note. The ordinary is accented by Germont's letter—much crumpled, read
and reread day after day. The extraordinary is Alfredo's return.

PREPRODUCTION

I was presented at my first production meeting with a fait
accompli. Already contracted for *Traviata* were the two leading
singers, the conductor, and a set and costume designer—a clean

sweep! Howard Bay and Patton Campbell respectively had been signed to design the sets and costumes with another director before I entered the picture. The defection of that director brought Bay, Campbell, and me together in a not unpleasant, shotgun marriage. Halfway through our preparations a painful back injury forced Bay to withdraw from the project, and a colleague, Robert Fletcher, was brought in to redesign the production.

Mr. Fletcher entered the fray at the eleventh hour, and thanks to his resourcefulness completed his designs at the stroke of twelve. The period chosen was Dumas's own time (1880s). I had made the following stipulations to the designer: the first-act living room was to allow plenty of leg room for the rowdy festivities, but a corner was to be created as a private area where the more intimate moments would be played out. A fireplace was to be kept burning to warm Violetta in her moments of illness and reverie. The fire would be a recurring motif, synonymous with the pangs of love that stave off the chill of death. Act II was to take place indoors, contrary to convention. It would be the living room of a country place outside Paris, very provincial, the kind of situation Violetta might have been born into. It would be the end of summer, a sudden chill in the air, falling leaves, a stove burning all day. At the moment of crisis with Germont, Violetta is to shut the French windows and seek warmth from the stove. The falling leaves would slowly lose their decorative value and become the falling away of her own life.

The third act would again reverse conventional practice and be set outdoors in the pavilion of Flora's summer home. The occasion: a *fête galant* around a Turkish motif, with a moon foolishly looking down on the lacquered proceedings. The final act would be the most intimate, all ashen gray. I asked that the room be stripped of furniture except essentials, and the outline of long-gone frames be visible on the walls.

As conceived, Violetta had to be devilishly well-acted as well as well-sung. Verdi had the good fortune to see and hear in his lifetime a consummate rendering of that role in the person of Maria Piccolomini. According to many critics of the time, her performance was shocking in its explicitness—a far cry indeed from the archetype in vogue by the turn of the century. Verdi adored Piccolomini, as I'm sure he would have adored her heir, Patricia Brooks. Miss Brooks is our Piccolomini, a true singing actress. With Patricia came total sympathy, involvement, and compatability with the role. Patricia was particularly remarkable in making dialogue of the notes. She had been trained as an actress and was skilled at isolating Violetta's various problems, such as her illness and private loneliness, developing them separately and then melding them to the music. Alfredo was to be Placido Domingo, the outstanding young tenor then on the threshold of an international career. Our conductor was the late Franco Patané. My first encounter with him was preceded by a warning from one of my colleagues: "Watch out. He never looks at the stage when in the pit." Initial preparation with the principals took place without his presence, but once he joined us, it was touch and go. The very first rehearsal with Patané proved a complete fiasco. Things were merely rocky until the first *lunga pausa* before *"Un di felice"* (One happy day) in Act I. By the time we had arrived at Violetta's *"È strano"* I was in the conductorial soup. Toward the end of Act I, my direction to Patricia was to pause for almost sixty seconds while she recovered from the ardors of the party. Only then was she to speak the words *"È strano"* (It's strange). Such things simply were not done, I was admonished. By the third rehearsal, I had been summoned to Rudel's office six times. A routine developed between us: "Well, what are you doing now?" Rudel would ask cheerfully even before I sat down.

Patané, although a most able musician, was simply unprepared for this approach to such an established repertory piece. Rudel became our mediator.

The chorus, bleary-eyed with fatigue after four new productions, at first hardly responded—they seemed listless and unwilling to accept the premise of the opening party as a debauch. One girl, dressed in male clothing, refused to behave in "butch" fashion on the ground that "George Sand was not a Lesbian. I looked it up!" Only after I had pulled the historical rug from under her and reassured her she was not playing George Sand was she willing to dig in her spurs.

The dress rehearsal of the opera was a nightmare. In addition to an invited audience, all the staff members of the City Opera were present in the bullpen. There was as much activity out in the auditorium as there was on the stage. Rudel and I went around during the opening scene throwing choristers into licentious positions. The conductor seemed flushed and suspicious. Pat was not singing at all. She was afraid he might stop her, as he had during rehearsals, frustrating her efforts to shape the musical line into real and specific emotional values. *No*, Patané insisted, she must *not* make laughter out of *"Ah, se ciò è ver, fuggitemi,"* (Leave me if this is so) and at the end of the first half of *Sempre libera, gioir* was not *martir*—the desperate connotation we had given the word "Joy." Every pause was an excuse for mayhem in the bullpen. Patricia was on the verge of tears. I pulled her aside and made her promise that on opening night she would do everything upon which we had agreed. The conductor would have to go along. I would assume all responsibility for falling objects. I had been forced to this deceit in a last-ditch effort to salvage the production as I had conceived it. The staff seemed incredulous of the proceedings. Alfredo's re-entry at the end of Act I was either in or out, according to the last authority consulted in the lobby. A pantomime I had devised during the fourth-act prelude, describing a creditor's removal of Violetta's last personal effects, was struck on the spot. This was the conductor's moment of glory. I was told, "Let Corsaro foul up everywhere else." Everyone complained when Alfredo held Violetta in his arms during *"Parigi, o cara."* How could he sustain it? Placido just kept singing, and the staff was still arguing long after the moment had passed. Dominic Cossa, who sang the elder Germont so beautifully, kept manipulating his padding every which way. At one point he looked more like Rigoletto than Germont.

On opening night things continued in this antic vein. A cat Gastone had carried to the opening party had survived the rigors of dress rehearsal, only to be attacked by first-night jitters: she puked over Gastone's beautiful costume minutes before the rise of the curtain. Up it went and out went Gastone, sans cat and in smelly disarray. The chorus seemed transformed. They were fantastic. Each member onstage was a person. I was seated next to Rudel in the observer's booth when we approached Violetta's pause before "*È strano!*" "What is Brooks doing?" he whispered harshly to me; "She can't pause that long—she'll ruin everything." The audience remained absolutely still. I could see Patané looking at the floor of the pit in resigned despair. Even from the back I could tell how flushed he was. Still the audience was deeply attentive. Rudel suddenly smiled. "A very interesting idea—yes, very interesting. . . ."

"*È strano!—È strano!*" Pat murmured. . . .

WORKING WITH THE SINGING-ACTOR

In my initial meeting with Patricia Brooks I offered the following picture of Violetta's character as a guide.

Violetta is a rebel who is too busy living to die. She is a *jeune fille de province* and, despite her sheen, will always remain one. She is basically religious, very superstitious, and filled with the dread of damnation. Alfredo is also a middle-class boy. What a contrast he makes to the city slickers! Violetta, recognizing his type, abuses him at first for the traits they mutually share. She is demanding but easily put off. She is an innocent voluptuary who has acquired her section of Paris only to throw it back in its face. Despite her licentious dalliances, she is remarkably unsullied. She has the ultimate courage to give herself to Alfredo totally, unselfishly, in contradistinction to her established code, which is only an exaggeration of the existing mores of her time. And within her frail body she eventually accepts, even wills, the consequences of her action.

As far as Domingo's Alfredo is concerned, Domingo preferred to "discover" the character as we went along. The first crucial revelation occurred at our third rehearsal together, which we devoted to the opening of the second act. At his rehearsal he sang the aria *"De' miei bollenti spiriti"* with great ardor, but then looked at me with a puzzled expression as he concluded.

P.D. *(in his delightfully fractured English that has since become unfractured):*   How you believe, Frank?

F.C.:   Almost!

P.D.:   How do you mean almost?

F.C.: I don't know what you're really trying to say.

P.D.: Well . . . what the words say—that Alfredo loves Violetta very much . . . and that he has never been so happy as at this moment.

F.C.: That's what the words say, all right.

P.D.: But you don't believe.

F.C.: Superficially I do.

P.D.: Yes, it is superficial. Oh, Frank, the trouble is . . . look at my score this moment. Here in the back. This is a list of all the times, the dates, and places I have done Alfredo. You see, over twenty-six times, in this country, Europe—all over. Each time I do my best. But I don't no longer know what to do with this char-acter. Twenty-six times, and maybe eight times I sing it to my satisfaction. The other times—all stupid! Alfredo seems so easy to play—but he is a difficult personage. He can be such . . . how do you say—a sap? Like this second act, I have tried everything. Directors say, just come in and sing, it will be sufficient. If I am still unhappy, they say, try coming in with a rifle, like the directions in the score say. I try that, but that doesn't help explain my *bollenti spiriti.* I don't even think Alfredo is a good shot. That doesn't help my spiriti either. I'm afraid I'm most tired of him, with or without a gun.

F.C.: Well, instead of a gun, you'll come in with a batch of posies. . . .

P.D.: Posies? What are posies?

F.C.: Flowers from the fields.

P.D.: Ah, yes, and then—?

F.C.: You and Violetta have been playing hide-and-seek. Let's begin the act by having you hide here in the room, while we see Violetta running past the French windows on the way toward the garden. Watch her trying to find you and then begin the recitative.

P.D.: If it will be that playful—I must sing it that way—not *alla tenore!*

F.C.: Exactly on target.

P.D.: And the flowers—?

F.C.: As you sing, put them in this little vase on the table behind the chaise.

P.D.: At what point in the music?

F.C.: You find it for yourself.

P.D.: Okay. Roll them, like they say. (*Placido executes the scheme. After watching Violetta disappear into the garden, he turns back into the room and starts to sing. He suddenly stops.*)

F.C.: What's the matter? You almost seem shocked!

P.D.: I am. Usually I place my gun down to face the public . . .

F.C.: And now?

P.D.: Now I turn from the game to face myself—not the public. (*He smiles.*) Okay, again! (*He repeats the action, and this time when he turns back into the room he begins to sing quietly, simply content to be happy with his own being. At the words "Ed or contento" (Now that I feel contented . . .) Placido finds the spot to place the flowers in the vase. This he does slowly, lovingly. Unwittingly he then heads for direct center to finish the recitative.*)

Frank . . . Frank . . . I feel stupid again. After such a good beginning . . .

F.C.: Just keep away from center stage at all costs. When you head that way, you automatically brace yourself and go into the tenor's fifth position.

P.D.: Don't tell me, I know—with my left foot off the ground. . . .

F.C.: Why do all you fellows do that? You all do it!

P.D.: It's the tension, and trying to be noble—like a leading man should look in the opera.

F.C.: But what's so noble about a dangling left foot?

P.D.: I don't know . . . just happens . . . *Misericordia!* [Have mercy.]

F.C.: Okay. But just watch that foot there. And after you place the flowers down—take a look around the room. Do you like being here?

P.D.: In the rehearsal?

F.C.: When you say that word *"rinasce"* [reborn], what or where does it take you in your imagination?

P.D.: Nowhere while I'm singing.

F.C.: Try thinking of a happy place you know—while you're singing . . .

P.D.: Without the music I can think of many places. . . .

F.C.: All right—pick one! Now!

P.D.: There is a spot in Mehico—but how can that really help? In the opera we are in Passy—a country house in France.

F.C.: All places where people are happy are related.

P.D.: That is true. Yes, we try! (*His tone becomes melting with this Mexican memory. He even takes more time and care with the phrasing. He is still standing behind the couch—miles from the vortex of center stage.*) Frank, I am feeling most excited! Now, what do I do with this *maledetto* [cursed] *bollenti spiriti?*

F.C.: Regarding Violetta, you mean? Well . . . What time is it?

P.D.: It is late afternoon. Violetta will find me—

F.C.: *and then* . . .

P.D.: Well . . . we will go and make love. Later, some wine and dinner—not out in the garden . . . it will be too chilly there for her. In her room. We will sit by her fire, and then I will read to her . . . from *Manon Lescaut*—you like the idea? And then make love again.

F.C.: Well, isn't that what your *bollenti spiriti* is all about? Make it the anticipation for the lovely evening to come. It certainly would help explain the "*bollenti*" part—after all, outside it's really a calm sunshiny day . . .

P.D.: *Bollenti*—Boiling, of course! If I start thinking these thoughts, where will I go with such a thing in my head?

F.C.: The more excited you become . . . well, let's put it this way . . . when you can't stand it any longer, just stretch out on the chaise full length, lean back, and let her rip.

P.D.: Let her what?

F.C.: Just sing out.

P.D.: What about the high B flat?

F.C.: You should have absolutely no difficulty in that position. You're just not used to doing it that way. You'll get used to it.

(*Placido tries, but interruptions have deflected his concentration.*)

F.C.: I think you need a little encouragement from the outside. Pat?

P.B.: I'm here! I'm here!

F.C.: We need you to help Placido focus his *spiriti*. (*I take her out of Placido's hearing and instruct her accordingly.*) Dur-

ing the two orchestral measures preceding Alfredo's aria, I
want you to call his name from offstage. Do it playfully and
invitingly.

*Pat does it precisely and beautifully. At the sound of her
voice, Placido's eyes light up. He moves to the doors,
shuts them quietly so that she cannot yet find him. He
then leans against them and begins his aria. It is all there
in a nutshell. Placido concludes his song.*

P.D.: *(Still seated on the couch, hugging one of Violetta's pillows as if it were the lady herself):* You know, Frank—this
Alfredo is becoming a most interesting fellow. I thought he
was when I first read the novel of Dumas fils, but Piave had
made such a weakling of him, I thought him hopeless . . . a
hopeless hero with beautiful music! Now, what do we do
with Annina who is coming in? *(Placido is rubbing his
hands together with positive glee.)*

A more detailed description of the actual production can be
found in the section of this book devoted to The Finished Productions of *La Traviata, Madama Butterfly,* and *Faust.*

6

Madama
Butterfly

PREPRODUCTION

Take a story by a Philadelphia lawyer, one John Luther Long;
generously sprinkle ingredients from Pierre Loti's novel *Madame Chrysanthème*, add the heavy batter of David Belasco,
theatrical *entrepreneur singulier;* pass on to Luigi Illica and
Giuseppe Giacosa, Italian playwrights, for the mixing; place
into Puccini's fiery furnace—and you have an international
bouillabaisse to gourmandize any gourmand. Perhaps there exists an equally exotic mixture of herbs and spices in operatic
lore, but I doubt if any can match this Puccini dish. Served piping hot on the night of February 17, 1904, at La Scala in Milan,
the immediate result of all this expertise was a painful and prolonged indigestion. Its failure to please traumatized an already
neurasthenic Puccini and marked the beginning of the break
between him and his librettists, Illica and Giacosa (who had
contributed mightily to the success of *Manon Lescaut, La
Bohème,* and *Tosca*). It further helped create the void of six
years between its première and that of his next opera, *La Fanciulla del West* (The Girl of the Golden West). It was also to
mark a musical transition for the forty-two-year-old composer.
The hints of Debussy and the school of impressionist painters
discernible in *Butterfly* were to broaden and deeply color the
landscape of *La Fanciulla* and *Il Trittico.*

After its première *Butterfly* was revised and in three months
was successfully mounted in Brescia. Puccini was to continue

his revisions for the next four years, and in fact was to lavish
more time and attention on this opera than on any other before
or after its composition. The opera became at once a favorite
child. He even pasted a picture of a mother and child in his
autographed score. The version now extant represents the con-
clusions he had reached by 1907. And, sans picture of mother-
and-child but still bearing discrepancies from the original edition, it has become one of the most popular operas of all time.

Now, alack, fifty years later, poor *Butterfly* appeared exhausted from her travels. She seemed ready to be wrapped in
tissue paper and locked away in Aunt Jessie's china closet in
Hackensack, New Jersey.

Several weeks after I was announced as director for the
forthcoming "new" production in the fall of 1966 I received an
intriguing phone call from Faubion Bowers. If anyone could ad-
vise me on *les choses japonaises*, it would be Faubion, who had
spent years in Japan during the Occupation as General Mac-
Arthur's cultural attaché. Agreeing that another traditional *Butterfly* would be a gross anomaly, Faubion insisted that I conceive the production in the light of the atom bomb dropped on
Nagasaki, the setting of the opera. In view of current history,
nothing else would be tenable, he argued persuasively. It
seemed a logical conclusion, and I even wondered why it
hadn't been done before. I had recently heard of an *Aïda* set
amid the war between the Israelis and the Arabs, complete with
Hatikvah finale. So why not *Butterfly* and the bomb? I hesitated
to employ a literal modernization, as I suspected that, once past
its novelty value, the music would fight back and cause an inevitable stalemate. Yes, I wanted to scrub the baby clean, but I
feared throwing her out with the bath water. A recently observed experiment had proved this point conclusively. A group
of singing-actors had performed the first act of *Traviata* at the
Actors Studio in New York City. Among other things, the characters had frugged to Verdi, and at the finale they piled pyramid
high on a motorcycle that had miraculously managed to get into
Violetta's apartment. The approach aroused interest in the work
of the actors and director, but defeated Verdi. Here was modernization full of ideas but without historical perspective. It was
as incompatible with the composer's purpose as the destruction

of Hiroshima would have been to Puccini. No, the bomb must
go. Yet Faubion's call echoed in my head.

In researching the opera I discovered that Puccini kept re-
ferring to Cio-Cio-San as his "tragic heroine." Butterfly is at the
head of the gallery of Puccini heroines for whom the fortunes of
love were disastrous. If one did love a man, she had to be punished. This was Puccini's archetype. Earlier in his career, he
had attempted a Carmen-like heroine in *Edgar*, his second opera. The character of the rapacious Tigrana was too much
against the grain and, coupled with a feeble libretto by Ferdi-
nando Fontana, failed to fire his imagination. *Edgar*, in fact, remains the only total flop in Puccini's oeuvre.

The original plan for *Butterfly* included a second act that
was to take place at the American Consulate. Puccini had urged
his librettists to lay particular stress on the East-West conflict
and to find every means possible to dramatize the disparate values of the two cultures. Eventually this idea was discarded as
the focus sharpened on Cio-Cio-San, who became the fulcrum
for this conflict. Even her musical sound was taking on a new
timbre. Yes, it suggested the delicacy of a china doll, but the
doll's *tessitura* was a cruel and demanding one, distinctly at
odds with the tradition of "diminutiveness" associated with her.
Puccini had obviously sensed this paradox, for pursuant to the
La Scala première (in which Rosina Storchio, a lyric soprano,
had created the role), *Butterfly* was entrusted at its Brescia revival to one Salomea Krusceniski, a dramatic soprano. Puccini
was to favor the latter approach in future productions. The
spinto emphasis lent a darker, more mature element to the role.
This dimension of majesty added credence toward Butterfly's
elevation into the tragic mold.

Psychologically, the most profound experience in the opera
is Butterfly's abandonment by Lieutenant Pinkerton. It is all the
more traumatic when one considers that her own father, forced
to commit hara-kiri, had abandoned her as a child. Pinkerton's
action has awakened the earlier trauma. Her final act of suicide
dramatizes her deep, inexpressible rage at these events. The
means employed for this self-punishment repeat her father's
action.

It is curious to recall that when Puccini was five years old

his own father had died, leaving a pregnant wife in desperate
financial straits and six mouths to feed. The scars from this period may have plagued him throughout his life and in part may
have been responsible for the long depressions and fits of melancholy that recurred until his death in 1924. Although attempts
to parallel artistic creation with the course of an artist's life
yield dubious rewards, there is a special bond between Puccini
and this particular creation of his that justifies such conjecture.

The specter of "abandonment" is presaged in the very first
scene of the opera. Intended or not, the well-laid plans of our
youthful anti-hero and acceptance by his Polonius-like American Consul present a pejorative view of Americans in foreign
parts. *"La comperai per nove cento novante nove anni . . . ,"*
sings Pinkerton. (Roughly, "The girl, Butterfly, is contracted to
me for 999 years with options to cancel.") "After all, we're in
Japan, where an expert can exploit his talents profitably," rein-
forces the Consul. Offering the older man a drink, Pinkerton
goes on to toast his American bride-to-be. This is one of Puccini's most devilish and playful ironies, particularly as the toast
overlaps the first notes of Butterfly's approach. In other words,
purchased for the price of wampum, she is a piece of Oriental
goods whose main function is to lie down and enjoy it.

I had read how Richard Strauss advised some conductor of
Salome to proceed as if he were conducting an operetta with an
unhappy ending. This light-textured approach could only make
an already sinister work more so. I began to regard Puccini's
ravishing score in that light.

Once past the picture-postcard entrance, Cio-Cio-San begins
to make herself seriously felt: *"Ieri son salite. . . ."* ("Yesterday,
I secretly went to the American Mission and asked to be con-
verted to Christianity so that I might start my life with you in
the proper manner. Neither my uncle nor my relatives know
about this, but, if forced to, I'm prepared to renounce everyone
and everything to stay with you.")

All sentimental connotations of the conversion aside, this
Butterfly hardly seems prepared to be added to anyone's collection. In her audacity she even appears a bit of a maverick off the
painted screen. When she is excommunicated by her Buddhist
uncle and deserted by her people, she reacts as any fifteen-year-
old might—or at least used to. How is she to bridge the gap of

her ostracism? How will she live as Pinkerton's wife? Will she retain her Japanese habits? Perhaps so, but they may be painful reminders of the past. As there seems little hope or need on her part for reconciliation with her people, the only future is in absorbing and being absorbed in her husband's way of life as an American wife. Everything in Act II indicates that she has fully accepted this fact.

Thumbing through an illustrated history of Japan, I came upon a charming and touching old print. It showed a Japanese woman at the turn of the century seated at an American sewing machine, stitching up the seams of an American dress. My first thought was that the dress belonged to an American customer. Why should that be? Get thee behind me, cliché, I muttered. Why shouldn't the dress belong to the Japanese woman herself? Imagine the minor revolution she would stir up, walking along the streets of Nagasaki! What a world of frustration and aspiration that gesture would imply! I knew I had found the extraordinary for my Butterfly. Seeing her in my mind's eye dressed in that American dress, facing the Consul, Sharpless, who is smoking one of Butterfly's three-year-old cigarettes, I began to wonder if I was not merely substituting one paper-doll cutout for another. Yet there she sat on her Victorian chair, facing the possibility of Pinkerton's desertion and giving herself alternatives in that eventuality: to return to her former life as a geisha—or to die. They seemed appropriate romantic gestures, but in not considering their utter seriousness I was denying her lifelikeness and condemning her back to the shelf.

Two world wars had left their mark since *Butterfly* first saw the light of day. In the wake of Japan's ignominious defeat in World War II we have witnessed the struggle of minorities to assert their identities and claim their share of the world's riches. Butterfly could claim no less. I had found for myself the necessary "extension" to make *Madama Butterfly* an experience for today. Cio-Cio-San's concern with becoming an American would define the East-West struggle that Puccini had seemingly lost in the struggle of revision. The problem of identity, so exacerbated in postwar societies, would be our main concern. It would dictate every detail of the stage action. And it would be accomplished within the compass of the score the composer had finally arrived at—with not a word or a note changed.

The East-West conflict is thus at the heart of Cio-Cio-San's identity crisis. This premise must be established immediately: To the Japanese, America means money. Goro and Pinkerton haggle over the price of the house for the new bride. The buying and selling of Japanese female flesh is being transacted all over the island. Pinkerton will be accompanied by three other naval officers who bargain with Goro for several of Cio-Cio-San's geisha friends. In fact, money is to be made everywhere, the place is crawling with foreign devils. It is apparent that the Japanese commissioner performing the marriage ceremony has only just concluded the same amenities for a British officer. The flag draping his chest will be reversed by Goro in mid-sentence to the Stars and Stripes, befitting the national anthem being played. Goro, the Commissioner, and the Registrar disport themselves in an uneasy blend of Eastern and Western dress. After all, they must go where the money dictates. Several other pantomime characters should be introduced at the wedding to lay the groundwork for the Americanization of Cio-Cio-San. Two young American ladies will accompany the Captain of the *Abraham Lincoln* (Pinkerton's ship). They will appear at the wedding party, a combination slumming expedition and courtesy call. The women will be dressed in the Western style of the period (the early 1900s). Butterfly will be fascinated with their appearance, and so the model for her own future dress established. To the wonder and confusion of the natives, rice is to be thrown by the Americans at the conclusion of the ceremony. A symbol of survival for one culture is a traditional but wasteful gesture by the other. All the well-wishings by the Commissioner and Registrar must be punctuated by the doling out of dollars by Pinkerton.

At the conclusion of the first-act love duet, Pinkerton will take the flower garland left by a geisha on the porch post as a symbol of happiness and transform it into a bridal bouquet. He places it in Butterfly's astonished hands and proceeds to carry her over the threshold, according to American tradition.

In the second act Butterfly will wear American dress. She will have styled her hair in American fashion, and her new garb will be accented by a brooch around her neck to suit the fashion. Some three years and much practice have modified Butterfly's geisha walk. Victorian furniture has replaced Japanese, and the tokonoma (a small partitioned area reserved for sacred objects) will become an American shrine. From the Japanese point of view such a conversion amounts to desecration. In the tokonoma we will clearly see the wedding photo surrounded by the American flag and a crucifix. Suzuki will retain her Japanese style in the household, which for the older woman becomes an armed camp. Cio-Cio-San's aspirations have created a schism between herself and her old servant that only the deep undercurrent of their love has prevented from becoming an open rift. The question of the use of pillows or chairs for their guests becomes one of the ways in which their conflict is dramatized.

The little son, Trouble, will be dressed as an American boy might be. In most productions Trouble, although three years old, is treated like an outsized Armour's Star Ham, trundled out of one pair of arms into another and expeditiously rushed offstage to avoid being trampled by the soprano's B flats. In the new version, Trouble will move about, perform, and participate in several significant actions; he will have an independent existence as a character.

One of the crucial moments in our East-West conflict will occur just before the vigil in Act II. Butterfly asks Suzuki to dress her as she was on her wedding day. She will be wearing her American dress and, as she begins to slip on her wedding kimono, she pauses, realizing her folly, and brushes the garment aside. Looking at Suzuki, she gestures at her modern clothes. She will appear *"cosi"* (this way), and with that single word she dashes Suzuki's hopes while imagining Pinkerton's delight and surprise as he beholds his "American" wife. Cio-Cio-San had further anticipated this reunion by arranging to have her son dressed in a navy officer's formal white uniform duplicating Pinkerton's own. In the final act the boy's appearance in white serves as a striking contrast to his father's dark blue.

When Cio-Cio-San, still dressed in American clothes, is confronted by the "real" American wife in the final scenes, she unconsciously reverts to Japanese behavior. From this point on she regresses, step by step, inevitably leading to her ritual suicide.

After many trials and errors, Francesca Roberto was chosen among several contending sopranos to sing the première performance. Placido Domingo was Lt. Pinkerton, and our conductor was again Franco Patané. The success of *Traviata* had done much to allay his doubts and even rally his interest in the "new" approach to the classics. It was a satisfying and touching sight to behold this hitherto hard taskmaster unbending and participating in evolving the new production. Throughout the *Butterfly* rehearsals we were *d'accordo*. This was to be our last collaboration. Patané was killed in an automobile crash in his native Italy during the late spring of 1968. In his own lifetime he was a conductor much underrated except by his co-workers, who recognized the first-class musician and devoted artist he really was. I shall miss the man himself as much as the poetic transparency of his intimately scaled *Traviata* and the tensile strength and melancholy of his *Butterfly*.

Francesca Roberto had sung countless Butterflys and was on the verge of cashing in her chips at the thought of still another interpretation. The unorthodox approach gave her new hope—Francesca has become one of *the* Butterflys of our time. Domingo was comfortable from the first—inventive, full of high spirits, and singing like an angel. Such a teddy bear of a bastard had never been seen in Nagasaki before. The chorus this time was prepared for every eventuality. I had to prevent many of them from improvising beyond the call of duty. As always, time with an operatic chorus is expensive and in their presence one works under the gun constantly. This time their enthusiasm and initiative were warming and encouraging, and a complex bit of staging was turned into a holiday.

The setting for *Madama Butterfly* must suggest a picture postcard gone wrong. It must make an absurd impact against the disaster it encloses. Lloyd Evans and I devised the two sets for the production. The first act emphasizes the garden of the house purchased by Pinkerton. A large bridge dominates the background, forming a connection between Nagasaki and the hilly area on its outskirts. A small section of the house itself is visible. The second and third acts occur indoors; the garden surrounding the house is visible on all sides. Its several statues of

demon gods strewn about will suggest an element of fore-
boding.

Contrary to most *Butterfly* first acts, ours was to be in per-
petual motion, a serpent winding and unwinding, restless, dangerous, and coming to rest at the love duet. Our dress rehearsal
took place during a union strike. All the props and Victorian
furniture for Butterfly's American home were unavailable. Further, Cio-Cio-San's American wig and dress were also missing.
Our outsized efforts to lengthen and shorten her eyebrows were
the only means we had of gauging if the transformation would
work. We were in a mild state of despair, since we would be
forced to open completely unsure if the Americanization would
prove credible. The strike was literally settled in mid-rehearsal.
Trucks rushed to the theater. Furniture, hand props, the new
dress—everything was unloaded and scrambled onto the stage.
While Francesca sang, we practically stripped her and poured
her into the new costume—in full view of the invited audience
who shrieked their approval. I distinctly heard a voice shout,
"Keep it in!" Ten minutes before the end of Act II, the furniture was being set in place, singers dodging the stagehands as
they maintained their beat.

In the original La Scala première, the opera had been performed in two acts; the second, in two parts. Subsequently Puccini revised the work into three acts by removing seven measures
that had connected the two parts of act two. We attempted to return the work to its original two-act form by reinstating that
seven-bar bridge, thus repeating the original faux pas. I had devised all sorts of action for Butterfly as she awaited her man,
but my inventions clearly indicated how interminable the La
Scala first night must have been. No wonder the last act had no
effect. Another idea of re-creating a Belasco trick had also fallen
by the wayside. During the vigil in the first staged production
of the play version, Belasco had wafted perfume or incense out
into the house to dramatize the flower-festooned abode, while a
small orchestra of samisens played behind the scene during the
eight-minute change. Air conditioning at the State Theater had
kiboshed that lovely notion.

Fortunately we were able to rework the second act after the
complete run-through. Time, besides the union, had played fair

for once, and we could approach our opening with a greater sense of stability.

The opening-night reviews were good but somehow disappointing. Several major critics had not shown up, possibly unable to face the rigors of still another *Butterfly*. It took two seasons for most of them to finally review it. I still consider *Butterfly* a favorite among my productions, and it has been gratifying to see this opinion corroborated by audiences and critics alike with each recurring season. In a recent telecast film version directed by Jean Pierre Ponnelle it was interesting to observe how many of the ideas stressed here were further developed to make an even more fervent case for opera as drama—a proposition that seems to be spearheaded by the stage director's work in this branch of the musical arts.

WORKING WITH THE SINGING-ACTOR

The day before starting rehearsals I pinpointed Cio-Cio-San's character as a guiding principle for the direction of the opera. The memo to myself ran thus:

First we must wash away all those tears . . . for at the slightest provocation every stage-Butterfly in captivity bawls. To develop her "extension" she must be made of firmer stuff. So, emerging from our cocoon is a species with steel-tipped wings. As a geisha of fifteen she is already resilient and resourceful, wise beyond her tender years and conversant in the ways of men. The child in her still lurks, with mischief always tinging her sudden bursts of affection and jealousy. Her aristocratic background, though now a thing of the past, has left its imprint in her unshakable pride and dignity, even though she is rejected by her own people. She is indeed her father's daughter and, like him, of a rebellious yet idealistic nature, continually in search of an object of faith and love. As in her father's case,* so in the daughter's; the object of the search proves unworthy of devotion. Curiously, however, her "Americanization" in some way represents an elevation back to her former state as the

* Historically his championing of a rebel cause that failed forced a royal decree to be issued against him, thus his hara-kiri.

daughter of a mighty lord, for it sets her apart and above her present fallen condition and makes her an aristocrat again. She can be vain and foolish and even snobbish; but pressed to the wall she can become a tiger.

At eighteen she is a woman and a devoted mother suffering from great loneliness and sustained only by her dream of a future with Pinkerton. Both these factors unfortunately blind her to the simple facts of life. She has created an imagined, if rarefied, climate for herself, and thus her world hovers over an abyss. During her long vigil she is not unlike a novice in a convent awaiting the vows that will never be bestowed upon her. In a deep sense her rejection is a fall from grace.

The first week was devoted to staging the opening act of the opera. The second Monday was reserved for work with Francesca Roberto alone.

F.C.: Before we begin to work, I'd like you to take a look at these magazines dated nineteen-ten. Look specifically at the pages devoted to the popular fashions in women's clothes— American style—of that period.

F.R.: What's that got to do with Butterfly?

F.C.: You're going to pick out a particular dress that hits your fancy—and you'll wear it.

F.R. *(with a squeal)*: An American dress? But how would she know about such things?

F.C.: You've seen them in Nagasaki. You've even picked up copies of American magazines at the Consulate. In fact, you will ask them to help you get a pattern and make the dress yourself.

(Francesca suddenly grasps the idea. She becomes very quiet, for she is apparently moved by the notion. Francesca was not prepared for this Americanization. I had decided to keep it a surprise.)

F.R.: What sort of dress will the Captain's ladies wear at the wedding ceremony in Act One? *(I open the magazine and show her two examples.)* Wouldn't you think Butterfly would want to imitate those? After all, they are Navy wives—or are they?

F.C.: Is that who you think they are?

F.R.: I'm not sure. . . .

F.C.: Make up a story for me about them.

F.R.: I figure one of them—an older woman—would be the Captain's wife. The younger one could be her daughter. Or even a sister, for that matter. No, it's her daughter. This is their first visit to Japan. My God—the younger one could be Kate Pinkerton herself! No, their marriage has already been arranged. Too bad—sounds like a good Corsaro idea gone astray.

F.C.: Nevertheless, the presence of the American guests should be grist for your mill. It should make Butterfly feel proud for landing Pinkerton for herself. In her own mind, she thinks Pinkerton prefers her to the home-grown variety.

F.R.: How would that help with the clothes?

F.C.: You tell me.

F.R.: I would probably want to outdo them on their own turf.

F.C.: Naturally. Why don't we construct a fantasy on that theme—using these pictures.

F.R.: First of all, the hair. I would like to look like this picture here. A different hairdo would be a radical change from the geisha look. Then there's underclothing, shoes, stockings. . . . What about the furniture in the house? Oh, look at this adorable neckband. Might she wear one?

F.C.: It's yours for the asking.

F.R.: It adds a dash of elegance to the look. These models all seem so tall in these pictures. I'm so short, won't I look ridiculous? (*Francesca is short, dark, with a madonna face. Byzantine.*)

F.C.: Not if we choose a style suitable to you.

F.R.: Will I have to move differently in such clothes?

F.C.: By the time of the second act, more than three years have gone by.

F.R.: It took me two weeks to learn how to move and gesture as a geisha. It's not the McCoy, but the few things we selected to do I'll keep working at. Will I have to give it all up by the second act?

F.C.: I doubt that you could relinquish such an ingrained habit so easily. You will adapt it to the new skirts. You will not have given up your walk, for instance—you will learn to

modify it. You are ostensibly still a geisha moving in Western clothes. It will add a special note of piquancy to the
characterization.

F.R.: Look at all these different poses!

F.C.: Take the magazine home and imitate them in front of
your mirror. With each pose construct a story for Butterfly.

*(The next day Francesca comes in with a rehearsal dress
and hair comb that will help suggest the new look. She
also brings some hand props with her to use.)*

F.R.: I've picked my three poses. It was a hard decision. I
tried them all before I made my choice. *(She demonstrates,
explaining as she goes.)* I found this old cameo pin at home.
It belonged to my grandmother. I haven't looked at it for
years. I thought Butterfly . . .

F.C.: No, remember it's Mrs. B. F. Pinkerton now.

F.R.: Mrs. Pinkerton, then.

*(Francesca sees Butterfly in her home in Newport, Rhode
Island. She places one hand near her throat, then spreads
her fingers delicately. One finger plays with the cameo.
One arm leans on an imaginary support, which she tells
me is a fireplace. Her head is erect, her chin tilted slightly
to the side. She has just finished the preparations for a
large dinner party and is waiting for Pinkerton to come
home. It is raining, and a cheery fire burns in the grate. In
Francesca's fantasy, it is their fifth wedding anniversary
and she is pondering what Pinkerton's gift will be this
time. She moves about the room and looks out through an
imaginary window in anticipation of his arrival.*

*Her second pose finds Francesca resting her chin on
two bent fingers on her right hand. Her head is thrust
forward. "Which dress shall I wear for the New Year's
ball?" She laughs silently to herself and thinks she senses
Pinkerton nearby stealing up behind to kiss her neck. She
suddenly breaks away from his imaginary embrace and
waltzes around the room; together they twirl about and
finally fall to the ground. She responds sensually to his
touch.*

*Third pose. She sits in an armchair, her head thrown
back proudly and her arms fully extended on the chair.*

*She is looking at a Christmas tree. Her boy Trouble, now
called Joy, is opening gifts. Pinkerton is helping the boy
unwrap them. Her face expresses her happiness as she
looks from one to the other. She rises and sails majesti-
cally across the room, then rests on all fours on the
ground in front of the boy. She places her chin in her
right palm, two fingers raised along her temples, then her
left hand to her chin in an identical pose, thus framing
her head cherubically.)*

F.C.: Divine. Now let's use these fantasies at the beginning of
the second act. Instead of a fireplace, we have the Oriental
hibachi—but let your mind remember those pictures you
saw. It will be raining to help you with the proper mood.
Work with each pose and sustain it for the duration of your
fantasy. Above all—take your time. *(She does precisely what
I ask, and unconsciously she modifies the geisha walk to
conform to the present demands. The effect is enchanting.)*
Now we'll repeat all that to the music.

F.R.: What about Suzuki?

F.C.: Let her do her own thing, which is always connected
with the old order in Japan. You've lived together a long
time. You're used to each other. When you sing your
lines, do them out of the particular reverie you're involved
with at the time. You are too busy living out the preferred
fantasies of an American wife to give Suzuki too much credence.

*(Francesca adjusts completely. She hardly looks at Su-
zuki, who is intent at her prayers and subsequent mending of the tatami. Instead, Francesca remains by the tokonoma, that honored spot in Japanese households here
filled with American objects—her wedding photo, an
American flag, a crucifix—objects that help her substantiate her dreamy state. By the time Francesca reaches "Un
bel di" (One fine day), the aria seems a natural extension
of her fantasy games. Her equanimity, tempered with a
little snobbishness toward Suzuki and Yamadori, the Japanese suitor for her hand, is finally broken when Sharpless suggests that Pinkerton may never return to her. Her
dreams collapse like a stack of cards.)*

INVENTING A CHARACTER:
THOUGHTS ON CONSUL SHARPLESS

At our first meeting together, the baritone Dominic Cossa seemed to be marking time before beginning the serious business of rehearsing. He protracted the dreaded moment by regaling the accompanist, Domingo, Nico Castel (Goro), and me with samples of his scatological humor. Gradually his one-hundred-percent batting average diminished and after three successive stories failed to wing home, Cossa threw up his hands and declared, "Okay, so we'll rehearse instead." His good humor disappeared and wearied lines of depression suddenly streaked his brow. The cause of this reversal was flatly stated. "Sharpless is a dull tool who sings some beautiful music. All you can do with the joker is look dignified and sing straight out. Yawn! Yawn!" I would encounter such apathy several years later with the tenors singing Don Ottavio in *Don Giovanni,* sopranos tackling Donna Anna in the same opera, and baritones, Silvio in *I Pagliacci*—all "dull tools" dramatically. They are vexing, creatures of uncertain profile, usually found in the "sympathetic friend" category. To merely sing their gorgeous music in conventional characterizations seemed to ring the private death knells to the imaginations of the artists concerned.

I dismissed the other singers for a half hour and dealt only with Cossa's disaffection with the "friendly" Sharpless. I asked Cossa to construct a life history for the character (even the name indicates devitalization). Cossa offered a series of dispirited clichés—homilies derived from the printed text. Without his active interest, I knew I would get a professional but empty-headed performance.

D.C: Do you know something I don't know about him?

F.C.: Tell me what makes you want to tell those jokes of yours all the time?

D.C.: I just have a zest for life—particularly where sex is concerned.

F.C.: What about Sharpless's sex life?

D.C.: I don't think he gets very much.

F.C.: How come?

D.C.: I've never looked at him from that angle because there's no place in the music or text that suggests sex of any kind.

F.C.: What about Pinkerton and Cio-Cio-San? Are there any such liaisons in Sharpless's life?

D.C.: I'm not sure.

F.C.: Quite a business at the time, wouldn't you agree? Arranging a quickie marriage seemed to be as easy as visiting one of our local massage parlors.

D.C.: It's practically legalized prostitution, but exciting—for tenors, that is.

F.C.: Why not for baritones?

D.C.: This baritone is always shaking his head and complaining about it.

F.C.: You mean he just . . .

D.C.: He's a walking case of *"giudizio"* (use caution)—that's his favorite motto in the opera.

F.C.: As the baritone, you obviously envy the tenor's opportunity in this case?

D.C.: The character doesn't, but I certainly would. Ah, what the hell, the baritones never get the girl anyway. . . .

F.C.: Then your resentment extends throughout the repertory?

D.C.: We usually turn out to be the villains. Villains? Take a look at this Pinkerton. He's having a slumming party. He's being careless with another human being for a few bucks. Butterfly is nothing but Kleenex to him. Talk about villains! Yet all the time Sharpless is handing out that stuff about honor. You know—

F.C.: You therefore are of two minds about the matter. Think of yourself as Sharpless in this instance.

D.C.: In that case, I would be saying one thing and thinking another.

F.C.: Very "consulate"-like—wouldn't you agree?

D.C.: But if Sharpless then were really me—I would be fiercely jealous of Pinkerton. I would want to insure part of the "fun" for myself.

F.C.: Yet you said he had no sex in his life!

D.C.: That's when Sharpless is not me. He's probably too scared of sex.

F.C.: How about love?

D.C.: Of that too!

F.C.: Could that help explain why he appears to be a bachelor? Does he like women, do you think?

D.C.: In his own stiff-necked way . . . I would say yes.

F.C.: Could he be homosexual?

D.C.: I don't think so. . . .

F.C.: But you're not sure. . . ?

D.C.: When you come to really think about it . . . I know several guys like him, though not with his class or position. Men from my old neighborhood. Men who stayed close to their mothers all their lives after their fathers died. They took over in a way. Very knockabout types—good-natured but weak inside. Frightened. Never sure of themselves. In a way mamas' boys, without looking like mamas' boys.

F.C.: I can imagine Sharpless fitting in that category.

D.C.: Poor bastards! One was a close friend of mine! I don't know whatever became of him. We lost touch over the years. It happened when I started to sing professionally. It made him not feel good enough whenever we would get together.

F.C.: Maybe Sharpless does not feel good enough?

D.C.: He could . . . couldn't he? Breeding or no breeding!

F.C.: Go on now—let your imagination take over.

D.C.: Okay. He probably had an important affair with a lady when he was younger, and was afraid to go through with it. He was all right in the bed department—but once emotional demands were made on him he found some excuse to break up the affair.

F.C.: What sort of girl was that?

D.C.: Like his mother, I suppose. I guess he couldn't risk the fear of losing her twice.

F.C.: Go on.

D.C.: He must have an occasional fling. A one-time sort of thing.

F.C.: With prostitutes?

D.C.: With prostitutes. Probably in the dark. He drinks a lot—socially and alone. He needs it to help him get to sleep at night.

F.C.: Any other reasons behind the drinking?

D.C.: He needs to numb his feelings. He's a compassionate guy—from a distance. If things get too painful he just walks away. Nobody who knows him guesses this. All day long he's immaculately tailored, wears a smiling face, and stands up for the underdog.

F.C.: Are you implying he's hypocritical?

D.C.: Certainly to himself he is!

F.C.: Ah, there you have invented the character's secret.

D.C.: But how can we begin to show all this?

F.C.: We must attempt to do it somehow. Invent bits of behavior to reveal him.

Cossa's "real" sympathies were now engaged, and together we tried to invent outlets for our mutually guarded "secret." I asked him never to discuss the character with the other singers, better to allow them to discover this new Sharpless for themselves. The revelations in the process of rehearsal were subtle yet telling:

1. The all-too-anxious acceptance and enjoyment of the drinks proferred.
2. Whenever things became too sticky with Butterfly, he would pull out his watch fob (we decided it was his father's one legacy to him) as a reminder of pressing fictive appointments.
3. Contemplating the flower petals on Butterfly's pallet, he picks up a handful absently and is transported back to his own failure at marriage long ago. When he comes out of the reverie, he throws the petals down with a gesture of bitter self-mockery.
4. Sharpless sees himself in Butterfly's son Trouble. The bliss of mother and son is recalled. The cry for the missing father stirs, and adds a special intensity to his resolve to reconcile Butterfly with Pinkerton.

Such were some of the details that helped us sharpen Sharpless—and lift him out of the torpor of the conventional "good guy" into a living, private being with a story to tell—or, better, a story not to tell as, all the while, he preserved the social "face" he was trapped with in his given profession.

7

Faust

The opera *Faust* is associated in my mind with second-rate traveling stock companies of *The Bells, The Count of Monte Cristo,* or *The Octoroon,* which preyed on our towns and hamlets at the turn of the century. Complete with slapdash rickety sets, moth-eaten costumes, and a wind machine, they represented last-ditch efforts of has-been hams to round out derelict careers. These farewell tours, hardly made to catch the conscience of the King, merely roused the ire of the local sheriff, and, two steps ahead of him, yet undaunted, these companies struck out toward the horizon to eventually founder this side of Albuquerque.

Gounod's *Faust* has been making "farewell" appearances for over a quarter of a century. Somehow, some way, it manages to pick itself up and press on. Eventually it may have to be clubbed to death as an act of mercy.

Gounod's opera is a curious anomaly. In part it is a success by default, for where angels feared to tread, there trod Charles François Gounod (1818–1893). Here is a veritable mountain of a theme—celebrated in literature by Goethe and Marlowe, among others—ripe for the musical picking. Yet only Gounod of the sugar palate was to win the day operatically speaking. Meyerbeer, musical *savant extraordinaire* and Gounod's contemporary, had turned hands down on the subject: "Faust is the Ark of the Covenant, a sanctuary not to be approached with profane music," he queezed. Prometheus himself, Ludwig van Beethoven, would not consider writing even incidental music for the play. Arrigo Boito managed a creditable, sometimes inspired *Mefistofele* (1868, revised 1875), but it is rarely performed today, and Ferruccio Busoni's fascinating *Doktor Faustus* (1925) even less so. The greats had avoided the great

challenge—Wagner, Liszt, Schumann, and Berlioz had preferred to comment on the legend in overture and oratorio. Master plays (or novels) rarely seem to travel well; they invariably
lose in the translation. One recalls Verdi's struggles with *King
Lear,* although his own *Otello* and, later, Alban Berg's *Wozzeck*
(1925, after Büchner's play) remain outstanding exceptions to
the rule. With the field wide open, Gounod had picked up the
gauntlet with his finely gloved hand and, as someone said, "A
first-rate opera by a second-rate composer" was born.

Completely devoid of any of the philosophic or emotional
complexities of Goethe, Gounod's *Faust* has held the boards for
over a century. As a sentimental pastiche it has few rivals.
Michel Carré and Jules Barbier, the librettists, had cannily emphasized Marguerite's story. It is much to the point that the opera travels under that lady's name in German-speaking coun-
tries, to distinguish it from its honored source. My only regret in
this whole turn of the wheel is that Alexandre Dumas and
Gioacchino Rossini, who had been proposed as a team for an
operatic *Faust,* had not taken up the challenge. Think what that
might have been—*Il Signor Faustino?*

The New York City Opera was about to celebrate the
twenty-fifth anniversary of its founding, and Gounod's *"dolce
far niente"* had been selected to commemorate the event. Beverly Sills was to sing Marguerite; Norman Treigle, Mephistopheles; and Michael Molese, Faust. Ming Cho Lee was to design
the sets, and Jose Varona, the costumes. I was to stage the work,
and Julius Rudel would hold the reins over the production.

"Gluck's lie" was not to have a wider berth than in this medieval horror story told in sweet song!

Dr. Faustus is a tired old man whose achievements in philosophy and science lie like ashes at his feet. Alone and in despair, he attempts suicide. Is it complete extinction he seeks?
Or is it perhaps a symbolic death he yearns for?—a release from
the life of the mind to the life of the senses! "Give me youth,"
he cries. "Girls, kisses, caresses . . ." As such needs are, according to Christian view, decidedly not divine, his only recourse is
to Satan, with whom he makes a pact. Faust, in selling his soul
to the Devil, re-enacts in miniature the fall of man from spirit-

ual grace. He is willing to throw over all spiritual aspirations (the Christian road to salvation) in order to abandon himself to a sensual life. This willful change of identity is contrary to the role assigned him in life and corresponds to Satan's own mighty transgression. In Western cultures the "life of the senses" necessitates ultimate retribution rather than salvation.

By denying his higher faculties, Faust not only denies, he kills, God! This choice allows the Devil greater power than the Deity. Today we live in a similarly iconoclastic era, where the power of magic, potions, and occult rites is peculiarly prevalent.

It is fascinating how, once past his transformation, one loses interest in Faust himself (at least in Gounod's version). Poor Charles François could do little with his marionette except feed him an occasional bonbon. Faust does not fit his new breeches. In fact, as sensual man, he is a flop. *"Salut! demeure"* (Haven of chastity) is the outpouring of a genteel soul. Was he ever a success? one wonders. Probably not. As we all repeat our errors, so must poor Faust. As a "romantic" hero he seems incapable of action except through the use of magic—the child's illusion of protection and power in a hostile world. As magic implies an escape hatch, Marguerite's final redemption through magic is merely adding fuel to the fire. God, the great conjurer in the sky, pulling His ace trick! This anachronism is acceptable only as "camp" in a contemporary frame of reference. Celestial fireworks seem to nullify Marguerite's all-too-human dilemma.

Marguerite's innocence places her nearer to God than is Faust. She has preserved her identity and suffers. She is accordingly capable of accepting her role in life and the consequences of her actions. She has killed her newborn child (and in Goethe's text, her mother). For this she must pay the extreme penalty dictated by society. Hence she awaits execution.

Gounod's final stage directions read: "The prison walls open. The soul of Marguerite is transported to heaven. Faust in despair gazes after her and falls to his knees in prayer. The Devil turns away before the glory of the archangel's sword." Goethe is hardly that explicit. Marguerite cries out Faust's name twice. Part one of Goethe's poem—the chief concern of Gounod's librettists—thus concludes. In Goethe, salvation is implied and there are no good guys against the bad. God and the Devil had made a gentlemanly pact during the prologue. Such cinemascopic demonstration of heavenly hosts ill befits the Patriarch. But of course Goethe is Goethe and Gounod is Gounod!

And today is today! We are now at a spiritual crossroads, where the ground for rejuvenation is uncertain and treacherous. The death of God—if temporary—seems a temporal certainty and *esprit du mal* rules unchallenged and unchecked. We have partly regressed to magical states and through analysis of past ills (we are all Freud's children) are cautiously attempting to create the basis for a new faith: in life, perhaps in God! The Faust legend was not just an eighteenth-century view of German life. It arose out of a people's basic needs. Problems of identity and personal fulfillment still plague us. To re-create a Victorian soporific—to re-create any soporific, past or present— seems futile and even debilitating when faced with a legend of this magnitude and scope. But Gounod's *Faust* is still in the repertory, and until a new *Faust* arises (at least musically speaking) we make do with its limitations.

Contrary to convention, which has Faust meditating in his study, we must create a man *in extremis* and establish a "dangerous atmosphere" suggestive of the Fall. The opening scene is basically about death and rebirth: the old Faust to the young. Within our new concept, Faust's rebirth is really his death.

Faust's study will become a scientific laboratory. There will be several corpses on slabs readied for dissection, as Faust frantically searches for the "secret of life"—*"En vain j'interroge, en mon ardente veille, la Nature et le Créature"* (In vain have I probed the mysteries of man and nature). His action borders on the unlawful—he consorts with grave robbers who abet him in his search. Here indeed is obsessional man at the end of his tether.

There is some precedence for this view of Faust. In Goethe, he stands historically as a necromancer and cabalist. The original model, a German schoolteacher who lived during the fifteenth century, was a paragon of immorality. He was a fortune-teller and sodomite capable of raising the shade of Helen of Troy and cohabitating with her.

Mephistopheles's first entrance is as a corpse. He rises from a slab and gradually emerges as the *"vrai gentilhomme"* from his shroud—a reminder that he is associated with the death of the spirit and the desecration of divine will. Faust merely prepared the ground for his coming. In most productions "Mephisto's" entrance is accompanied by some kind of sulphuric explosion—but let's leave that to the traveling gypsy companies.

Faust's transformation should be witnessed by the audience. It is the ritual release from the mind to the chrysalis of the senses. There must be no total darkness, no hasty tossing of cap and gown behind high-backed chairs. The change will be facilitated by Mephisto—in a womblike re-enactment. Even Faust's voice must be transformed, and not until the final duet of Scene 1 is Faust to be in full-throated estate. The trick is how to get a pugnacious tenor to suggest vocal *faiblesse* without sounding like vocal mayhem. In the past it was not unusual to have two men play the roles—a sort of before-and-after Faust.

Let us then give the Devil his due as the greatest con man in and out of captivity. His opportunistic spirit is prepared to travel anywhere at any time to achieve his aims. We will emphasize this evanescence by changing his physical appearance in each scene. It takes a real con artist to appreciate the value of integration with one's landscape. There is nothing more ludicrous than the sight of most Mephistos at the Kermesse. One look by any lame-brained peasant and who could mistake his profession.?

The idea that "God is dead" and His earthly institutions a long day's dying will be dramatized in the following ways:

1. Instead of causing wine to flow out of a barrel, Mephisto will prompt blood to gush from the wounds of a Christ figure in the town square during the Kermesse. He will then drink this "wine" in the name of Marguerite.
2. At the moment of the sword chorale, Mephisto, instead of cringing before the sign of the cross made by the soldiers, will spill the last drops of blood (wine) to the ground, throw the cup aside, and push the cross away from him. This move creates panic and scatters the soldiers. God is silent! Amulets and beads cannot invoke His presence against such a "living" adversary.

3. The next and most frightening of Mephisto's desecrations comes during the cathedral scene where, dressed as a friar, he officiates at the mass. Standing in the pulpit, he has the audacity to make his own sign of the cross with a clawlike hand. In a Black Mass ritual, the sign of the Christian cross is reversed—the gesture from left to right is made at the bottom of the crucifix (pelvic level) instead of at the top (shoulder level). The acceptance of this blasphemy by his fellow prelates implies that they are in league with him, suggesting further chaos within the religious order.

Faust as anti-hero must surprise even his mentor. Mephisto literally guides Faust's every move in courting Marguerite. In fact, Mephisto derives more satisfaction from these encounters than does our erstwhile hero! What price freedom? Once in Marguerite's garden, Faust seems full of compunctions. At one point, trying to countermand Mephisto's orders, Faust will try to leave the garden. He will be compelled back by the urgings of his new-made choice. Supernatural aid does not, however, guarantee finesse in the art of lovemaking. Poor Faust will appear the adolescent boy in his best Sunday suit concerning *les choses féminines*. He at least finds the appropriate words to bow out of a clumsily managed seduction—*"Divine pureté. . . . chaste innocence . . . J'obéis"* (Divine and chaste woman . . . I obey your will and leave). Again demonic intervention is needed to affect consummation. Later on, during the duel with Valentin, it will be Mephisto who guides Faust's unwilling hand in striking the deadly blow.

Marguerite, as the stage archetype of "the eternal feminine that leads us on" (Goethe's *Faust:* Part II), is a beguiling idea. But in practice the symbol drowns the reality—she is all overspun sugar and no spices. We must avoid the smothering blandness that has afflicted her breed. The country-bumpkin aspect should also be minimized. She is obviously capable enough to fend for herself. Had her brother, Valentin, thought otherwise, he would have made different arrangements before departing for the wars. She is looked in upon by a neighbor (Marthe Schwerlein), but she lives her life pretty well as she sees fit. Heavily circumscribed by church attendance and polite social affairs, this new independence is her first taste of real freedom. She is not a nun, as many Marguerites would have you believe, but a young woman with budding sensual appetites and a vivid imagination. Externally she makes a model appearance. Once past her initial caution, she abandons herself completely to Faust. Left pregnant and husbandless, responsible in part for her brother's death, and already warned by Mephisto of her impending damnation, she escapes into madness. Her insanity reaches its apex when she murders her newborn infant. Although we have argued against Gounod's magical solution for the finale, we cannot divorce ourselves entirely from the notion underlying it: namely, the need to be whole again—to be reconciled to the spiritual order of things.

The new interpretation would develop in this manner: At the beginning of the final scene we would discover the crazed girl fondling what looks like an infant in swaddling clothes. On closer inspection we will observe that she holds nothing but an improvised bunch of rags rudely patched together, and that the child is a tuft of hay. We will see her first playing with the child contentedly. She will then pantomime the killing of the child by drowning. This is a ritual scene (the ordinary)—daily re-enacted since her imprisonment. Following the offstage cry of *"Sauvée!"* (She is saved!) Mephisto and Faust will hide in the shadows as a group of nuns and monks enter the prison cell. Their voices blend with the offstage chorus proclaiming the salvation that will be bestowed on her in Christ's name. A priest will give her holy absolution through the last rites. Seeing her awaiting executioner, she looks at the straw child in her arms and slowly unravels it. In this gesture she penetrates her madness, and, through the holy office of communion with God, acquires the strength to accept the consequences of her action. Her punishment, accepted consciously, becomes an art of self-expiation. It is now possible to face the idea of salvation with faith and conviction.

PREPRODUCTION

Our *Faust* was to be a "dance of death," bringing to mind
Brueghel's celebrated vision of chaos. Fantastical as those
paintings are, they are composed of singularly realistic details—
the ordinary and extraordinary fused, real people in real landscapes suddenly overwhelmed by horror . . . Death intervening
in the middle of a card game and lovers surprised in embrace.

A laboratory filled with realistic, albeit terrifying, details (the
corpses for dissection) becomes a total nightmare when one of
those corpses rises from its slab to address Faust.

The Kermesse, viewed in an "All Fools' Day" atmosphere of
license and ribaldry, is a carnival scene—full of itinerant jug-
glers, tumblers, fire eaters, and gypsy fortunetellers. Several
booths and a wagon are set up in the town square around a
large-sized crucified figure of Christ. Mephisto, appearing as a
fortuneteller, seems indigenous to his surroundings. We participate with him vicariously in his new role and are shocked only
when he summons blood from the wounds of the crucified
Christ. This compounds his victory over the cross. It is an unexpected reversal—contrary to the convention set up in our minds
concerning the balance between matters infernal and celestial.

The Garden scene usually fits the description of it in the
printed scores, with a tiny window facing the audience. Our
new setting was to emphasize Marguerite's house. We would
see both inside her bedroom as well as the surrounding gardens, which would include a well and a religious icon. This division would permit us to achieve two things:

1. to focus on details of the ordinary of Marguerite's day, and
2. to enable the lovers to visibly embrace and fall quietly on
   the bed while Death itself, in the guise of Mephisto, disports
   in the garden, adding another notch to his long line of desecrations. This is the extraordinary of the scene and should
   have impact for the audience, long accustomed to a discreet
   accounting of this moment in conventional productions.

In the final act the cathedral will be stark and gray, dominated by a large pulpit and some scattered chairs. It is filled

with the silent movement of monks preparing a vesper service. One monk is indistinguishable from the other until the extraordinary revelation of Mephisto as presiding head of the service. The ordered world of religion is turned upside down. How did he get there? Or, better, how is he allowed to remain there? Can he be stopped?

We have further reversed the convention of having Valentin's death take place in a street outside his house. The main action will occur in his own front yard, with the street adjacent to it. As head of his regiment he could receive the honors bestowed on him by local dignitaries on home ground. The division of the stage allows for greater counterpoint in action.

The final prison scene would be the barest of the sets: a long stairway leading to a door at top, a bench, and some straw.

Rudel and I had discussed the production minutely—and with minor exceptions saw eye to eye in all its details. The cast, only collectively available for two weeks of solid work, had been briefed as to the approach. They had performed their roles countless times all over the world in mostly conventional productions. The first phase of rehearsal revealed the mannerisms and clichés they had accrued. Beverly Sills was particularly amazing, revealing depths of feeling hidden beneath those conventional attitudes. In performance she would be absolutely radiant. Her vocal line, conceived as chamber music, was all dialogue suffused with a warm and continuous emotional life. She managed to humanize this much-abused heroine. Hers remains one of the most subtle and beautiful performances I've witnessed in an opera house.

Norman Treigle's Mephisto, already considered the finest of our day, artfully combined his vision of the role and mine. I had anticipated a difficult collaboration, but such was not to be the case. He was a patient and consummate artist, and his Mephisto emerged as one of the grand performances of our time. It was the essence of the demonic spirit—part tiger, part harlequin, and part Don Juan.

Michael Molese at first suffered severely the slings and arrows of tradition, but he made rapid strides toward achieving the desired effect. Faust is a problematic role under any circumstances—the soprano and bass usually take the lion's share of the applause no matter what the tenor does. It is a credit to Molese's imagination and capabilities that he never balked at what might be for any red-blooded tenor a somewhat onerous view of his character. He was to capture the idea of the anti-hero exactly. It was unfortunate that most of the critics tended to fault Molese for what was unorthodox interpretation.

Rudel in the pit was exemplary—stressing the youthful ardor and thrust of the music to great effect. This was our first collaborative effort at Lincoln Center, and without his spirit of adventure, his willingness to open new horizons in the world of opera productions, this *Faust* would never have come into being.

The dress rehearsals presented few hitches. The shroud for Mephisto kept being changed at each rehearsal, and only on opening night was the desired garment available. The blood gushing out of Christ's wound worked at the final dress rehearsal—and only then. Perhaps we were hexed by a higher power for such an attempted bit of sacrilege. From opening night on, only the implications of this action were clear.

Our final moment had never been completed in either of the two dress rehearsals. Marguerite, after climbing the stairs, was to be seen under the gallows rope—surrounded by the executioner and a few monks. As *Faust* is an inordinately long opera, even in our cut version, rehearsals always stopped at this crucial point: overtime again. I was not sure of the effect. I feared it would be obvious, but try it we must. Unfortunately, we gambled with it on opening night, having had no other means or time to judge it properly. I eliminated the tableau subsequently, leaving us with the last view of Marguerite ascending the steps to meet her fate. It was a fortuitous decision.

REHEARSING WITH BEVERLY SILLS:
"THE JEWEL SONG"

B.S. (*arriving punctually and plunking herself down in a chair*): Okay, Corsaro, on which side do I wear my braids? Right or left?

F.C. I don't get it.

B.S.   I favor the right side—and how long do you want the braids to be? (*She bursts into loud laughter at my puzzled expression.*)

F.C.   I still don't get it.

B.S.   Listen, I've done umpteen *Fausts*—and the major problem I've had to face each time was where to put the braids. Where's your sense of humor, Frank?

F.C.   What if I told you there'd be no braids?

B.S.   You mean I'll be in the nude? Frank, what are you doing to me? My mother warned me about directors.

F.C.   Tell me, why do you favor the right side for the braids?

B.S.   They're easier to toss (*another burst of giggles*) . . . in moments of ecstasy. The left side means no ecstasy—very serious, so no tossing.

F.C.   And what if I tell you there's no spinning wheel?

B.S.   That means I really have to act. So how do we start, now that you've taken away my props?

F.C.   First of all, you're sitting on the wall. Come over here and let Patrick (Bakeman, my assistant) finish setting up the set.

B.S.   A set yet! Usually I have only a bench, my spinning wheel, and, if I'm lucky, a flat with a window painted on it.

F.C.   Actually, we will be seeing the inside of your room overlooking the garden. Your room will have a four-poster bed in it. There will be a screen behind which you dress. There's even a little bird cage.

B.S.   No live birds, please. One at a time is enough. Listen, the stories I could tell you about live birds onstage!

F.C.   The garden is surrounded by a stone wall. Onstage left there is a bench, behind which is a statue of the Virgin Mary. Flowers are growing everywhere.

B.S.   Sounds very homey. I'll enjoy living there for once, tanks Gott. No braids. What do I do with my feet then? Usually with the braids comes a duck walk. (*Beverly demonstrates the guileless movements of a village virgin.*)

F.C.   Save it for some Donizetti comedy or a Von Weber heroine.

B.S.   Tell me! Tell me the whole scene first and then I'll do it.

F.C.   Okay. Marthe comes in ahead of you, walking rapidly.

You're lagging behind, daydreaming. She stops at your gate and takes a look at you. You come out of your romantic cloud for a moment, kiss her on the cheek, and bid her good night. Marthe walks offstage. You come through the gate. . . .

B.S. That's new. Never had Marthe with me before. Oh boy— no braids and with Marthe. I'm breathless.

F.C. You linger a moment. You look down the road behind you and say your first line, thinking of Faust, naturally. You next take a look at your room. Then a short look back down the road—then a long look back at your room, and heave a heavy sigh.

B.S. Why, she hasn't paid her rent?

F.C. After having had that delightful encounter with Faust—to go back to the drudgery of being alone—?

B.S. I get you!

F.C. During the orchestral introduction to the "King of Thule," you go inside your room. You stop by the bedpost and start disrobing. . . .

B.S. I knew it! I knew it!

F.C. Do you object?

B.S. I love it!

F.C. As you sing, you are naturally thinking of Faust—longingly.

B.S. You mean sexy? I'm allowed?

F.C. Why not? Marguerite may be technically a virgin—but she does have a fantasy life. She's heard what goes on in the village. Any number of other girls have told her stories. Now she's alone—and she has encountered a man who has stirred up all those conflicting daydreams—not to mention night dreams.

B.S. Just as long as I am still a technical virgin.

F.C. Technically, yes. Well, then she slowly drops her outer garment at the line *"ses yeux se remplissaient de larmes!"* (his eyes would overflow with weeping!), sighs again, and with the resumption of the orchestral material, picks up her skirt and takes it behind the screen. You resume singing out of sight. And emerge with a hairbrush in your hand—then sit at the window seat in your night shift. Your longing is increased by the melancholy music you sing.

B.S.   Longing and melancholy in a night shift—lousy bed companions.

F.C.   You move over to the trunk, where you finish the song. Incidentally, it should be handled like a folk song. Too often it's made to sound portentous—like the willow song in *Otello*. She's just singing in her shower, so to speak.

B.S.:   I never feel melancholy in the shower. Longing—that's something else.

F.C.:   Just give it a momentary emphasis on the *ses yeux* line but don't ride it too much.

B.S.:   I understand.

F.C.:   When the Moderato resumes, you get up, place your hairbrush on the little night table, singing your next line to your little bird.

B.S.:   I beg your pardon (*giggling uncontrollably*).

F.C.:   And cover him up for the night.

B.S.:   You're darn right (*more laughter*).

F.C.:   You turn back the covers of your bed on "*cher Valentin.*" . . .

B.S.:   Does that have a double meaning?

F.C.:   No. You lie down for a moment, but you're restless, you get up and wander out into the garden.

B.S.:   In my chemise?

F.C.:   Why not? It's your own private domain. . . . It's a soft spring evening . . . you're absolutely alone. . . .

B.S.:   I'm panting! What do I do?

F.C.:   You genuflect in front of the Madonna.

B.S.:   Poor girl. I mean Marguerite, not the Madonna.

F.C.:   You see Siebel's bouquet and start to pray.

B.S.:   I'm excited and I start praying?

F.C.:   Out of habit—but what do you think she's praying about?

> (*Beverly's throaty laughter is her answer. As she kneels she sees the jewel box Mephisto has planted there, opens it impulsively, and gets up. Automatically she starts to go to Marthe's with her prize. She changes her mind and sits on the edge of the well instead. She puts on the first things she sees—earrings and then a tiara. She picks up the small hand mirror. Her reaction is to laugh at what*)

she sees reflected there. The musical scale beginning with the trill on the word Ah *must express this astonishment and high spirits.*)

Don't turn melancholy on *Ah s'il était ici!* as every soprano tends to do. Sustain the buoyancy instead. The repeated *réponds* (answer me) must be still a child at play.

B.S.:   That's easy.

F.C.:   At the orchestral interjection, you rush back into the house, close the shutters against prying eyes—real and imagined—and, kneeling against the trunk, you really dive in and complete the metamorphosis. The cold touch of the bracelet should not elicit fear, but is almost the sensual high point of the aria. Marguerite's suppressed desires are beginning to show. She rises and dances about the room. Leaning against the bedpost, the *réponds* become alluring, self-tempting. . . . The run on the word *Ah* is now tinged with an unforeseen touch of invitation. In her ecstasy . . .

B.S.:   I don't toss my braids.

F.C.:   Better she climbs onto the bed and frames herself between its posts—a queen of longing and desire. In the orchestral coda she falls down onto the bed, laughing in sheer delight.

B.S.:   I'm exhausted!

F.C.:   Shall we start?

B.S.:   Are you sure this is *Faust*? Don't answer that! My imagination is tripping over itself. Let's get started.

And we began to work.

8

The Night the Roof Fell In, or Mozart's Don Revisited

Among the miscellany of lumber-and-canvas productions created thereafter, two are of special significance for me. Mozart's *Don Giovanni* and Debussy's *Pelléas and Mélisande* have been called the worst and best of my total output to date. Both operas point out several telling lessons to the wary young director, besides dramatizing the insane inconsistencies between life and art: Pelléas was created during a depressing period of personal loneliness and frustration; *Don Giovanni* was blissfully conceived during a summer hiatus in the Poconos. Unending days of sunshine complemented the dizzying spirals of my mind. I have since vowed never again to conceive anything remotely in or near the Poconos.

During the run of *Don Giovanni* performances my controversial status was rained on incessantly. I became the bull's eye for the critics' collective gun sights!

The trouble started with Rudel's decision to mount two

productions (Italian and English) of the *Don* simultaneously. We were given three weeks to stage both—turning the whole enterprise into a monster rally. Imagine: two complete casts, plus covers, plus thirty-two supers—and all with their preconceptions of the work.

The results met with the kind of fulminations that could have saved Con Edison a month's service in lighting the city. The *New York Times* screamed "Vandalism," *New York Magazine* echoed with "Travesty . . . an act of perversity." One critic faulted me for daring to sexualize Mozart, whose music he considered totally unsensual (I wonder what country matters he thinks are being discussed in *Figaro* and *Cosi*?). Anyway, the dam had burst, and it was *Get Corsaro Week* in the press. For I was due to be gotten—my past productions had trod on too many traditionalist toes. One impresario outside New York tried to lower my fee during negotiations following *Giovanni*; I took an old friend's counsel and instructed the manager to take my contract, and . . . .

Don Giovanni (subtitled *Dramma Giocoso*) is the most sacred cow in the operatic pasture, enshrined as one of the great masterworks of Western art. In its wake, the reverence, deference, and downright worship lavished on the mighty mite of Salzburg have put him on a pedestal beyond the reach of mortal man. As a result, his music has in some mysterious way become the most difficult to perform. Its perfect symmetry creates an a priori blockage in the performer. One's rude human impulses, the puny reach of any single imagination, seem unworthy of grappling with its bunched perfections. Accordingly, the cult of perfection has made Wolfgang music's most perfect symbol. I have seen such an elegant musician as Claudio Arrau actually sweat while discussing a Mozart concerto.

What is the real nature of the unattainability of Mozart's music? It seems to be nothing more than its infinite humanity—a humanity so rich, so tactile, so beautifully strung that one does not know where to begin dealing with it! Here, also, temporal musical forms further confuse the issue: the mores of the eighteenth century (the ordinary of Mozart's life) have tended to obscure the extraordinary—a vision of the ultimate reconciliation of all things so vast and far-reaching as to make the vision perpetually contemporary.

The nineteenth century was responsible for turning *Don Giovanni* into a moralistic tract. Its Good Housekeeping Seal of Approval was stamped by the great Gustav Mahler. As conductor of the Vienna Opera, he was the first to eliminate the final scene of multiple ironies, thus leaving the audiences suspended over the burning pit of late Victorian guilt. In no time the kit and caboodle of Freudian shop talk accrued around the work. This new moralistic look tended to load the guns against the *"dramma"* ever being *"giocoso."* The Don, in such a context, is ultimately impotent—a sexual loser, a fading fop on his last legs! The killing of the Commendatore is stressed as Oedipal guilt—and the operation of irreversible fate becomes the dominant theme. Chunks of Hamlet and his father's ghost are thrown in for good measure to thicken the psychiatric stew. This is all chazerei, but it has become the stuff and nonsense of tradition! Most such performances are nothing more than soberly staged concerts in fancy dress, whose characters, stripped of their complexities, have become stereotypical arms of the law. Subtle and difficult people such as Donna Anna and Ottavio turn into ludicrous bores. These characters merely serve to underline the correctness of the theme of heavenly intervention, and so we are guaranteed a *Giovanni* on the dependable level of the yearly Christmas pantomime. It has become serious opera's own *Nutcracker*—with all the nuts already cracked. The view of the failing Don seems completely at odds with the proclivities of composer and librettist. I doubt that either Mozart or Da Ponte could ever have interested themselves in such a sexual imposter. Taken in that light, the whole machinery of the plot, borrowed or not, becomes academic. There would be no earthly reason for heavenly intervention. The Don would collapse of his own petard, or lack of it. Surely heaven would have made a bigger splash setting its foot in the door at around the five-hundred mark in Leporello's accounting. A penny for the old man would appear more appropriate than celestial retribution.

My preparations were long and painstaking. I left no stone unturned—I read everything from Da Ponte's original libretto, republished in New York City during his encumbency at Columbia University—through the various analytical theses on Don Juanism as homosexuality in reverse, past E.T.A. Hoffman's imaginative essay, and on to Brigid Brophy's re-eval-

uation of *Mozart as Dramatist.* I heard every recording—foreign, domestic, commercial, and pirated. I even listened to Dar-
gomijsky's *The Stone Guest* (lately adapted by Peter Schickele
into the more viable *Stoned Guest*). Matters cleared up considerably after this sifting and sizing. I said good-by to the traditional son of guilt and welcomed Lulu's older brother instead! A
new rake walked into my imagination—the ideal sensualist
seen as social samaritan . . . the dispenser of the Big O—an image that tends to make us all sexual Walter Mittys. Giovanni
emerged as a culture hero whose brand of heroism made him a
menace to that culture. He is chaos incarnate and archetypically
romantic. In a society like that of Giovanni's (Spain recovering
from the Inquisition), the myth of such a free spirit naturally
grows. A man who can pursue his self-ordained destiny is a figure to be feared and envied! "Ladies, I show you yourselves!
Come, I am at your disposal." *Don Giovanni,* then, is the male-
chauvinist opera for all time!

Giovanni's sexual mishaps onstage are merely the result of
clever contriving. The plot is the stuff of comedy—based on the
assumption that outside the dictates of happenstance our hero is
perfectly capable of having his way. The balance of tensions in
the opera (both *dramma* and *giocoso*) depends on that proposition.

In my stage production the world reflects Giovanni's private
vision of it. The making of his myth becomes part of its fiber.
Giovanni is a movie star with his personal press representative,
Leporello, in tow! Therefore the beautiful, the old, the ugly, the
large, the small, and the tall are all given their chance with him.
The fête at the end of Act I becomes a veritable feast of those
had and about to have. Sometimes a mere embrace, a kiss, is
enough for the lucky lady. Giovanni understands his image and
the power of its suggestability. Not all sensual interaction requires sexual fulfillment! Like a gorgeously hosed humming
bird, he spreads his good cheer indiscriminately and with grace.
Penetration is only required for hard cases—or as he purposes.
Leporello's Catalogue Aria becomes a scurrilous Sermon on the
Mount, a bit of black-comedy evangelism. Leporello addresses
Elvira and a street crowd all rapt with the wonder of it. The
sermon naturally preaches the glories of a palpable heaven—

physical submission and conquest—versus the intangible hypocrisies of the socially prescribed one.

Donna Anna is without doubt a hard case—and it must be clear in the first scene that the lady doth protest too much. At the moment she is discovered by her father in Giovanni's arms, having suddenly broken off her tirade to silence Giovanni's lips with her own, she yells bloody and bloodier murder. This repressed sexual hunger is Anna's beacon light throughout the opera. Because of it she will lie and seek revenge. In her final solo aria she faces her duplicity and tears up the letter she is writing to Ottavio (in my version, he is not in attendance). She finally makes a realistic choice to marry Ottavio—in the name of money, position, and sexual second-bestness. It is the crowning irony of her life. Ottavio's acute sense of his secondary position in Anna's affections adds enormous gallantry and pathos to *"Dalla sua pace"* (For her sake). His character takes on dimensions not usually associated with this traditional stick.

On the other hand, Donna Elvira simply knows what she wants and, poor ex-novitiate, she is a plucky, foolish fey. She is a comic yet touching forerunner of womens' lib and a walking put-down to the institution of marriage. Zerlina, next to Giovanni, is the most natural and therefore the most dangerous character in the opera. Like the Don, she would have her cake and eat it too. Masetto knows this but is helpless. Both he and Ottavio are seen as psychic cuckolds in the free world of Giovanni's making. They can eat only crow off his table. Zerlina's abilities to improvise her situation and rationalize the results in terms of her workaday world bespeak a healthy sensual nature. She is prevented from slipping into the literal hay with the Don only because of comic intervention—Elvira's perfectly timed entrance. How cleverly Mozart parodies Elvira's castigation of the Don. *"Ah! fuggi il traditor"* (Run from this betrayer) is old-time Handel. Its lovely pomposities are the most delicious of hypocrisies served in pokerface style.

In fleshing out Giovanni's society, I introduced three ladies of the day, noon, and night—courtesans of various ages with whom Giovanni often relaxes. They are not for his bed. They are soulmates who understand him perfectly, since they too share his life of existential pleasure.

In 1971, when Julius Rudel introduced me to the late Bruno
Maderna, our conductor for this double-header, I felt I had
found a soul mate. One meeting and we had agreed on everything. We both shared the knowledge of the libretto's secret
language—its double meanings hiding scatological jokes and
sexual images so dear to the Mozart and Da Ponte who emerge
from their letters. All the ribaldry would be projected in a light,
fluid musical approach—a reflection of the divertimento style of
the eighteenth century rather than in the more romantic style of
the nineteenth. The physical production would cross the sunlit
terrazzi of Goldoni with the masked twilight streets of Pietro
Longhi. How delighted Mozart was with these Venetian mas-
querades, for their nocturnal prowlings could afford chancy
pleasures. His letters to his sister Nannerel bubble over with
such excitements.

Interestingly enough, most of the opera's subterfuges are
made logical and plausible in this world of masked encounters
and for once Leporello is forced to become the Don Leporello
of his own imaginings—There, but for the grace of God . . .
Forced to imitate his master, Leporello must be skilled enough
to persuade Elvira, who, after all, has known the genuine article. As early as the first scene, Giovanni appears as a masked
intruder in the Commendatore's house. He could be any one of
many overrunning the town. Giovanni avoids a duel with the
old man until the latter strips him of his mask. Thus exposed, he
has no other recourse but to defend himself. Later, at
Giovanni's improvised *ballo,* the appearance of the vengeful
trio (Ottavio, Anna, and Elvira) *en masque* is merely adding
spice to the nightly sauce.

The cast gathered for the two *Giovannis* included some of
City Opera's best talents. A miscalculation on management's
part had the redoubtable Maralin Niska essaying Donna Anna
in the Italian version and, three nights later, Donna Elvira in
English. A delirious exercise of the ensemble ideal—but Niska
was caught in the rapid-fire switchover. Pat Wise, the Zerlina in
the Italian cast, was just plain difficult. She is a fine little artist,
but fought tooth and nail to preserve the traditional view—the
pert peasant girl next door, the eternal soubrette and darling of
the crowd. Her personal need to be loved by the audience far

superseded the demands of my idea of Zerlina as a cunning little vixen. This was particularly true of all the Zerlinas who appeared in either production. Some even rehearsed the role as I envisioned it, pouring lotions of sex and savvy into the little hoyden. Once before the public, however, they reverted back to the standard prototype of countless pastorales. Robert Hale as Giovanni began promisingly. He had a natural matinee-idol quality—and he seemed to be reveling in this celebration of the hard and soft of manhood. But from the first run-through on, he was intimidated by all the secret forces that permeate an opera house. By opening night he was unable to fit the pieces together. I had instructed the casting department that Leporello should be chosen as the shadow image of the Don. Spiro Malas looked no more like Hale than Falstaff could resemble Valentino! Previous contractual agreements, made a year before my ideas on the opera had jelled, prevented a proper adjustment. Malas was winning, but within the mold of Baccaloni and Corena.

With Maderna at the harpsichord, time was taken to make the recitative function as true dialogue and not the six-o'clock rush hour to the next hit number, as per usual. The chief musical difficulty lay in Maderna's failure to realize his musical approach. It was a sophisticated and mercurial one, and, frankly, few of the singers were truly equipped to execute it. The singers wanted to sing! Maderna wanted a *concertant* effect! The score was studded with musical haymakers, and he was asking them to breeze through them. They could not hear themselves in the house—the singer's odd barometer of self. Soon suspicion and doubt as to the efficacy of the musical approach developed in their ranks. Maderna's mistake was not to accept the danger signals: He trusted implicitly that they would catch up to his lead. But such was not to be.

We discovered early that, rather than creating two versions of the same production, the English one was imposing its own special demands. There were large variances between the implications of the original Italian and its translation. This is always typical, but under the pressured circumstances it became an unforeseen liability. Hours were spent retranslating and adjusting.

By this time we were in the theater. The set had arrived and promised to be a disaster. I had not kept abreast of the designer's alterations from our original concept to its realization. Somewhere communication between my trusted designer and me had gone awry. How? I am still wondering. The costumes were an attempt to glitz up inferior material chosen for budgetary necessities. It did not help matters that most of them did not arrive until opening night.

The première was actually our dress rehearsal. We had never been able to run through onstage until this inauspicious moment. Naturally, the public cares nothing about such problems—and so, despite my reassurances to the cast, there was terrible tension backstage. The physical production had yet to come together. Before the entrance of the Commendatore in the last act, we had constructed the door and adjacent wall so that it would crumble. It never crumbled. The substitute laser beams were to make up for the loss of the desired effect. On opening night, the first sight of this purportedly awesome moment practically turned into a laugh riot. I joined the laughter wholeheartedly myself. What else could I do?

At the curtain calls Maderna and I were roundly booed and bravoed. Next morning the press had its field day. They were right in that the production was not ready to be seen, wrong in that they seemed unwilling to recognize our reading of the opera in its own light. Yet the music and libretto have been the source of intensive argument and interpretation since the opera's première in Prague in 1787. Our production was offering its own insights, but unhappily was condemned in the cradle. Ultimately, in the eye of the storm I was forced to integrate both productions. They righted themselves only gradually, and every change along the way was fussed over and re-reviewed. Chances of survival were minimal, however, for they had been given the kiss of death. Rudel himself, very much a nineteenth-century man regarding *Giovanni*, did not support me or the productions. He asked me to reconceptualize them, something I was in all good conscience unable and unwilling to do. Julius withdrew the production a year later and substituted a "corrective" one shortly thereafter. The embarrassments compounded one another, and the two *Giovannis* were put to rest in the warehouse.

At a luncheon meeting with the *New York Times* critic Donal Henahan, who supported my approach to the opera, if not its execution, he remarked: "You know, Corsaro, if this had been your first directing job in opera, your career would be over!" I had directed fifteen productions for the New York City Opera prior to *Giovanni*. Rudel would complement Henahan's remark by concluding, "After the number of successful productions he's given us, Frank is entitled to a flop."

I still maintain that, despite the clumsy physical production, it would have been possible to achieve my purposes in the long run. In time, its so-called perversities would have been viewed objectively, and the true intent of my approach would have revealed itself. Invariably the critic asks, "Have you changed anything in the meantime?" The answer is invariably, No! As it was, *Giovanni* enjoyed a sort of underground success. When I'm spoken to directly, the voice of approval is usually lowered, as if some Big Brother in the Sky were listening in. Recently I received a call from the President of the Colorado Opera Society. In passing, he mentioned that in their recent mounting of *Don Giovanni* the director had used many of the details of my production. He hoped I didn't mind. He said all this in a sudden *mezzo voce*, adding a chuckle or two in conspiratorial delight.

9

Pelléas and Mélisande

Debussy's opera is one of my desert-island choices. As an adolescent I was tantalized by the excerpts on RCA records featuring Charles Panzera and Henri-Bertrand Etcheverry. *Pelléas*, of all operas, is the least excerptable—and there I was, with a handful of recorded pinnacles, lusting for the valleys in between. I can't recall ever hearing the opera in its entirety in my youth. I have since acquired a pirated set of discs dated 1934 featuring Lucrezia Bori as Mélisande, Edward Johnson as Pelléas, Ezio Pinza as Golaud, and an unidentified prompter who was its fourth star. During *mon heure en claqueur* I witnessed several revivals at the Met with Bidu Sayao, Lawrence Tibbett, and Martial Singher. Later came Victoria de los Angeles—an artfully sung and subtle Mélisande. Pierre Monteux conducted once, I think—but all I can recall of it onstage is the overwhelming sense of pistachio ice cream in slow motion. The Maggie Teyte version at the old City Center was *recherche du temps perdu* in vanilla white—made palatable by Theodore Uppmann's Pelléas. His was the best until that of Richard Stilwell, and Jean Morel's conducting the most luminous until Julius Rudel's. In college I learned that French Gramaphon Records had finally issued a complete performance under the direction of Roger Désormière, recorded during the Occupation. This still remains the most viable of all available on disc. To satisfy my unquenchable thirst, Martha Sykes, wife of a college chum at the time, lugged the complete 78 r.p.m. twenty-four records from Paris back here to the States; I have never forgotten her for that act of charity. She is now one of the pillars of the Opera Guild at the State Theater, and to this day, when we encounter each other, that lovely memory lingers in the air between us.

In 1971, I heard rumors that Julius Rudel was planning a new production of the work but was contemplating another director to mount it. I have never presumed to do again what I did then. I asked for a meeting with Julius and told him head on that I wanted to direct it! Julius seemed rather surprised at my interest. "Why would you, of all people, want to do *Pelléas*?" Of course he knew to whom he was talking—old Kid Verismo himself! Give me a Russian peasant or a sprightly whore to conjure with and we're home free—but heaven protect the likes of Mélisande from my sweaty embrace! I concluded an ardent pitch, and without a pause Rudel gave me a bemused smile and his managerial blessings.

Ten years in the composing, *Pelléas* reveals the creative mellowing process to perfection. Debussy bears the souls of his characters in the very palm of his hand. He knows the meaning and implication of every word they utter and do not utter and he has measured out their anguish with extreme compassion and cunning. Part of the drama lies in the ambiguity of the literal word itself. Behind this ambiguity lurks continual danger. In a way, *Pelléas* is early Harold Pinter. As in Pinter's world, we are forced to navigate a field of treacherous ice floes, the true destructiveness of which lies in the invisible depths. When produced "symbolically" the result is stasis. The ship and the ice do not exist. There is no need for navigation—all is ordained, and the figures become mere pawns manipulated by an indifferent fate. This represents the theoretical approach to Maeterlinck's esthetic. All the singers can do in such interpretations is to stagger about stiff-legged, with staring eyes. Accordingly the opera's power is diminished and the burden is placed on the orchestra to project "mood" as substitute. But mood itself is a prelude or foreshadowing of a particular human condition. If that mood does not burst into life, it cannot sustain itself. It will be eternally promising an event that never takes place. This moody or benumbed effect has unfortunately become accepted as the correct style for the piece—particularly by the French themselves, strange to say.

Understatement is the other word associated with *Pelléas*. But understatement implies a statement, a certainty somewhere. Without the latter there is no possibility for the former. We are back to the vague caresses of mood again. In such productions, the characters grace the landscape but never illuminate it. No wonder *Pelléas* clears out the house after its first two acts! It is a masterwork that fails in opera houses, already too remiss in dealing with the realistic values of most veristic works. Adding *Pelléas*'s "mystique" in such circumstances is like adding insult to injury.

The following synopsis of the plot is derived from my production for the New York City Opera. Most of the action takes place in and around the castle of Arkel, King of Allemonde. In it live Arkel's ailing son (whom we never see); his daughter-in-law, Geneviève; and her two sons, Pelléas and his older half-brother Golaud, a widower with a small son, Yniold.

Act I—Scene 1: Lost in a forest while on a hunt, Golaud comes upon the frightened and disheveled Mélisande, who will tell him nothing about herself except her name. She refuses to go with him out of the forest, but when he leaves she follows him.

Act I—Scene 2: Months later, Geneviève reads Arkel a letter Pelléas has received from Golaud, asking that Pelléas signal him if he and his new bride, Mélisande, will be welcome in their grandfather's castle. Pelléas has also received a letter from his closest friend, Marcellus, who is at the point of death. Arkel refuses to grant Pelléas permission to go to his friend but allows the distraught youth to light the signal for Golaud's return.

Act I—Scene 3: Deep in melancholy after his friend's death, Pelléas avoids all company. Mélisande offers him her friendship in an attempt to cheer him.

Act II—Scene 1: Pelléas, Mélisande, and the young Yniold stroll near an abandoned fountain in the castle park. Yniold wanders off, leaving the two alone. Playing with her wedding ring, Mélisande accidently drops it into the fountain.

Act II—Scene 2: Golaud, injured while hunting, is tended by his wife. When he notices the loss of the ring, Mélisande lies to him, telling him it must have slipped off her finger in a grotto by the sea. Golaud insists that she find the ring immediately, and suggests she enlist Pelléas's help in the search.

Act II—Scene 3: Pelléas leads the hesitant Mélisande into the grotto, explaining that she must be able to describe it to Golaud if the occasion arises. The moon breaks through the clouds, revealing several men seemingly asleep in the cave. Their presence frightens Mélisande, who begs Pelléas to take her away at once. He tells her that a famine in the land has probably caused the men to seek shelter there.

Act III—Scene 1: Pelléas discovers Mélisande combing her long hair by a tower window. When she leans out the window and her hair envelops him, Pelléas refuses to let it go. When Golaud sees them he chides them for their childish behavior.

Act III—Scene 2: Exploring a subterranean vault of the castle, Golaud is aware that Pelléas is standing dangerously close to the edge of a precipice. He overcomes the temptation to push him, and follows Pelléas who, sickened by the stench, makes his way out of the vault.

Act III—Scene 3: Golaud warns Pelléas to avoid Mélisande.

Act III—Scene 4: In front of the tower, Golaud questions his son about the actions of Pelléas and Mélisande. The child's prattling increases Golaud's suspicions.

Act IV—Scene 1: Pelléas informs Mélisande that he must leave the castle; they agree to meet that evening for the last time by the fountain in the park.

During the brief ceremony of thanksgiving for the recovery of Pelléas's father, Arkel assures Mélisande that everything will now change for the better. Golaud enters and in a frenzy cruelly seizes Mélisande by the hair, tormenting and ridiculing her.

Act IV—Scene 2: Yniold is unable to retrieve the ball he has been playing with when it falls behind a large stone. He is distracted from his search by the sound of sheep approaching. When he asks the shepherd why they seem frightened, he is told they will not sleep in the stable tonight, but he receives no answer when he asks where they are going.

Pelléas and Mélisande meet and bid each other farewell, acknowledging their mutual love. Golaud approaches quietly; although hearing him, the lovers embrace passionately. Golaud reaches them and, in a brief scuffle, kills Pelléas.

Act V: Though uninjured in the struggle between Pelléas and Golaud, Mélisande nonetheless lies dying. When Golaud questions her about her love for Pelléas, she replies that it was not a guilty love. Her baby daughter is brought to her. Mélisande dies . . . Golaud has received no satisfaction for his tortured mind. The little baby must now live on in her mother's place, to take her turn in the world.

Characters

Arkel, King of Allemonde .... Bass
Geneviève, mother of Pelléas and Golaud .... Alto
Pelléas ⎰   ·············· Tenor
Golaud ⎱ King Arkel's grandsons   ·············· Baritone
Mélisande .... Soprano
Yniold, Golaud's son by his first marriage .... Soprano
A Physician .... Bass

Place: The mythological Kingdom of Allemonde

Before official staging rehearsals, the singers were asked not to be coached outside the environs of our facilities at the New York City Opera. There are ten musical mavens per square block in New York, and all are experts in *le style français.* For to all intents and purposes we were mounting a veristic opera—with the substantial inner work that approach entails.

A summary of our approach as compared with other practices might be enlightening.

Act I, Scene 1: A forest

We developed the story behind Mélisande's mysterious presence in the woods. I've escaped from somewhere far away, is all she will admit. Where did she come from? Why was her elegant dress in tatters, and her crown at the bottom of a pool of water? Maeterlinck's play, *Ariadne and Bluebeard,* offers some clues.* In the latter play, Mélisande, along with other female prisoners, attempts to escape from Bluebeard's castle. Since *Pelléas* does not follow from the action of its predecessor, I allowed my imagination to improvise on the intervening events immediately preceding the action of the opera.

Bluebeard has set his knights out in pursuit of the ladies.

---

* The composer Paul Dukas set this play to music. His opera is full of direct quotes from Debussy's opera as related to Mélisande, who also appears in the Bluebeard play.

The soldiers run drunken riot and, ambushing the escapees in the nearby woods, proceed to ravage them. Mélisande manages to hide and crawls furtively away during the melee. She falls exhausted in a traumatized state by the time Golaud comes upon the scene. She suspects he is one of Bluebeard's cohorts, and her first words, *"Ne me touchez pas!"* (Don't touch me!) are fraught with that particular anxiety. Mélisande is almost persuaded to follow Golaud until he picks up his spear resting against a tree. This reminder of her frightening experience forces her to flee again. Golaud, himself lost and weary, is ready to accept his encounter with Mélisande as a figment of his exhaustion. He leaves the secluded spot and tries to retrace his steps. Far behind, Mélisande appears, following him stealthily.

In some productions Golaud first enters either a stalactite forest that would adorn the shop window of an elegant couturier on Fifth Avenue or a neo-Bayreuth disc redolent of Wagner—the fairy tale abstracted and even made chic. Mélisande is usually in gorgeous array, having just left her dressing room and the make-up artists rather than Bluebeard's castle or any reasonable facsimile. Following my own veristic view of the fairy tale, I opted along with our designer, Lloyd Evans, to create a series of realistic landscapes bathed in the glow of the pre-Raphaelite painters.

Act I, Scene 2: A chamber in the castle in Allemonde

After Genevieve has read Golaud's letter to Arkel, Pelléas makes his forlorn appearance. His friend Marcellus is dying and Pelléas asks leave of the old king to go to him. Arkel refuses, giving the illness of Pelléas's own father as the reason. The old couple leaves and Pelléas remains alone. He rereads Marcellus's letter. Then he burns it by a flame from the brazier nearby and collapses, weeping in helpless despair.

In most productions, the chamber hardly exists at all. More abstracted space, with or without a chair. In a recently mounted production, Arkel pontificated from an arbor that seemed composed of cellophane strips, he himself looking very much like a medieval Santa Claus taking requests for the holiday.

In our version we are trapped in the last chill of winter. A fire burns against the encroaching dampness of the castle keep. This brief scene is usually dreamlike in its effect, and in it Pel-

léas maintains his inky suit of melancholy. I preferred to charge
it with Pelléas's anger at Arkel's refusal to allow him to go to his
dying friend, and the old man's contumely thereon. When
Geneviève says her last line in the scene—"Light the lamp tonight, Pelléas"—she is preventing a possible altercation between the distraught youth and his grandfather. The chantlike
quality of the music does not dilute the strong pull of tension.

Act I, Scene 3: In front of the castle

Our setting was part of a ruined bridge leading to a beach
overlooking the sea. Time and the recent wars had wreaked
their havoc on this lonely place.

Pelléas is still in his sullen mood. At the opening of the
scene he is visible onstage (contrary to the score). Hearing approaching footsteps, he attempts to escape, but is seen by Mélisande and Geneviève. He remains polite but distant. "I'd like
to sail away tonight and never return," he mutters with intense
bitterness. The two women are alarmed and Geneviève attempts to alleviate the gloom by suggesting that Pelléas accompany Mélisande back to the castle, while she attends to the
young Yniold, playing nearby. This is the crucial moment in the
first act. The usual assumption is that Pelléas and Mélisande are
already in love and disguise this love with their weather reports: in short, that love is never seen to happen onstage. In our
production, Pelléas offers Mélisande his arm in deference to
Geneviève but he is still morosely concerned with his dead
friend. Suddenly, with tears in his eyes, he says, "I think I'll
leave tomorrow," but he knows it is already too late to help
Marcellus. Mélisande asks, "Oh, why are you leaving?" Pelléas
rushes off to hide his pain, but Mélisande's restraining gesture
stops him. He keeps his eyes averted until she offers him her
hand in friendship and understanding. Pelléas recognizes the
charity and grace behind that gesture. He sighs deeply and
smiles for the first time. "Forgive me," he seems to say, "I have
not been myself." He leads her off gently, and we see them in
the background, walking along side by side, as he begins to
unload his heavy heart. We can still see them after the music
has ended—their colloquy an extension of the stage silence following.

Act I, Scene 4: A fountain in the park (marked Act II, Scene 1 in the score)

Pelléas enters, carrying the boy Yniold on his shoulders. They play together briefly with a ball, which Pelléas tosses into the woods for Yniold to find. Mélisande enters and it is immediately evident that her relationship with Pelléas is on an easier footing. They are both out to enjoy this summer's day. Twin slabs jut out over a large fountain. Pelléas invites Mélisande to sit on one, and he takes the other. They relax by the water, which, as Pelléas avows, is ever cold as winter's ice. Mélisande, lying back on the lower stone, looks up and sees Pelléas gazing down at her from the upper reach. There is a long pause in the music as they look into each other's eyes. A pizzicato in the orchestra breaks the silence and Pelléas begins questioning Mélisande. Mélisande avoids the consequences of that shared look by pretending to play with her wedding band, which inadvertently causes disaster.

In most other cases, we are faced with a small well (a glorified hole in the ground) on whose edge Pelléas and Mélisande perch precariously; Mélisande's ring play seems another arbitrary distraction rather than a psychologic necessity.

Act I, Scene 5: A room in the castle

The set represents a bedroom—specifically, Golaud's and Mélisande's. Golaud, supported by a huntsman, is taken to his bed. In attendance come Geneviève and the serving women of the castle, ever hovering around the misfortunes of their masters. The reappearances of the main characters in scenes in which they do not sing is my attempt to fill in the sense of the life at Allemonde. None of this supplementary action is indicated in the score. Pelléas and Mélisande enter the chamber last. Golaud reassures the assemblage that, despite his accident in the woods, *"Tout va bien!"* (All goes well!). When Golaud tells Mélisande his fall occurred as the clock was striking noon (precisely the moment Mélisande lost her wedding ring), the two young people exchange a hurried glance. The group leaves, but Pelléas lingers and approaches Mélisande hesitantly. "Can I be of any help?" he seems to be saying, but Mélisande gestures for him to leave. She watches him go and suddenly cries out, as written in the score, unwittingly declaring her love for Pelléas. The force of this private admission astounds and confuses her. *"C'est quelque chose plus fort que moi"* (It is something much stronger than I), she readily admits, trying to bury the full import of her secret. She lies down next to Golaud and tries to comfort him. Some local critics have thought this intimacy too realistic for such an ephemeral creature. But this elfin being, we will soon learn, is about to bear a child. We can always reinvoke the stork to rationalize this rationale, I suppose. When Golaud discovers the ring is missing, it comes as a surprise, not as a melodramatic certainty. Superstitious fear seems to erupt; a familial connection with the ring, dear to this man who feels out of place in the family escutcheon, is hinted at (Golaud is a stepbrother to Pelléas). As terror mounts, he moves from his bed and orders Mélisande to find the ring, which she claims she lost during a search for shells by the grotto. A stylized moment occurs as Mélisande slowly slips from the nuptial bed and leaves—a gesture suggesting her emotional divorce from Golaud.

In most other productions, Golaud, as the scene begins, is already lying on a pallet somewhere in the castle. I'm sure even the Allemondans could afford better accommodations for a grandson of the king, particularly in his condition. During the entire scene he remains prone on this medieval stretcher, while Mélisande gyrates about him. The scene cries for violent movement. The wounded man strikes out in his passion, unmindful of physical pain, only to suffer more intensely from this action. The wound itself is deeper and more piercing than its physical source. Golaud is a sort of French Amfortas. Even the opening measures of the interlude preceding this scene allude to Wagner's *Parsifal*.

Act I, Scene 6: The grotto

The chief function of this scene, I believe, is to dramatize Mélisande's confrontation of her hopeless love for Pelléas. This is characteristically accompanied amid symbolic images of death.* Pelléas gently touches the frightened girl, *"Venez!"*

---

* The *Tristan and Isolde* syndrome that Louis de Rougement contends in his book, *Love in The Western World*, has dominated the imagination of man since medieval times.

(Let's go!) he urges. *"Laissez moi . . ."* (Let me go. I'll get back by myself.) Again she lies, unable to express her real feelings. As Pelléas looks back into the cave, Mélisande stares directly at him. Her love is in full view—unseen only by Pelléas.

The scene concludes the curve of Act I in the City Opera's production, with Mélisande's silent confession as its climax. Without some equivalent reality dramatized, the scene becomes all gauze and sea sound, and no matter how ravishingly played, makes a weak finale to the act.

Act II, Scene 1: One of the towers in the castle (Act III in the score)

Mélisande's deeper feelings for Pelléas are as yet unrecognized by him. The tower scene is their first genuinely romantic encounter. Ours is not a Rumpelstiltskin tower out of Arthur Rackham, as I have seen attempted in several productions. There are no legendary tresses falling from a tiny aperture fifteen feet above ground. The hair is waist length, the tower a window off Mélisande and Golaud's bedroom overlooking a private entranceway overrun with vines and tendrils. The little courtyard below is surrounded by a wall, which becomes a playful obstacle course in this moonlight game. The two banter, and Pelléas tying Mélisande's hair to the climbing ivy becomes a logical part of their sport. When discovered by Golaud, their behavior is a combination of amusement and terror. It is actually Golaud who forces Pelléas to see the serious implications of this nocturnal colloquy. In the short postlude to the scene, Pelléas gazes at Mélisande shutting her window and suddenly faces the truth of his feelings for her, while Golaud continues to mumble weakly at their childish folly. Mélisande remains to observe both men from behind her latticed window.

Act II, Scene 2: The vault to the castle

The most cryptic scene of all, in which it is suggested that Golaud unconsciously threatens his half-brother's life. The older Cain has taken his Abel to face the terrors of the dungeon vaults. On a challenge? Forcibly? It is not clear. Pelléas kneels on a buttress suspended over the stygian depths. Golaud holds his arm to steady him as the younger man observes the slime below. Golaud is tempted to push him over the edge, taking advantage of a dizzy spell that hits Pelléas. Only at the last mo-

ment does Golaud change his mind. He pulls Pelléas back violently, causing the lantern to swing about wildly in his hand.

Act II, Scene 3: A terrace at the entrance to the vault

Another elusive scene filled with Golaud's vague threats to
Pelléas's life. Instead of the usually wide empty space called
for, the men emerge from below onto a courtyard where a medieval catapult stands—another reminder of the recent siege. As
Pelléas sits on it contemplating Mélisande in the distance, Golaud, puttering with one of the war machine's ropes, informs
Pelléas that Mélisande is pregnant. Pelléas descends from his
perch in astonishment. Golaud, continuing to toy with the rope,
passes in front of Pelléas and, with a sudden jerk, pins him
against the catapult's side. Golaud's previously veiled threat becomes an open one.

Act II, Scene 4: The tower

Again we are outside Golaud and Mélisande's tower. The
entrance has been boarded up at Golaud's command, as an express warning to Pelléas. The boy Yniold is playing with his
bow and arrows. He shoots one of them at Golaud's feet as the
latter enters. Throughout the ensuing exchange Yniold sharpens
his toy arrows. Golaud treats his young son as a military man
might. Don't cry! Stand up straight! Be a man! When Yniold
climbs the tower to observe Mélisande in her chamber, Golaud
becomes enraged at his son's unwillingness to tell him what he
sees. He finally applies a switch to the boy's legs. The lad
pleads to be let down from his perch and finally escapes in terror before Golaud collapses in helpless despair against the
back-door entrance.

Yniold is traditionally played by a soprano rather than by a
boy, as originally intended. It is difficult accordingly to create
this hazardous father-son relationship. Politeness and consideration for the female-pants role creeps into the proceedings, and
usually not much happens either physically or emotionally between Golaud and his son. The boy who originally created the
role of Yniold, a M. Blondin, is now an old man who, I am told,
still drives a cab, giving guided tours of Debussy sites while
describing his own participation in the première performance.
Soon after the opening, an ordinance was passed against chil-

dren appearing on the stage, and hence another pants role was inadvertently added to the rather slim repertory. Ours was the first reinstatement in this country of Debussy's original intent—a practice that proliferates with each new mounting of the opera.

Act III, Scene 1: A room in the castle (Act IV in the score)

The setting of this scene is perhaps the most adventuresome of this production. The "room" in the castle becomes a ceremonial chamber, dominated by a neo-druidic monument and sacrificial stone. The provocation for this setting derives from Arkel's first line in the scene: "Now that Pelléas's father has recovered," bringing to an end a long vigil. A ritual of thanksgiving is about to take place. Present are Geneviève; Mélisande, bearing a floral offering; the servants of the castle; several attendant high priests; and Arkel, officiating the event. Except for Mélisande and Arkel, the other people here do not figure in the original score. Pelléas and Golaud are noticeably absent, although it is apparent that both men have already paid their respects (Golaud's sword rests ominously by a prayer stall where he left it). The entire scene evolves around this propitiatory event. Golaud interrupts the ritual, dismisses the servants and priests, and ultimately cuts short Arkel's final prayer by attacking Mélisande. At the height of his fury, he grabs her by the hair and thrusts her upon the sacrificial stone. He is about to kill her when Arkel shouts "Golaud," bringing him temporarily back to his senses. In an interesting way, this environment, and the action it generates, intensifies the sense of a harsh society and its mores, made translucent in this pre-Raphaelite rendering.

Act III, Scene 2: The park with the fountain

Also reinstated in this production was Yniold's solo scene. In it the boy continues his lonely games, battling with the recalcitrant stone that holds his ball prisoner, stalking the approaching sheep herd, until darkness suddenly envelops him and the lad is forced to return to the castle.

In the following scene between Pelléas, Mélisande, and Golaud, careful attention is paid to the constant play of light and shadow called for in the text. When Golaud stabs Pelléas upon discovering the lovers, Pelléas dies crumpled on the fountain where he first drew close to Mélisande on that faraway summer's day. His arm hangs limply down over the fountain, his blood dribbling into the water that still claims Mélisande's wedding ring.

Act III, Scene 3: The bedroom (Act V in the score)

To sustain dramatic tension this final act is played without an intermission. The room is recognizably Golaud and Mélisande's bedroom, seen earlier. In most productions this setting appears for the very first time at this juncture. Mélisande lies in bed on the point of death. Geneviève brings Mélisande's baby into the chamber. After Mélisande dies, Arkel takes the child into his arms and, following his final line, "It's now the little one's turn," the following pantomime concludes the opera. Golaud rises from the bedside and starts to leave. He sees Arkel with the child in his arms and turns away, as he did earlier when Geneviève proffered the infant, for he believes the child is not his, but Pelléas's. Arkel now again gently offers to entrust the infant into Golaud's care. Golaud first regards the child, then the dead Mélisande. At the muted trumpet, suggesting the wailing infant (much like the closing bars in *Butterfly*), Golaud reaches out and takes the child. Slowly he follows Arkel out of the chamber room, cuddling the infant to his chest. The servants gather round Mélisande's bed, cover it with the overhanging drapery, and kneel round it as the opera ends.

There are no arias per se in this opera. It is one long series of recitatives. The tendency among singers is to compensate for the lack of arias by oversinging or overdeclaiming the vocal line. We sought a middle ground wherein actual speech and singing interlaced imperceptibly. This does not, however, relate to the problems of *Sprech-gesang* (as in *Wozzeck, Lulu,* etc.), where speaking lines are specifically pitched on the musical staff. Once the private sorrows and frustrations of the characters were explored as usual, the stage was suffused with a torrent of feeling that I proceeded to lid and even repress. The result was not unlike watching a sea of dangerous ice floes. The peril was all below the surface. This weight of emotionality was carefully maintained throughout, and the use of a front-scrim gauze diffused matters further, while lending the opera a patina of long ago and far away.

My production of *Pelléas* has been blessed from its inception with the best casts of singing-actors now available to do Debussy service. The last revival in the fall of 1976 was in fact an ideal one: Glynis Fowles and formerly Patricia Brooks as a sensual but tormented Mélisande, Stilwell's yeoman and beautiful Pelléas, Michael Devlin's infinitely human and poetic Golaud, and Ara Berberian's ineffably compassionate Arkel were all remarkable creations.

Julius Rudel has nowhere demonstrated his special gifts as conductor and collaborator as in this production. If there is to exist a "Method" conductor in opera, Julius Rudel has beaten him to the punch with his handling of *Pelléas*. Throughout rehearsals he was part of the total picture, in perfect accord with the plan of action. His conducting was in the best sense a true extension of the stage. It was as if he had directed the production himself—breathing along with the characters, seeming to follow their thoughts, while maintaining his own tale to tell with the orchestra. I know of no impresario or *intendente* or what-have-you with his special insight and skills. In time the proper assessment of his regime at the New York City Opera at Lincoln Center may reveal, for all its shortcomings, a true and simple fact: that it was Julius Rudel who set the pace for the latter-day reawakening of opera as musical theater in America, while discovering, for his company, the finest flowers in the field. This includes not only the performers but the superb technical staff: John White, the wily and scholarly associate artistic director; that firm rock among technical administrators, Hans Sondheimer; and the genial, patient master of the slippery art of rehearsal programing, Felix Popper.

10
Working
with the
Live Composer

Shortly after the première of *Traviata* it was a pleasant surprise to find myself a much sought-after director in opera.

In the theater, new scripts are typed up and presented in spanking covers for one's perusal. Holed up in some comfy den, one can evaluate their merits at leisure. Not so in opera. Except in the case of electronic or similarly geared compositions, a typewriter does not yet exist for the more conservative musical notation. One is inevitably forced to contend with the original piano vocal score in its customary black cover, scrawled in the composer's spidery handwriting. It is almost impossible to read through such material on one's own. (Is this a quarter or a half note? Which line of the staff is this note on? What is that word?) And so the composer invariably comes into the picture as his own best—or worst—exponent. This situation creates obstacles and frustrations galore. About one out of every ten composers can actually sing his materials—the rest is jabberwocky: a blend of squeals, shouts, and snorts. This "composer's voice" is found in the talented and untalented alike. In either case one must grin and bear it—for, as they say, it comes with the territory.

Carlisle Floyd does not have a composer's voice. In fact he has no voice at all. When playing through a score, one simply plucks out the vocal line while he accompanies. It's a form of piano three hands that might tickle Charles Addams's fancy.

Lee Hoiby sings in a gentle simulacrum of a voice. It's rather like contemplating a water lily by Monet—very restful.

Thomas Pasatieri straddles the fence. His upper range soars and sounds rather like a lynx in heat, while his middle and lower ranges whine and cajole simultaneously.

As for Alberto Ginastera—that is a special tale.

In 1958 (the year of my operatic plunge) Carlisle Floyd's work *Susannah* had just about become an American classic. Mine was the third production of it in as many years. It rather reminded one of the joke about the lady demanding that the tenor sing the aria again and again until he got it right. My production was invited to represent the United States at the Belgian World's Fair that year. Carlisle was not to see my mounting of his work until then.

Neither *Wuthering Heights* nor *The Passion of Jonathan Wade* that followed were to enjoy the celebrity and popularity of their predecessor. In 1962 or thereabouts, Carlisle decided to rethink and restock his larder, and so took a sabbatical from the American operatic scene. In 1966, *Of Mice and Men* was ready to roll, but the City Opera had moved to Lincoln Center and premières of American opera did not figure as prominently as before. When they did occur, the results tended to be disastrous. By the time Hugo Weisgall's *Nine Rivers* had permanently rolled over to Jordan, new works were totally suspect, if not occluded from consideration.* As kith and kin, Carlisle had been part of the City Opera's birth pangs, so it was a natural assumption *Of Mice and Men* would be given every consideration there. The opera would arrive at its maternal doorstep quite independently, however.

* The atonalist schools were still exerting enormous influence in musical America. In fact, the eye of the Schönberg storm had shifted from the European scene to our own universities and conservatories. In the process melody—opera's mainstay—had all but been throttled. Up to the mid-fifties, the première of a new opera was a welcome event. Soon thereafter the tide began to turn. The reason was obvious: atonality was not God's gift to the singing heart; the liver maybe, or better still, the spleen. Its two greatest achievements, Alban Berg's *Wozzeck* and *Lulu,* have never found a mass audience. Yet two out of every three new opera scores suffer their hangover. Unless something really new or better comes along, we may yet live to hear an atonal *Our Town.*

Carlisle had been commissioned for a new work by Kurt Adler, the impresario of the San Francisco Opera Company. *Of Mice and Men* was summarily composed for and rejected by it. The commission had been made prior to the Douglas Moore-Berkeley incident.** Completed in *Carrie Nation's* wake, it presented Kurt Adler with the possibility of another anachronistic work, for it seemed doubtful that Carlisle would subvert the strong bent of his lyricism and jump on the dodecaphonic bandwagon. Forced therefore to deal with the increment of the Berkeley bunch's wrath, Adler, either for artistic or political reasons, or both, gave up prime ownership of the new work. Meanwhile, back at the ranch, Julius Rudel's company, badly in need of a prestigious winner to counteract *l'affaire Weisgall*, quickly gathered *Of Mice and Men* to its bosom and prepared to realize its première for the spring '68 season.

In Carlisle's original plan for the work, it was axiomatic that the bass Normal Treigle and the tenor Richard Cassilly would respectively play George and Lennie, the two itinerant farmhands. Until Treigel's death in 1976, the leading roles in Floyd's operas were conceived with Treigle as a model. Both Rudel and Floyd felt the score was right up my alley, but Treigle's loyalties lay elsewhere, and as he had been a staple of every Floyd première, his predilections spelled gospel in the instant. An attack of Jordanitis à la Weisgall and an overtaxed schedule gave Rudel pause in mid-rehearsal and he opted for postponement, the better to implement the many revisions proposed to the composer. Floyd, surfeited with delay, would have none of it, and he issued an ultimatum to that effect. Rudel promptly dropped the work, thereby making it available to the Seattle Opera, which had lain in wait. Carlisle then designated me as director.

In meeting Carlisle, the last thing you would imagine him to be is a composer—a teacher, the proprietor of a sporting goods store, maybe an airline captain—for there is something deceptively square about him. He is almost down-home folk—affable

** Moore's last opera, *Carrie Nation*, was premièred in San Francisco in 1967. The Berkeley music students picketed the opera there—objecting to it as a musical anachronism.

and obliging, with just the right touch of taciturnity. This is all homeopathic stuff born out of a diehard Methodist upbringing and a decent respect for its mores. The other side of the Janus head reveals a nature of guarded, even feral, circumspection that belies his usual bonhommie . . . for Carlisle cannot quite quit on the notion that Southern men are not supposed to be composers. Yet Carlisle finds that among other things he *is* one—and in that fraternity he is almost nonpareil in his pursuit of the theme of brotherhood and the ineluctable musical passion he brings to that vision. This combination of old flapjacks and tender grapes is both unexpected and endearing.

The first order in the new Seattle regime was to rewrite the role of George—transpose him from a bass to baritone. This change brought the disparity between George and Lennie into line, as a low rumbling bass line against Lennie's stratospheric tenor made for an almost insouciant kind of grotesquerie.

Carlisle has always been his own librettist, and his version of Steinbeck's play was his best achievement to date but for a couple of ill-advised improvements over the original. Chief among these was an extended bordello sequence, introduced to (I cannot resist) broaden the play's all-male horizon. There was justification for it in the original play, where Madame Rosa's place was the sole source of recreation in the local podunk. If you wish to curry favor in the movies, add children and/or pets. If you want to curry favor in opera, write a whore-house scene. Truism or not, Carlisle seemed wedded to this material, for it represented his libretto's most original inspiration, and what's more, it had been entirely sanctioned by Steinbeck. While the brawling in Rosa's flophouse created a striking choral ensemble, it seemed a gratuitous interruption of the main action. The felony was compounded by a long confrontation between George and the ranchhand's foreman, Slim, that nestled in the middle of all these shady doings and represented a high emotional point in the opera. It took a fifth of Jack Daniels and the timely complicity of Carlisle's wife, Kay, to finally excise the scene. At my suggestion, Carlisle transposed the confrontation scene to the bunkhouse, where it belonged—and there, free and clear, it made a powerful effect.

All these new arrangements created pandemonium in Seattle. The house conductor, Henry Holt, had been rehearsing the denizens of Rosa's fancy house, and the scene shop was putting the final coat of paint on its roof. Glynn Ross, the managing director of the company, asked us to reconsider our cut and allow the opera to proceed as it was. In other words, *mucho dinero* had been spent! Floyd, tempted to reinstate it all, gave himself a brief amnesty to reassess the opera in the light of my suggestions. Meanwhile the Seattle doxies were cooling their whatses, and when Carlisle concluded I had advised him correctly, Rosa's girls found themselves out in the streets again. As for Elaine Bonazzi, the artist who was to portray Rosa, this was the second instance of her being hired for a Floyd première only to be written out before she could get in.

When staging rehearsals got underway, they would be a model of their kind. Carlisle had been quite explicit in his stage directions, but as a true professional he knew such to be grist for the director's mill. Allowing me and the actors free rein, we often improvised and sought fresh solutions for each scene before making any definitive choices. Sometimes these possibilities had not been conceptualized by Carlisle, but once they met his approval he would revise bits of music and text to accommodate them.

On opening night, Carlisle and I sat side by side dressed in mufti, eating it all up. Carlisle's pen had touched rock-core realities, and his musicalization of this tale of alienation and loss transcends the play's limitation and lifts it into the area of high art. The opera has yet to make its New York debut. To date, sundry complicated reasons, too involved to go into, lie behind that lamentable fact.

Following its triumphant première, Carlisle insisted that my stage directions supplant his own in the published edition of the score. I implored that he keep the record of this particular performance down to a minimum. To have it represent the sine qua non of his concept seemed complimentary yet ultimately obfuscating. The Seattle production was an idiosyncratic effusion—which perforce must alter with new actors in new circumstances. To attempt to define stage action on paper without the supportive tissue of motivation is a complex procedure, worth a volume on its own. It is certainly beyond the ken and interest of present-day music publishing. I was grateful for Carlisle's discretion in this tricky area. The present published edition suggests what was accomplished in Seattle, without nailing future artists down to its specifics. I have always been leery of stage directions postulated in published editions of operas. These have often helped proliferate the kind of traditions best dispensed with in our day and age. They tend to be equated with holy writ, as the composer's final say in the matter, rather than being the record of a one-shot deal that the pressures of publishing have rendered immortal.

Alberto Ginastera, the eminent Argentinian composer, may or may not possess a composer's voice. We never got that far. During the winter of 1971, we had had several sizing-up sessions in New York and decided to make a team of it. His new work, *Beatrice Cenci,* would be my first foray into atonality, and its première would be part of the festivities opening the Kennedy Center in Washington. The date had been set and a production concept agreed upon—all based on conjecture, for there was neither music nor libretto. There was a librettist, a poet and teacher named Alberto Girri,* who was chiseling away at his task somewhere in Argentina. This chimerical being and his nonexistent text had been the subject of frustrating discussion for months, until I began feeling we ourselves were protagonists in a libretto by J. Borges.

I had been working in London with the authors of *Jesus Christ Superstar* when a call came from Ginastera, who was also in London. He had just received the completed libretto in the morning post. Would I join him and some friends for dinner and a subsequent reading of it? It was the eve of my departure back to the States, and I was pressed to accomplish last-minute chores. But of course! Looking more than ever like the president of the grandest bank in Argentina, Ginastera introduced me to his new wife, as we, along with the composer's publisher and producer, sat down for a quick sup at a Soho bistro. Wearied by recent pressures, I abstained from an after-dinner cordial, knowing the irrevocable price of such pleasures.

Back at Ginastera's suite, the composer, straight-backed and

* Later joined by William Shand, who collaborated in finishing the libretto.

bespectacled, sat on a rococo bench, ready to unleash the horrors of the Cenci household. The "lee-bretto," some forty-odd pages, was typed in red lettering on what looked like processed iguana skin. Obviously somewhat unnerved by his task, Ginastera manifested this state by intoning the text with mesmerizing deliberation. As hexameters spilled over and through the Renaissance gore, I gradually abandoned all attempts to overcome my fatigue and fell soundly asleep. From a distance my somnolence could be mistaken for inner absorption: Fortunately I did not snore—some shred of professional courtesy mastered an otherwise nightly wont. We must have made a remarkable sight: Ginastera's solemn recitation and my own defection (or is it submersion?). Ginastera, as I soon learned, had been too preoccupied with his own performance to sufficiently notice mine. As the other listeners were seated behind me, I had managed to eat my cake and have it too. Solipsistic delights of this order come but rarely!

I awoke as the final pages were read. Pleased with himself and the text, Ginastera muttered something in my direction sounding like the South American equivalent of *nu*—and we were off. I had heard enough of the libretto to know whereof I zonked. In my submerged state, my uncertainties about this project had crystalized, and I now knew I wanted out. This entropic poem called a "libretto" was as silly as they come, and with all due respects to Ginastera's musical genius, I launched an all-out attack on Girri's text. Like a kamikazi pilot I dove unerringly at my target, sure of its destructability and my own. As my philippic wound down, we all egressed to the bar. I felt immensely refreshed and feisty as we drank a final *"a votre,"* and with promises to meet again in New York I made my way back to the hotel. On the plane next morning I paid the piper his—or in this case, her—due for my opprobrium. I suffered Beatrice Cenci's penultimate revenge—a savage bout of food poisoning, and needless to say I did not etc., etc.

I will always harbor affection for Ginastera, *la Cenci* notwithstanding, for, besides being a composer of enormous talent and panache, he paved the road toward my meeting my future wife.

Mary Cross Lueders, a young mezzo on the New York City

Opera roster, was appearing in the final performance of Ginastera's opera *Bomarzo* at the State Theater in Lincoln Center.
The last-minute unavailability of Joanna Simon had summoned
Mary from her Philadelphia home to save the day. She had sung
the role of Pantisilea a year before, but had neglected to keep
abreast of its vocal demands, since it had been a one-time deal
with no promise of a return engagement. Now, without rehearsal and peremptorily shoved into an ill-fitting costume, she
was hustled onstage to literally face the music. *Bomarzo* is a
thirteenth-century horror story set in a twelve-tone scale. It is a
nightmare for singers accustomed to the home comforts of the
usual repertory. Its musical line is, to say the least, difficult to
negotiate, and its pitches and intervals require an ability to escalate like an electric saw.

As Pantisilea the courtesan, Mary was discovered onstage
seated in an imitation of Cellini's shell. She had been instructed to strike an opening pose that demanded she point one
foot toward the ceiling while her toes gripped a cluster of dripping pearls (delightful debauchery, no?). Gravity being what it
is, the pearls loosened as she sang. Catching them in midair
before they settled ludicrously in her crotch, Mary kicked them
as she rose from her semirecumbent squat. The strands broke
and pearls shot in all directions. The tenor playing the hunch-
backed Prince Bomarzo made his usual hasty entrance, unaware
of what had transpired. He found himself sliding across the
stage and finally landed in a thud on his hump. Attempting to
help him rise, Pantisilea executed a similar pratfall (which she
attempted to convert into dance movement for the audience's
edification) and flattened herself beside him. The prone position seemed their safest bet, and so, prematurely horizontal, the
courtesan and her lover began their duet, punctuated by the
ping of little pearls as they slid into the orchestra pit. Ping!
Ping! Ping! As pearl followed pearl into the tuba, celeste, and
percussion, Mary lost her vocal nerve and began to major every
minor interval. The tenor, unable to maintain his pitch, tried to
move away—causing another disaster that noticeably shifted his
hump to the opposite shoulder. Julius Rudel, conducting that
night, simply stopped beating at this point, leaving Mary to
fend for herself. Her improvisation, spiced with the echoes of

her last Italianate role, lent a measure of musical conservatism hardly to be anticipated in such a recondite score. Onstage was a night at the opera with the Marx Brothers. In front nothing had been noticed—not a titter in the house. Only Mary saw the shifted hump; the pearls sounded like another aleatoric device.

Later, backstage, tripping over her apologies and some last-ditch pearls, Mary was caught twixt tears and laughter. When Ginastera himself appeared in her dressing room, her remorse at having botched his music overcame her and she broke down. Ginastera, always the impeccable gentleman, took Mary's hand and kissed it gallantly. "But your music, Maestro," she pleaded, "I'm truly sorry." He looked at her with a thoughtful gleam and furrowed brow. "No, no, my dear," he protested. "I like it that way too"—and meant it! When Mary's old teacher at the Curtis Institute heard what had happened, he sent her a note—her final exculpation. "Jews and pessimists cannot sing major intervals," he maintained, "while Protestants and optimists cannot sing minor ones." Knowing this, how could a good Wasp lady from Philadelphia expect otherwise?—And so we were wed.

Bonnie and I planned our marriage on Memorial Day in 1971. When the day arrived, it rained incessantly—a good omen in the theater but a bad one for my in-laws on whose Philadelphia lawn the ceremony took place. In a momentary pause in the deluge, we all dashed out into the garden and faced the minister by a small fountain filled to overflowing. A prop sun, complete with smiling face, had been rigged on a pole. Suspended over our heads, it became our sole protection and canopy. Two seconds after the final "I do's," it downpoured again and we all dashed back into the house. That night we drove in the torrent to New York. Holding hands, we both fell fast asleep in the back of the limousine hired for the occasion. It was a Jacques Tati wedding. The very next day I embarked on directing the world première of Lee Hoiby's *Summer and Smoke*. For the next few weeks Bonnie and I basked in a fitful sun by a St. Paul, Minnesota, hotel pool. Each day between eleven and one we pretended to be in Bermuda on our honeymoon.

Lee Hoiby does look like a composer. His image has stared out at me from woodcuts of medieval trouvères, their heads bathed in lambent light, strumming chiterna and lute. Hoiby's dulcet personality has as sidekick a wanderer's mentality. Were he a monk he would naturally belong to some mendicant order where Franciscan concerns are tempered by uncontrollable wickedness. Shortly before I met him, Hoiby had been asked to compose incidental music for Tennessee Williams's *Absurd Tragedy*. I can see him now, shuffling toward Williams in soft-sandaled feet and proposing an operatic *Summer and Smoke*. Horrors!

During the late summer of 1959, I had spent time with Tennessee at his home in Key West as we worked on revisions of *Night of the Iguana*. We had intermittently discussed the viability of his plays for opera. Several blowsy evenings were whiled away imagining Blanche du Bois in full operatic flight—"I Have Always Believed in the Kindness of Strangers" in D minor. In the spirit of pure scatology, I had improvised Hannah Jelke's monologue in *Iguana*, irreverently called "The Salesman, The San Pan, and Me," in C major. Otherwise the subject of Williams in opera was strictly *noli mi tangere*. Why he consented to Hoiby's request is a moot point. He probably liked Hoiby's looks and felt beholden for having taken up his time composing for a flop play.

Hoiby's opera, beautifully adapted by Lanford Wilson, was given its world première in 1971 by the now defunct St. Paul Opera Company. I directed it as if it were a sung play, with Mary Beth Peil and John Reardon giving exquisite performances as Alma and John.

Lo and behold, Tennessee appeared at the opening. Looking startled and visibly nervous, he seemed a fish out of water. What had he wrought? The character of Miss Alma is his quintessential heroine! He felt mercilessly exposed in enemy waters. When I asked if he would take a curtain call, he huffed uncertainly and said he would see. Echoes of Maeterlinck and his denunciation of Debussy's *Pelléas* ran through my head. At the conclusion of the first act, Williams remarked pitifully, "It's such a little play, and there's so much music. Poor Alma, I never thought she could sing worth a damn when I wrote her." During intermission he seemed to shrink in his own limelight, confused and even annoyed by the audience recognition of his presence. Everything in the opera was familiar, yet everything had been vertiginously changed. That curtain call was still doubtful.

By the final scene it was evident that we had, in show-biz parlance, a hit on our hands. The ovation was unanimous. To no one's surprise, Tennessee came bounding up the aisle like a puppy and took his place with the company. When I went to take his hand to lead the company forward, he withdrew from my touch. Looking at him grinning sheepishly at the audience, I could see, however, that stunned look in his eye, more distant than usual: envy, resentment, awe, a feeling of being superseded, disappointment—what did it import? Any one or all of them—for the kid with the handsome face had been as good as his word: Hoiby had managed to turn this lovely wisp of a play into a haunting, timeless epiphany of love lost and life regained. The power of music had penetrated the soul of Miss Alma, where words hang mute.

Like the play, Hoiby's opera has fared best in intimate surroundings. Forced to fill the reaches of the State Theater, it was heard at a disadvantage and did not survive its outing there. The opera has a special charisma when it is heard under propitious circumstances. For my taste it represents one of a handful of really successful works written for the lyric theater in America. And I place it lovingly among my favorite American operas, which include, to date and in no particular order of preference, Gershwin's *Porgy and Bess*, Blitzstein's *Regina*, Joplin's *Treemonisha*, Floyd's *Susannah* and *Of Mice and Men*, Barber's *Vanessa*, Ward's *The Crucible*, and Pasatieri's *Sea Gull*.

Chekhov offers unique challenges to a composer contemplating him as librettist. Besides being the single greatest playwright of the twentieth century—a formidable enough obstacle—the nature of his genius lies in the power of his indirection, and his ability to create drama out of undramatic situations. These elements basically spell anathema to an opera composer. Easy enough to trade on are the celebrated Chekhov melancholy and the occasional surges of lyric passion that burst through his twilight landscapes. Much has been made of Chekhov's Russianism, another potential hurdle for a non-Slavic composer. But Chekhov transcends his mother tongue and, working with the precise tools of a naturalist, he has gracefully led his characters through their ambiguities to make finite statements of their humanity in the face of ontologic truth—the real basis for his universality. Chekhov's effects, if they can be called such, are accomplished with a minimum of fuss and exaggeration—antithetical to opera's tendency toward the broad stroke. There had never been a successful opera based on a Chekhov play until Pasatieri's *Sea Gull*. It is a first in this division.

Tom Pasatieri, among other *wunders*, is the youngest composer I've ever worked with. In that regard it's the closest touch I've made with a child prodigy—no aspersion intended. That was over five years ago—now Tom is an old man of thirty or thereabouts, but no less prodigious.

Chekhov's *Sea Gull* was our meeting ground. The play's basic premise concerns art and the artist's effort to realize and nurture himself and his capabilities in the daily grind of living. Tom's own young battle *in excelsis!* The characters' frustrations and rebelliousness echoed his own sense of ardor and despair. The play's combination of introspection and flamboyance fed his theatrical fires, and in the figures of Arkadina and Nina, he could revel in his madonna-bitch obsession.

I became acquainted with the score as it literally came off the Steinway. Kenwood Elmslie's already completed libretto seemed to have artfully caught the play's essentials. Our only disagreement concerned his short-changing of the famous final scene between Nina and Constantine ("I am a seagull—no, I'm an actress"). Elmslie had underplayed his hand here to a fault. The reshaping of this material was my chief service to the author, and in the process a beautiful musical theme was rescued from oblivion. Tom was almost profligate—with tiny gems tucked away in all the corners of his score. A theme used briefly in an introductory prelude to the Nina-Constantine duet became a recurring motif in Nina's final aria of self-acceptance.

Tom's other gifts include a sure sense of casting, and he has a huckster's ability to make his dream come true. He always composes with particular voices in mind, and before one note had been put to paper he had handily gathered such rosebuds as Evelyn Lear (Arkadina), Fredrika von Stade (Nina), Richard Stilwell (Constantine), and John Reardon (Trigorin) to help insure the opera's success. Each had worked with Tom before and was cognizant of the young composer's propensity for the romantic vocal line—and grateful for it.

The production of *Sea Gull* was as close as I've gotten to a Stanislavski ambience in opera, and it proved a resounding success at its Houston première (for which it was commissioned by the enterprising impresario, David Gockley). I was much relieved to hear that Seattle and Washington, D.C., had picked up the gauntlet of this fine work. Would that opera impresarios follow suit, for it has become clear that, with the rise in the price of apples, the longevity of new operatic works in America is less certain than ever. More's the diabolical pity! This lamentable fact of life does not seem to daunt Tom entirely. Although he often threatens to defect to Hollywood and make a 3-D living, I see that he is busily arranging for the première of two new operatic works in the near future and contemplating the schema for two others already commissioned. Tom is preoccupied where he should be. *Pax vobiscum!*

Floyd, Hoiby, and Pasatieri are the three living composers whose operas I've been involved with from beginning to end. Whenever I have an idea for an opera subject, I will usually seek out one of them. If the idea does not seem suitable for any of this triumverate, I try to farm it out elsewhere. Of late Pasatieri asked me to write a libretto for him based on the Eugene O'Neill one-act monodrama, *Before Breakfast*. It has since been completed and scored. We hope to add two more short works and create a latter-day *Trittico*. I am itching to try my hand at a full-length original libretto. I recently approached the composer Domenik Argento with the notion. His two extant operas, *Postcard to Morocco* and particularly *The Voyage of Edgar Allan Poe*, both fascinate and delight me. Another highly individual talent is Conrad Susa, whose *Transformations* and *Black River* have raised hopes for a new voice among the younger generation of opera composers. A fond wish is to lure the brilliant John Corigliano and Stephen Sondheim into the field of opera— grand, medium-grand, or whichever way I can get it: two first-rate composers in a field where they are needed.

Another wish—to work with the Polish composer K. Penderecki—almost became a reality. When he asked me to direct his upcoming version of Milton's *Paradise Lost*, I felt I was approaching the *pointe finie* of my career. Penderecki and I met over coffee in a little greaser near Steinway Hall and discussed the problems entailed by such an undertaking. And then we hit one stumbling block. . . .

F.C.: There is a problem we must address ourselves to, however. . . .

K.P.: Yes?

F.C.: Adam and Eve and Lucifer and his cohorts lived natural lives before the Fall. . . .

K.P.: How do you mean this . . . natural?

F.C.: Well, among other things, they were naked in one another's sight—right?

K.P.: I think so . . . of course, what am I thinking?

F.C.: How do we make that dramatic distinction—physically— without being silly . . . I mean we can't add feathers to a body stocking . . . in fact, a body stocking would be self-defeating in this instance.

K.P.: Yes—I see what you mean.

F.C.: Then think of most operatic bodies!

K.P.: Must I?

F.C.: We could use multimedia and project the leading characters. But that would make for one helluva tough job of synchronizing the singing filmed images with the orchestra.

K.P. *(after a pause):* Maybe we should do it as a collage, with the singers in the pit and. . . . No, I suppose not. . . .

F.C.: Besides, it wouldn't be much fun, would it?

K.P.: No—not very much.

F.C.: It's a ticklish subject—at worst, the whole venture could end up being super kitsch, and that must be avoided. What's the solution?

K.P.: It is difficult, isn't it . . . ? No matter which way you look at it *(turning ashen at the thought of the money already paid in commission by the Chicago Lyric Opera Company)*. Sometimes I wish I had not thought of the idea in the first place. Opera! *Ya barza zemartyuma!*

We said a mournful good-by and I've never heard from him since.

American opera has had, contrary to general opinion, a very continuous line of action in its behalf. Its two major champions in this country have been the Metropolitan Opera Company and, since its establishment in 1944, the New York City Opera. Between the two houses over fifty premières of new American works have taken place. Add a large sprinkling from such other major houses as the Chicago Lyric and San Francisco Opera Companies, and one can safely say that at least one brand-new American opera a year has seen the light of day since the turn of the century. The following is the historical record of works produced in the United States at the Met and City Opera—the granddaddy companies.

PRODUCTIONS BY
THE METROPOLITAN OPERA COMPANY:

1909–10   *The Pipe of Desire* by Frederick Converse
1911–12   *Mona* by Horatio Parker
1912–13   *Cyrano de Bergerac* by Walter Damrosch
1913–14   *Madeleine* by Victor Herbert
1916–17   *The Canterbury Pilgrims* by Reginald De Koven
1917–18   *Shanewis* by Charles Wakefield Cadman
1918–19   *The Legend* by Joseph Breil
1918–19   *The Temple Dancer* by John Adam Hugo
1919–20   *Cleopatra's Night* by Henry Hadley
1926–27   *The King's Henchman* by Deems Taylor
1930–31   *Peter Ibbetson* by Deems Taylor
1932–33   *The Emperor Jones* by Louis Gruenberg
1933–34   *Merry Mount* by Howard Hanson
1934–35   *In the Pasha's Garden* by John Lawrence Seymour
1936–37   *Caponsacchi* by Richard Hageman
1937–38   *The Man Without a Country* by Walter Damrosch
1937–38   *Amelia Goes to the Ball* by Gian Carlo Menotti
1941–42   *The Island God* by Gian Carlo Menotti
1946–47   *The Warrior* by Bernard Rogers
1957–58   *Vanessa* by Samuel Barber
1963–64   *The Last Savage* by Gian Carlo Menotti
1966–67   *Antony and Cleopatra* by Samuel Barber
1966–67   *Mourning Becomes Elektra* by Marvin David Levy

PRODUCTIONS BY
THE NEW YORK CITY OPERA:

1948 *The Old Maid and the Thief* by Gian Carlo Menotti
1949 *Troubled Island* by William Grant Still
1951 *The Dybbuk* by David Tamkin
1952 *Amahl and the Night Visitors* by Gian Carlo Menotti
1953 *Regina* by Marc Blitzstein
1954 *The Tender Land* by Aaron Copland
1956 *Susannah* by Carlisle Floyd
1958 *The Ballad of Baby Doe* by Douglas Moore
1958 *Tale for a Deaf Ear* by Marc Bucci
1958 *The Good Soldier Schweik* by Robert Kurka
1958 *The Taming of the Shrew* by Vittorio Giannini
1959 *The Scarf* by Lee Hoiby
1959 *Wuthering Heights* by Carlisle Floyd
1959 *The Triumph of St. Joan* by Norman Dello Joio
1959 *Six Characters in Search of an Author* by Hugo Weisgall
1960 *The Cradle Will Rock* by Marc Blitzstein
1961 *The Crucible* by Robert Ward
1962 *The Passion of Jonathan Wade* by Carlisle Floyd
1963 *Gentlemen Be Seated!* by Jerome Moross
1964 *Natalia Petrovna* by Lee Hoiby
1965 *Lizzie Borden* by Jack Beeson
1965 *Miss Julie* by Ned Rorem
1967 *Servant of Two Masters* by Vittorio Giannini
1968 *Nine Rivers from Jordan* by Hugo Weisgall
1971 *The Most Important Man* by Gian Carlo Menotti
1977 *Lily* by Leon Kirchner

11
Media Productions

A MEDIA SHAVING

Jacques Brel protests that "Children are Bored on Sundays." That may be so today, although I dread to think it. In my childhood and adolescence, the weekend was a golden time. Pennies had been hoarded—stray dimes from Mother's purse or Dad's pocket—and the Friday dismissal bell signaled the end of schooltime supervision and the beginning of a two-day orgy of movie-going. Occasionally extra dimes were cadged from indulgent parents to pay for impecunious companions. Accompanied or *a cappella*, my course was set. I was directing even then, for I devised an arbitrary system of entertainment. A month of Saturdays would be parceled out to Leo the Lion at the Loew's Fairmount, and a month of Sundays to the plane circling the globe at RKO Chester. My steadfastness to this form of prepubescent repertory was unswerving, despite the programing. Admission was 15 cent on Saturdays and 20 cent on Sundays. Armed with potato knishes and Milky Ways (when they were really Milky Ways—in which you could lose a tooth), who cared about the movie fare? It was just being there, liberated and gorged, that counted. I would sit rapt and ignorant before Norma Shearer in *Rip Tide* on Saturday, then watch Sonja Henie skate her cute dimples off in one of her Baked Alaska* musicals on Sunday. Rub-a-dub-dub, one smart kid in a tub!

* A description first used by James Agee.

Sailing out on a sea of adventure. I suppose this is all part of growing up absurd—but it was an inestimable spur to the imagination while providing very little balm for my budding soul. Yet in memory the times glow magically and to a degree I understand and sympathize with the present wave of film nostalgia where Cary Grant and Carole Lombard, among others, have been practically raised to the level of culture heroes. The Saturday Metropolitan broadcasts soon augmented my filmic diversions. If any weekend was overloaded with treasures, I would reposition Leo to midweek and make a mad dash downhill after school to beat the price hike at three P.M. Some measure of my innocent merriment has lingered over the years of moviegoing—but the magic circle did not complete itself until I found myself at my first multimedia rehearsal. There I was, now in blue jeans, with a pocketful of Milky Ways (the new variety, but still wolfed for the sake of that oldtime religious feeling). I was about to mix the chief pleasures of my youth into one miraculous soufflé. As the old song says, Who could ask for anything more?

12

The Makropoulos Affair

The title of the play by the Czech playwright Karel Čapek, on which Janáček based his opera, is *Věc Makropulos*. Translated literally, it reads as "The Makropoulos Thing"—a psychological dangler of a title that squirms uncomfortably. Christened and rechristened thereafter, it has emerged as *The Makropoulos Story/Secret/Case/* and *Affair*. At the New York City Opera, we were in a quandary as to which Makropoulos to make it. "Case" implied another courtroom drama and "thing" aroused expectations for a horror show. "Story" was too general (everybody has one). "Secret" and "Affair" ran neck and neck, with "Affair" winning, since it implied "secret" while exuding the aroma and spice of the boudoir.

Leoš Janáček (1854–1928) is probably the most original of all Czech composers. While sharing the romantic ideology of compatriots Dvořák and Smetana, his pursuits of folklore far transcend their comparatively bland nationalism. Janáček's index of speech patterns, codified into musical notation, is a Czech Baedeker of sound derived from man, nature, and even electronic phenomena (for example, the telephone in *Makropoulos* has its own vocabulary). His research in these areas represents a form of monomania that has no peer in operatic history, and *Makropoulos*, spawned in the fens and byways of Bohemia's meadows and forests, is his love child. Written to his own libretto, it is an almost complete rendering of Čapek's diatribe against longevity in life (Čapek's answer to G. B. Shaw's more optimistic *Back to Methuselah*). Janáček's ultimate compassion for Čapek's 342-year-old heroine, however, raises the play out of its despair into a sphere of metaphysical speculation and longing. What ends cryptically in the stage version becomes apotheosis in the musical one. Once considered the least successful of Janáček's six major operas, it is rapidly taking its place, along with *The Cunning Vixen* and *Jenufa*, as his most accomplished.

Julius Rudel's first intention back in 1969, when the subject of Janáček at the City Opera arose, was to mount *The Cunning Vixen*. The sudden availability of the English soprano Marie Collier (who had made a smashing Met debut that year in Levy's *Mourning Becomes Electra*) caused a switch in management thinking to *The Makropoulos Affair*, a vehicle she had triumphed in at Sadler's Wells. Agents and stars, being the flaky combination they invariably are, caused this prospect to mire and founder—money, international schedules, and fickleheartedness prevailed in negotiation, and the notion of Collier was dropped in favor of a home-grown fair lady, Maralin Niska.

In my salad days I had been bored by a stage revival of Čapek's play, presented at the Phoenix Theater in its Off-Broadway home. It starred Eileen Herlie, giving of her sibylline best under the direction of the illustrious Tyrone Guthrie. The play, for all its titillating sci-fi overtones, seemed terribly mittel-European. The thought of its operatic treatment did not raise my blood pressure in the least. On first acquaintance its musical language struck me as a form of epilepsy, and the hope of projecting a coherent English text through all its standing, jumping, and racing rhythms seemed sheer folly. I cannot recall how all its frenzies finally coalesced, but within a week's study I was hopelessly captivated and completely unable to comprehend the reason for my former incomprehension. It was love at second sight! Yet this new-found appeal did not dispel my qualms or unlock the door to the opera's peculiar difficulties. Chief among these was its overall form. *The Makropoulos Affair* is three acts of continuous exposition. All significant action having occurred before curtain rise, its protagonists are left chewing the cud of the labyrinthian events. This is anathema to opera, which thrives on a straightforward narrative, with plenty of leg room for vocal display. Čapek himself had argued this point with the composer, even volunteering to write a complete new libretto, but Janáček, refusing the offer, proceeded to set the play as it stood.

On one level, *Makropoulos* operates realistically. The over-stuffed filing cabinets of a lawyer's office jostle with the flotsam of backstage debris and, later, with the peeling wallpaper of a seedy hotel room. Yet Emilia Marty, its principle catalyst, is often directed to appear within mysterious green lights that cast a pall of other-worldly dread over the proceedings. Stylistically, the story draws a fine line between its mundane preoccupation with legal documents and its storming of the infinite, where it concludes. How to balance this tightrope act remained prob-lematic.

While *The Makropoulos Affair* takes place in 1913, the events leading up to it really begin in 1587 at the court of Ru-dolph II of Austria. The Emperor, fearing death, orders his Greek physician, Hieronymus Makropoulos, to provide him with an elixir of life. When the physician believes he has suc-ceeded, the suspicious monarch insists on its being tried first by the physician's daughter, sixteen-year-old Elina. She falls into a fever and appears to be near death for weeks after taking the preparation. The physician is executed by the enraged Ru-dolph, but the girl survives and secretly leaves the court, taking with her the formula, a prescription for three hundred years of life.

Elina Makropoulos develops and ages normally until the be-ginning of middle age, but then never grows older. Fearing the suspicions of those around her, she proceeds to move from place to place, changing her name, her profession, and her per-sonality, but always retaining her irresistible beauty and her in-itials E.M. Thus, at various times, she is known as Elsa Mueller, Eugenia Montez, Ellian MacGregor, and, finally, Emilia Marty, the famous opera singer of 1913.

The events of her life as Ellian MacGregor have particular bearing on the predicament of Emilia Marty, for in that guise, in 1806, in the course of a love affair with the Baron Josef Prus, she bore an illegitimate son. She did two things that altered the course of her life. She deliberately named the boy Ferdinand Makropoulos to hide his illegitimacy, and gave the formula for immortality to the Baron. He never used it but left it well hidden in his home, and now Emilia Marty (having had three hundred extra years of life) must try to find the formula through the heirs of Baron Prus or she will, finally, die. The matter of gaining access to the Prus estate is complicated by the fact that a legal battle for it has been going on for more than a century.

The curtain rises in Prague, in the law office of Dr. Kolenaty, where Albert Gregor, claiming legitimate descendancy from the Baron Prus, is about to lose his case, since no valid will has been found to substantiate his cause. Emilia Marty appears at the law office and divulges information to Albert Gregor and his lawyer that a valid will does exist in the Prus house (now occupied by the great-grandson of the Baron Prus) in a filing cabinet marked with the year 1806. It is there that she hopes the formula will be found, together with the will. At first Kolenaty is skeptical but he goes off to make the search. In his lawyer's absence, Emilia Marty's great-grandson, Albert Gregor, bewitched by his mysterious benefactress, tries to woo her. She at first rejects him but then treats him tenderly—treatment he mistakes as passion. For one moment she lifts her veil. Magically, her face is transformed and Albert sees an old wizened woman. Emilia takes advantage of his confusion to try to gain some information about the document, but Albert appears to have none.

Act II finds Emilia exhausted after a performance at the opera. Prus, his young son Janek, and the latter's girl friend Christa, who longs for a career in opera, have come backstage to pay her homage. Marty is in a foul humor and when an old man, Hauk, appears, insisting she is the exact duplicate of his long-lost love, Eugenia Montez, she shocks everyone by speaking Spanish to him and kissing him shamelessly. She is finally left alone with Prus, who has found not only the will, but love letters from Ellian MacGregor to the Baron, as well as the baptismal certificate that has Ferdinand as "Makropoulos" rather than "MacGregor." She realizes that Albert Gregor's case is thus destroyed and so now tries to deal directly with Prus for her father's formula, but Prus refuses.

Albert Gregor is now useless to Emilia Marty and she coldly rejects him. He tries to choke her and to destroy his passion. Marty bares the scars and mutilations on her body, tokens of her past loves. He leaves, and Janek, Prus's smitten son, enters, de-

claring his love for her. She can use him and plots the theft of
the formula from Janek's father. But the father is also infatuated
by now and he, being the most direct route to her immortality,
obtains an assignation with Marty after she has exacted a promise that he will give her the document.

Act III finds Prus and Marty after a night of love in her
apartment. He is horrified by her indifference; nevertheless, he
gives her the document. Cataclysmic events follow. Janek,
Prus's son, has committed suicide; Hauk is led off to an asylum.
The others: Albert Gregor, Kolenaty, Christa and her father, Vi-
tek, and Prus converge upon Emilia Marty and demand to know
the truth. She takes refuge in her bedroom and, while she is
gone, the others examine the contents of a trunk full of letters
and articles of her past. They force her from the bedroom where
she has been drinking, not the elixir, but alcohol. She
drunkenly unravels the Makropoulos story, proclaiming that she
is Elina Makropoulos and that she is 342 years old. She faints,
and there appears the strange beckoning figure of Death. The
formula in hand, she accepts her mortality: "There is no joy in
goodness, no joy in evil, just a vast eternal loneliness." Mysterious voices echo her sentiments. The dying Emilia Marty hands
the document to Christa, enticing her with a promise of a great
career and eternal life, but the terrified girl sets it on fire. With a
cry of *"Pater Hemon"* (Our Father), Marty dies and fades back
into the limbo of time.

Through the dense conversations, Janáček's orchestra edges
and insinuates its way. It punches, stabs, ejaculates, and
caresses by turns. Ever murmuring prophetically, it is grim-
visaged; its antecedent is Dostoevski. Against this orchestral
tide, the voice rises in mostly parlando fashion, creating myriad
melodic fragments that never once break into a conventional
aria.

In rehearsing the piece, I leafed through many of Janáček's
letters to friends and colleagues. One was addressed to a stage
director named Ota Zitek, the man responsible for the mise en
scène of the première held in Janáček's hometown, Brno.

Dear Friend,
    One unusual chord can save a composition, if the chord
is a real bleeding knot of feeling. Your idea of the pro-

jected shadow in the second act brought the mystery of
Emilia Marty to unexpected heights. Thank you for your
work in The Makropoulos Secret. But especially for this
idea. You have greatly helped the work.

Yours sincerely

Brno, Dec. 24, 1926.   Leoš Janáček, Ph.D.

Later, when this shadow had been implemented in a performance elsewhere, Janáček would bemoan its effect: "It's not
long enough . . . not nearly long enough." Reading these letters
and reminiscences, I seemed to drift off somewhere, until a
voice within me stated clearly, "Make the shadow longer." The
voice was unfamiliar, and in my transport I eerily supposed it to
be the composer's own, agitating from beyond. The voice became insistent, a vision flashed through my imagination, and—
call it inspiration or Round One of madness—my media approach to the opera was born. As I toyed with the notion, I
could feel it was integral to the subject and a justified counterpoint to Janáček's neurasthenic score. I say "justified" because
I have grown in the conviction that the use of motion picture—
itself a modern concoction—should extend in opera production
primarily to those works created in the twentieth century.

The Makropoulos Affair had been given its world première
in 1926. Films were still silent. The flickering shadow world of
D.W. Griffith and *The Vamp* had reached its heyday and Al Jol-
son's *Jazz Singer* would usher in the advent of sound a year
later. I've always wondered what might have been playing at
the Loew's Brno in Janáček's time, and what impossible dreams
lay behind the shadow that was not long enough. Certainly the
figure of Emilia Marty belongs to the movie tradition of the
femme fatale. Even the opera's setting "somewhere in the early
part of the present century, in an old European capital" was
redolent of fustian and dripping candles. The play is a Haps-
burg mirage, trembling on the brink of Sarajevo. It should have
been produced by the old UFA* Studios in Germany (precur-
sors and specialists of the Gothic film) and the vulpine Pola
Negri could have been its star.

Casting myself as a latter-day Von Sternberg, sans puttees or
Dietrich (now, there's a bit of casting), I began fashioning a

---

* UFA: a film company that flourished during the twenties and thirties.

scenario for such a hypothetical film. How this would translate
to the stage was not yet clear to me, although the general corre-
lation between film and live action was. The film would represent the past and the stage the living present. Mounds of expos-
itory material would be enlivened and clarified while adding a
new tension to the stage action.

When I proposed such a treatment to Rudel, he grasped its
principles immediately, and we were in business. There had
been multimedia productions before (henceforth, "multimedia"
signifies the melding of film images with the stage) but not in
American opera houses. It was still a new technology here. In
Europe, Josef Svoboda had made extensive use of the technique while we were still playing hide-and-seek with it. Media
icing had decorated such Broadway musicals as *The Apple Tree,*
Jimmy, and *Happy Time.* One example stood apart as a serious
and bona fide achievement on the burgeoning horizon. During
the winter of 1969, the Robert Joffrey Dance Company was offering its startling and revelatory "Astarte"—a pas de deux with
a psychedelic film continuity. Santa's workshop had sprung
loose two of its finest elves, and the dance world had pushed
theatrical history up a peg.

Gardner Compton, cinematographer, creator of "Astarte,"
and his associate, Emile Ardolino, film editor, had their studio
on West Forty-sixth Street. When I sounded them out on the
subject of a media opera, they seemed puzzled and uncertain.
Opera and film? Whoa! Trim and mod in blue jeans, Compton
and Ardolino were dance freaks. Compton had been a member
of Martha Graham's company until a leg injury pushed him into
film-making, and Ardolino was a fresh-faced aficionado with a
background as an actor. What they encountered when I stepped
into their office was a slightly manic salesman eager to make
contact with their special sorcery. But I was an emissary from
the world of opera, and through their eyes I saw visions of
bulky thighs in sagging tights and kingly crowns askew. Reassuring them that opera was no longer the gravesite of the singing Brontosaurus, I ravished them with visions of things to
come. Pioneering was in their blood, and within an hour we
had become collaborators. I would not meet up with Ronald
Chase, my chief collaborator in media, for another year, when

our staging of Delius's *Koanga* in Washington, D.C., brought us together. If Compton and Ardolino had turned the project down, I most probably would have abandoned a media *Makropoulos* and settled for a traditional staging. Outside of Chase, Compton, and Ardolino, artists of their caliber in this area of endeavor exist on three fingers of your right hand. With the involvement of Compton/Ardolino, a festival opera (*Makropoulos* was planned for only two performances) became a major repertory item.

Our work developed in easy stages. Janáček's work was already done; ours was just beginning. The first order of the day was the completion of the film scenario. Out of it would grow the concept for the physical stage production. Ultimately, the role of the conductor would have to be aligned with our scheme. I encouraged Gardner and Emile to write separate scenarios based on my given lead. We would meet, compare exercises, then put the whole thing into a blender.

The film portions, as I indicated earlier, would represent Emilia Marty's past. Each of her impersonations would be realized physically and her flight through time would be our leading motif. As the opera begins, Marty is at the end of her rope. Death is at her elbow. She must find the Makropoulos document and secure the "fix" that will guarantee her another three hundred years of life. The film would reflect her memories of past events. To better dramatize Marty's agonized search, I invented the figure of her chauffeur—Death incarnate, patiently awaiting her surrender. In re-creating Marty's history, this apparition would first appear to her in her days as Elina Makropoulos. Then he would be disguised as a monk, whose grasp she has been eluding since the court of Emperor Rudolph II of Austria. Now, in the time of electricity, the automobile, and Emilia Marty, he has re-emerged as her chauffeur. In the singing text, the lines assigned to the stagehand in the second act were adapted to suit this fictional creation. Little is lost in the transition—the brief exchange between the wardrobe mistress and the stagehand is a dull effort to spark the play's humor (Čapek actually calls his dour play a comedy). Much is gained by anchoring this sinister character as more than a poetic figment.

Marty's progression through her various transformations

would be treated surrealistically on film. Fractured images would be revealed out of time sequence. This collage would finally clarify itself in the dénouement. The stage environment grew out of this idea. Marty's disconnected memories would be part of the vast jigsaw puzzle of her life. Accordingly, Gardner invented a series of nine screens, in the shape of jigsaw pieces, on whose surfaces we would project her splintered history. The images would be capable of moving from screen to screen. Their rhythm would be spasmodic—complementing Janáček's score and an exact reflection of Marty's paranoia. Slides of still images would be projected alongside the film, often overlapping or being overlapped by the motion-picture material.

Gardner's environment would constitute one half of the stage design. Unfortunately not a member of the scenic designer's union, Gardner could not supplement his creation with a matching stage setting. We would have to bring in another artist to round out those needs. Several designers, when approached, were unwilling to play what they considered second fiddle to him. Finally, in Patton Campbell—who had done the costumes for *Traviata*—we found a colleague who was both officially licensed and eager to broaden his own creative horizons. Our setting was to be drenched in the vat of German expressionism (circa 1910) as seen through the eyes of Antonio Gaudi, the Spanish necromancer whose architecture, sculpture, and artifacts are the final flowering of art nouveau. I specified the stage details (furniture, props, etc.) and Patton Gaudi-ized them, *igitur* coordinating their curves with Gardner's jigsaw contours. The results are three somber panels that perfectly reflect the necropolis of Čapek's universe. The surface material covering all stage furniture would be the dead-eyed gray of film negative, corresponding to the color of the adjacent screens. All costumes would be in period, with an extra tilt toward the bizarre in Marty's wardrobe.

Six months from my initial meeting with Gardner and Emile, we were ready to shoot our scenario. Patton's costumes and hand props had been prepared months in advance to facilitate initial photography. Our stage rehearsal was less than two months away. The only members of the cast who would appear both on and off screen were Maralin Niska as all the E.M.s, and David Rae Smith as her nemesis: Death incarnate. Actors, rather than singers, were auditioned and hired for Dr. Makropoulos, Elina Makropoulos aged sixteen, Emperor Rudolph and his retinue of depraved courtiers, several royal guards and monks, a pair of naked bodies to re-create two of Marty's affairs in former centuries, and one medium-sized snake to beef up the occult overtones.

None of the actors involved was a member of the Screen Actors' Guild, but performed for the camera to full program credit and an equitable wage. I can't recall what the equitable wage was for the medium-sized snake, but I'm sure it has doubled by now. A signed contract stipulated a waiver of all subsidiary rights (read royalties). As I will elaborate in the chapter on *Superstar*, the various unions were hardly cognizant of or, if so, indifferent to, our little backwater operation. Taking a tip from MGM's Leo the Lion, it was *Ars, Artis, Gratias* all the way. We next reserved space at an east-side film studio, where we spent three hectic days. One night alone was devoted to outdoor shooting. We scouted the mid-sixties and seventies between Fifth and Madison Avenues before finding the right location for Baron Prus's house, in which the legal will and the pharmaceutical treasure were hidden. Its façade reeked Old World. It was replete with stone gargoyle sentries at the entrance and mullioned windows in the upper reaches. At the tail end of a heat wave, Niska and Smith donned their unaccustomed suits of solemn black and played out their little drama of flight and pursuit on a blocked-off street (courtesy of Mayor Lindsay). Our only difficulty that night was preventing an overcurious tenant from constantly peering out of her second-story window within camera range, thus spoiling the mystery with her plastic hair curlers and nylon nightie.

The studio work had been scheduled down to the last detail. The only open-ended aspect concerned the so-called "porn" sections of our tale. Not ever having directed a skin flick before (my sober experiences in film and television had not prepared me for this personal breakthrough), I was at a loss as to what I could request of our nude actors at the going prices. We had decided to play this one by ear. On the last day of shooting, we dismissed the bulk of the cast by lunchtime. All hangers-on and potential voyeurs were sent packing, and the set declared closed. The two actors chosen were in the musical *Oh! Cal-*

cutta! and had been swinging their parts at audiences on both coasts for over a year. The distaff side of our duet had the most lustrous skin tone I had seen in many a moon, besides delectable breasts. Other cast members managed a sneak preview as they made their way out of the studio. Stripped for action, hours before her call, Miss Calcutta sat in the green room, cross-legged, eating a sandwich and talking to two of our crew members in dungarees. From a distance the scene bore a rough-shod resemblance to Manet's *Le Déjeuner sur l'Herbe.* Sans *l'herbe.* The male member of this pas de deux *au naturel* had doubled as a royal guard in the morning's takes. Now divested of armor and halberd, he bounced onto the set beaming, sans everything. Home at last!

The filmic episodes to be conjured with concerned Ellian MacGregor and "the secret practices" alluded to in the letters in Prus's custody. One was a no-nonsense tableau of lust (with Spanish shawl) between the Gypsy Eugenia Montez and Hauk Sendorf. The Montez episode was a study in Gypsy abandon (all Italians sing, blacks have rhythm, and Gypsies have abandon). Since this was silent-film stuff (though in color), I stood on the sidelines, with hands cupped to my mouth, instructing them on the particular disposition of limbs—when to, when not to, and occasionally stepping in to show them how to. The hitch came with the secret practices. I had decided Ellian MacGregor had often attended the gatherings of the notorious Medmen-hamites—a private English club that flourished in the eighteenth century (the period in which Ellian lived). It was situated just outside London in a Gothic setting—ruined towers, ivy-covered arches, the works! You packed two suitcases for the weekend: one for your clothes, the other for your leather. It was *the* exclusive sado-masochist club of the time. An appetizer was served up in London proper, for as part of the long weekend extending into the countryside the rites of Medmenha would be preambled by an evening at Charlotte Hayes's. A celebrated debauchee, she was wont to issue invitations of the following order:

Mrs. Hayes commends herself respectfully to Lord/ Lady ——— and takes the liberty of advising that on Fri-

day evening at 7 o'clock precisely, twelve beautiful
nymphs, spotless virgins, will carry out the famous Feast
of Venus as it is celebrated in Tahiti under the instruction and leadership of Queen Oberea (whose role will be
taken by Mrs. Hayes herself).

Small potatoes compared with the ceremonies at the Gothic ab-
bey, but no doubt a suitable warmup for the jaded palates of
Georgian rakes and their ladies.

When the moment arrived to wield the whip in the film portion, Miss Calcutta backed off and looked stricken. "Look
here," she said, "this is a pretty heavy scene. You're going to
have to up the ante. You guys have no idea what this sort of
thing can do to a girl." How does one convince a perfect
stranger (particularly a nude one) to simulate bestiality at
AGMA minimum? Perhaps someday, given the similar circumstances of compressed time and budget, I may resolve the problem more adroitly. Needless to say, we upped the ante and proceeded. The ante had an electrifying effect on Miss Calcutta's
swinging arm; thrashing about with eye "in a fine frenzy roll-
ing," she was a perfect Medmenhamite darling. No blows
were actually struck, but the foreplay enacted was fraught with
promise. The only ingredient missing to add authenticity to our
Satyricon follies was body sweat. Unfortunately, the make-up
department had not provided for this contingency. Through the
lenses, the liquid substance improvised looked like castor-oil
blobs, and dousing the bodies with water might bring on a chill
in the air conditioning. We solved this problem by shutting off
all ventilation and waited for the proper degree of swelter. The
studio became a mini-hell, while our eyes remained riveted on
naked buttocks for the first telltale glistening signs. We shot our
primordial fun fest in one squishy take, while I shouted dripping instructions from the sides.

The finished results took a week's development in the laboratory before we could run the processed film through the mov-
ieola. We had shot over twenty thousand feet of film, and in the
next few weeks we played the footage in all kinds of combinations, watching on multiple miniature screens that duplicated
the nine facsimiles shipped from Germany for the State Theater

production. Alongside these images we ran a taped performance of the music. Our conductor, a young Hungarian named
Gabor öTVoS, had not yet arrived in the country. Against that
day we allowed ourselves a degree of latitude regarding tempi
adjustments until his own designated ones came our way. We
did set the exact position of the stage screens during this time.
The screens themselves were of different sizes and shapes,
ranging from three to twelve feet in length. They were composed of a plastic screen fabric stretched onto aluminum framing and suspended at uneven distances from one another. Next,
the interplay of slide projection and the filmed portions was sta-
bilized. These screen arrangements would vary with each
act, creating new balances and perspectives. öTVoS finally
arrived and prepared a piano tape of the overture for our use,
thereby giving us the exact timings needed for a cutting
of the film.

The opera itself was staged within three weeks. The acting
style would be realistic, with touches of stylization to underline
the macabre moments. The cast was an ideal City Opera combination, which means high individual excellence and a strong
sense of ensemble. When not involved with the actors or our
technical setup, we were concerned with Norman Tucker's English adaptation. Geared to a British public, it often seemed less
direct than the original would indicate. Whole passages were
reconceptualized and rewritten. During all this hustle of activity, Niska and öTVoS were embarked on private warfare. His
rigidity in musical matters equaled her own free-wheeling approach. öTVoS could not speak English. Niska could, all too
clearly. Our *lingua bellum* became Italian, which öTVoS and I
could manage and Niska could not. I became the aide-de-camp
between them—translating and expurgating tirades as the occasion dictated. Eventually peace was restored, although öTVoS
never really found his way with the score. Niska's Emilia Marty
was and remains a splendid jewel of a performance—combining
a grand style with a sense of truth that is formidable, to say the
least. Meanwhile Gardner and Emile would attend the fiery
run-throughs, to insure that our film calculations were correct
and apposite to the devised stage action. We were given one
whole rehearsal in the theater to run through film and slides,

with the conductor and a pianist in the pit. Three dress rehearsals then followed, with the entire cast onstage. Only the final
rehearsal would be with orchestra. On this occasion, the orchestra's time superseded any other concern. All technical problems
would have to be attended to between the acts or after the rehearsal. *Makropoulos* easily became the most complicated show
to run backstage in a repertory of twenty operas. It required
trigger-sharp attention and interaction between the stage and
camera crews. All signals emanated from the stage manager's
desk. Gardner, Emile, and I would station ourselves in the auditorium, checking the media sequences from different vantage
points. Often a projector positioned too high for its respective
screen would cause headless images to appear. A loose or tan-
gled bit of stage masking would blot out all images from several
screens. These were remediable, but a burning slide was irre-
placeable in performance. Moisture sometimes accrued overnight between the slides, and what looked like a strange but
arresting effect out front was for us sheer disaster. To add to
such hazards, a lamp in a projector might begin to lose its watt-
age in midscene, and the image would begin a slow fade to
oblivion.

As I had suspected, the conductor did not maintain the same
tempi in any two performances. What conductor worth his salt
does? Slide cues could be managed, but there was no monitoring the motion pictures; once they had been cued, nothing
could stop them. Rarely did the musical cue match the corresponding movie image. It was always approximation time
USA—a fact we had anticipated. There was an inbuilt sense of
improvisation in the proceedings that was refreshing. All motion pictures and still slides were rear projected. The projectors
were mounted backstage behind the nine screens, and a black
velours curtain served to mask them from the audience. Slots
cut out of this masking served as apertures for the camera
lenses. In toto, we used eight projectors: four Buell slide projectors and four Quartz sixteen-millimeter ones. Out of the
twenty thousand feet originally shot, exactly three thousand feet
were finally used (about twenty minutes' worth of film). Over a
hundred slides in glass with metal binders were mounted in
carousel trays. The film had cost $30,000 to shoot and the physi-

cal stage production another $40,000. These figures became
pretty standard for future media operations.

A GLIMPSE AT THE
FINISHED PRODUCTION

After the conductor has taken his place at the podium, the
curtain rises on an ostensibly dark and empty stage. A single
large structure looms in the upstage area—one of the nine jigsaw screens. An image begins to glow on it—a fractured piece
of the Makropoulos document written in Greek. It fades slowly
as the film overlaps the document. In slow motion the figure of
Emilia Marty is running toward us from afar. The overture begins. As the ostinato continues in the orchestra, the remaining
eight screens begin their gradual descent, singly and in pairs, at
varying intervals. They pick up Marty's image in passing until
her flight covers all nine surfaces. Prus's house materializes on
one of the screens, and we witness Marty's frantic attempt to
gain entry (at regular speed). The sought-after formula (a slide)
appears again, along with a close-up of the door knocker marked
with the Baron's name and family seal. A pair of headlights
shines through the document and obliterates it. Simultaneously,
on one of the central panels, the chauffeur is seen pursuing
Marty as the chase moves from screen to screen. Huge still
close-ups of the chauffeur, Dr. Makropoulos, and Emperor Ru-
dolph flash subliminally in counterpoint. Marty is dressed completely in black, with a large picture hat and a veil covering her
face. As she continues her headlong flight, her other aliases follow. Each character appears in respective period costume,
working backward in time to when Marty was Elina Makropoulos, aged sixteen. For a moment the jagged pace slackens as we
study the young girl, but several rows of candles begin an ominous progression across the screens at various angles, and we
are at the court of Rudolph II in the year 1587. The ritual of the
potion-taking is under way. Elina is brought under guard to face
her father, who administers the drug while the crazed courtiers
assail her with mocking laughter. Each screen presents a con-
trasting view of this event. The effect is a surrealistic compos-

ite. Above this panoply, on the highest screen off center, we see a still of Emilia Marty as she contemplates her sad history on the lower screens. The film lurches and blurs as Elina drinks the formula and falls to the ground. We next see her on a bier, surrounded by gutted rows of candles. The camera moves into a close-up of her eyes, which suddenly open, then pulls back as she rises and descends from her elevated sarcophagus. She rushes to the portals and throws the doors open. In the dim light she notices the crumpled document on the floor where Rudolph had thrown it in despair of its efficacy. Stooping to pick it up, Elina becomes aware of a hooded monk walking toward her out of the shadows. Clutching the document, she runs from his outstretched arm as he begins his inexorable stalking of her through centuries to come. Elina's girlish figure, clad in a light blue gown, again merges with her other selves until a gigantic close-up of the terrified Marty dominates the screen in a freeze frame. This is the final tableau of the overture. Practically all the jigsaw pieces of the puzzle have been revealed. It will take the course of the evening to fit them together.

As the stage lights brighten, the nightmare images have left the screens and in their place we see still projections of bookcases and cabinets that amplify the stage picture. This is another function of the screens: besides reflecting Marty's torment, they help establish time and place. When Marty enters Dr. Kolenaty's office, she is dressed as we had seen her during the filmic overture. She steps out from behind one of the screens upstage, as if out of the void of history. While the law suit is discussed, the screens reflect her memory and several images of the overture are replayed in a new context. The hidden document keeps making tantalizing reappearances. The most telling use of the motion-picture clips occur in the following places:

a) As Gregor mentions his threat of suicide, Marty sees herself lying in death. The still figure of Elina Makropoulos surrounded by candles appears behind her. Marty is about to faint, but she recovers herself and the memory vanishes.

b) A few minutes later Gregor, questioning Marty, begins to handle her roughly. She seems to fall apart again, and as he apologetically leads her back to a chair, an enormous close-up of the monk springs up, his arms outstretched in her direction. In such instances, past and present become one, and the primary role of the film as psychic biography is entrenched.

The above sequences are entirely our invention. The first act provides an interesting solution to one of Čapek's built-in horror effects. Marty, wishing to discourage Gregor's amorous pursuits, attempts to reveal herself as she truly is. The script calls for a greenish light to flood the scene. In our version Marty raises her veil. Behind her a film unravels, exposing her as a 342-year-old hag.

In the second act, the slides are again used to implement stage reality. We are backstage at the theater after one of Marty's performances. Stagehands are seen storing several bits of scenery. One item is an Egyptian mummy case. On the screens we project some Ionian funeral statuary that complement it. This projection repeats itself ad infinitum. The screens are now farther upstage and even less visible than they were in the first act. A series of pulley ropes hang in front of them, helping to demarcate the backstage storage area from Marty's dressing room. The two erotic film passages mentioned earlier (Montez and Hauk Sendorf, and the Ellian MacGregor "secret practices") are played against the pleadings of the now senile Hauk and the investigations of Baron Prus. I've often wondered what our *Oh, Calcutta!* pair must have thought of these truncated but highly suggestive simulations of their own simulations.

The single most dramatic use of slides in the opera happens at the conclusion of this act. As Prus leaves to secure the desired document, Marty laughs triumphantly. She sees the predatory chauffeur contemplating her from behind the stage ropes. The Ionian reliquaries dissolve into full-length stills of the chauffeur staring down at her from on high, as Marty sinks back against the mummy case in an act of hysterical defiance.

Act III is pure Gaudi. The screens now huddle over the action. A series of assorted Gaudi prints create the bizarre wallpaper of Marty's private domain. The jigsaw puzzle is about to complete itself. While Marty recounts the story of her three-hundred-odd-year life, the central-screen images parallel her narrative exactly. The film episodes fit together at last. When

Emilia collapses, smoke begins to seep onto the stage, and the chauffeur, now changed back in time to the monk, makes his way to claim his prize. Instead of transfiguring Marty into a hag à la *Lost Horizon* (as per stage directions), I preferred she round out her own cycle and return to a lost moment of innocence. She drops the gaudy trappings of Emilia Marty and, before our eyes, she becomes Elina Makropoulos once again. Dressed in the identical blue gown we had seen on screen, she seems to glide joyously toward her rendezvous with death. After her long peroration, she offers the Makropoulos secret to any of her earthly pursuers in attendance. She has no further use for it. "Take it! Take it!" she cries, and the girl Christa seizes it and puts it to the flame of an oil lamp. Marty cries out *"Pater Hemon"* and dies. The cue for the final curtain is given at this point in Janáček's score. Since the orchestra continues to play for another minute, I preferred to utilize it up to the last chord. As Marty falls into the arms of the monk, the central panel discloses the document being destroyed by flames. All of Marty's past aliases spring to sudden life, running like moths toward the licking flames in an orgy of immolation. The hungry fire becomes a conflagration that bursts over all nine screens. As the monk carries the body of his quarry through the smoke and fire, the orchestra thunders its final amen. Slowly the retreating apparition becomes one with the enveloping smoke of time as the curtain falls.

13

Jesus Christ Superstar

When the phone rang I was resting comfortably in a hospital bed in Poughkeepsie, New York. A storm was raging outside, but my steady dosage of Valium made it a thing of childhood, where storms underlined the blessings of home and its protection against all trolls, real and imagined. My lawyer was at the other end of the wire informing me I was no longer to be director for *Jesus Christ Superstar*. An automobile accident had put me out of the box. A fractured lower vertebra would not be healed in time to support the director part of me. In my tranquilized state I barely grasped this news and, lulled by the sputterings at my window, I fell into a deep sleep. I awoke in time for supper—my head automatically full of *Superstar*. For months now my brain had become a proscenium arch under which the entire roster of *Superstar*'s characters danced madly. At the time of the accident on the Taconic, I was similarly occupied and hardly aware of the moment of impact. A year's preparatory work had come to a screeching halt—not with the proverbial whimper, but with an unforeseen bang.

It was July 1971. I had been married not even two months and had just left an audition for rock singers at the Mark Hellinger Theatre in New York. We were on the brink of final casting decisions and I was obliged, that fateful weekend, to be upstate to supervise a run-through of *La Bohème*. A summit meeting of *Superstar* personnel had been set for the coming Monday to iron out troublesome production details. It would be the final powwow between management and staff before embarking on the golden road to Samarkand. My friend and publisher, Bob Holton, had volunteered to drive my wife Bonnie and me upstate, en route to his own destination farther north. We were all seated up front while the back was occupied by luggage and two of Bob's black poodles. Just before the accident, the dogs set up a premonitory yowling. The car radio had just relayed the landing of our astronauts on the moon. Later I was informed that the superterrestrial event had sent shock waves into the stratosphere sufficient to cushion the impact of our simultaneous collision. Ergo, not extinction, but a fissure of bone and tissue (or so the celestial tea leaves would indicate). I should know better than to believe in such hocus-pocus, but it is my problem that I doubt yet dote.

Neither Bob nor Bonnie suffered more than minor whiplash, and the dogs went unscathed. Yours truly was fortune's plaything and I was hospitalized for almost two weeks. I returned to New York in an ambulance and spent two more recumbent and moribund weeks in bed. During this siege I was fitted for a corset to help support my spine for limited peregrinations. The corset affected my entire musculature and I became a walking ramrod. Stiff-necked and dour, I acted a road-company Von Stroheim minus the monocle. The illusion was further enhanced by an enforced renunciation of the taxi for the upholstered security of the limousine. From its windows I gazed sad-eyed but chin-high at the passing scene—a perfect counterfeit of my Prussian model. Eventually I was permitted to supervise the revival of *The Makropoulos Affair* at the City Opera. It was ironic indeed to return to my 342-year-old heroine. A new horizon had opened up for me with the mounting of the Janáček opera in 1970. This, the first major-scaled multimedia staging in New York, had broken with operatic traditions and it was this approach that had attracted the authors of *Superstar*. I learned that Tom O'Horgan was my replacement as *Superstar*'s director. His ascendancy was not entirely a surprise, for we had been the main contenders for the directoral reins. O'Horgan's preference for a more conventional theater approach threw the rest of my team of media technicians into a cocked hat. He demanded

a clean production slate and got it. All sorts of rumors were rampant concerning this change in leadership. Many implied I
had been on my way out long before the accident. In fact, it
appeared the accident may have been contrived—an almost
baroque bit of face-saving. Years later, in the midst of legal
proceedings stemming from the accident, the *Superstar* management would come to my defense and insure us a belated
victory.

While the gossip spread, my depression was somewhat alle-
viated by a return to the more humane pursuits of repertory.
There is a singular kind of joy involved in this—a super sense of
accomplishment as productions appear, disappear, and resur-
face years later on the agenda. This is not to deny that each time
a production is taken out of mothballs one still feels like a fish
swimming upstream. The repertory system, at least in opera, is
not necessarily a mellowing process. The original cast of any
given production has usually dispersed by the time of revival,
and the new cast is required to grasp immediately what originally took weeks of assimilation. A revival is mostly another
opening night, with all its perils revisited, and only incidentally
a growing experience. Still, it's your baby, and it has survived
the mildew of storage and other corruptions of time. While I
practiced Janáček that season, my inner mind was still grooved
to the problems of *Superstar*—now rehearsing down the block,
yet a million miles away. What the hell, it was just another
show, I argued. But it was not just another show!

On the surface, *Jesus Christ Superstar* seemed a brash, ir-
reverent view of the greatest story ever told. It was a wild blend
of soft and hard rock, cross-pollinated by classical wildflowers—
take your pick: Vivaldi, Dvořák, Prokofiev, et al. One evening
Andrew Webber, its composer, sat at my Yamaha and demonstrated his skills at gleaning the best of the classical cream.
Nothing in life springs full grown from Jove's brow, except Mi-
nerva. Webber was merely reaffirming an artistic prerogative:
Borrow if you must, but only from the best. His mad conglomer-
ate of musical styles still managed to get under the skin and
convince that something of this spirit had been afoot B.C. For all
its cynical high-stepping, its true rock core was innocence—a
desire to retrieve some kind of belief out of the hard core of

existence. It has since been mistaken for high camp. That's okay too, if you look at camp as the cry for help it invariably is. Listening to *Superstar*, one immediately summoned up a double vision—a watery-eyed H. B. Warner, the Christ of De Mille's *King of Kings*, thrown into a Dali-esque landscape of limp watches and wearing a Pierre Cardin caftan. One image presupposes the other and both are necessary for the work's effectiveness—the dominating image depends on which generation is looking through the stereopticon. The most original aspect of the work is the emergence of Judas as rock hero. Part lover and part inquisitor, he is the voice of our time interpenetrating history—and posing all those damned impossible questions again in the glare of our disaffection.

Superstar was a natural for multimedia so I had immediately enlisted the aid and collaboration of the *Makropoulos* team, Gardner Compton and Emile Ardolino. We went about creating the special world of Tim Rice and Andrew Webber much as we had for Janáček. We began by initiating a film scenario that aimed at an amalgamation of the New—and newer—testaments.

The recording had already been released in the States to wild acclaim, and all three of us had caught the *Superstar* fever. We were hungry to update the faith of our childhood, and since we had given up on temples and churches somewhere in adolescence, *Superstar* seemed an indirect road back. We refused to accept it as the show-biz send-up it was purported to be. How marvelous, we felt, to have plucked this theatrical plum, which both danced the soul around and helped fill the coffers. The whole world seemed to be singing *Superstar* that winter of 1970 when we began our work.

An overnight trip to London round Christmastime confirmed my engagement with the management. The authors and their producer, Robert Stigwood, agreed to conjoin with the American team the following April, when we would unveil our production scheme. What had been accomplished in opera was now to take a giant step forward on Broadway. As I have indicated, there had been attempts at multimedia on the Great White Way—but such had been the icing on the cake, never the cake itself. Compton and Ardolino (why do most last names, when coupled, sound like a team of lawyers?) had devised the media for the porn musical *Oh! Calcutta!* The filmed portions were actually blowups of the actors performing onstage. Compton was contracted to reshoot each time there was a significant cast replacement—a process accomplished in a day. The scale of wages for the performer was circumscribed accordingly. Union regulations governing such matters were either nonexistent or extremely tensile. When it came to opera, they were mostly nonexistent. Opera, after all, is art—and art is always in some presubsidized panic—which is to say very few make much money in art. Unions, which had tended to be lenient and even disinterested in such media pursuits, were now on the verge of a possible confrontation. *Superstar* was a presold blockbuster. It could easily become the ideal precedent the unions were looking for in multimedia practices. In the light of this possibility, Stigwood was understandably apprehensive. Union interference might escalate costs astronomically, thereby making operating costs prohibitive. Not unlike a television commercial, it was conceivable that a stray thumbnail in close-up might be the pretext for a royalty payment to the invisible owner attached to it off-screen. Think of crowds at Jersusalem's gates—and other such effects both grand and intimate! These considerations were much in mind as we developed the film scenario. We were forced to second-guess union attitudes. In the long run we managed to steer our course expeditiously, with no loss artistically. The media technique would have saved the production enormous sums of money, besides creating a new standard for budgeting in future. To further the media approach, we asked Robin Wagner to create the stage surfaces on which we would cast our magic lanterns.

Compton, Ardolino, and I met with Stigwood and the authors as prearranged. We spent a week at Stigwood's baronial estate outside London. Dogs, ping-pong, a Gypsy wagon, and an army of hangers-on dotted the manicured landscape. These gentlemen had a disconcerting habit of popping out from behind bushes, singly and in clumps, until one felt policed in some way. It rather resembled a sinister turnout by Edward Gorey. Notwithstanding the seriocomic atmosphere, our plans were enthusiastically endorsed. Compton and Ardolino flew directly to Israel for a week's shooting and I returned to work with Robin Wagner in New York, besides monitoring singing auditions. The block outside the Hellinger was lined daily with scruffy young hopefuls—with or without beards and guitars. Often the contestants extended from the stage door near Eighth Avenue down to Broadway, a block away, and around the corner. Wagner was developing his marvelous design and our only major hang-up was the placement of a network of microphones needed for amplification. We were on the verge of a solution when dissolution struck in the form of my accident. Stigwood would have been forced to proceed without my key presence in what, for him, were then unchartered waters. He chose an alternate course and revamped *Superstar* as another extension of *Hair*—a less risky but commercially proven commodity. Thus O'Horgan became the new Merlin. The media materials were scrapped and the films shelved. What could have been a breakthrough became another exercise in lumber and canvas.

O'Horgan's production opened in late September to mostly scurrilous reviews. It ran less than a year and was not toured in that version thereafter. Rice and Webber both felt that, had our media version been mounted, *Superstar* might still be running. Anyway, the films still exist in a vault somewhere, and Wagner retains his model of the stage setting we had devised for the superproduction that never was.

14

The Dormant Masterworks of Frederick Delius

On March 2, 1884, the ocean liner *Gallia* departed Liverpool bound for America. Two weeks and a stormy crossing later, she docked in New York Harbor. With not a single celebrity aboard, the arrival passed unnoticed by the press but for a brief item concerning George Paynter, the *Gallia's* barkeep. Duly noted was the fact that this trip represented his five-hundredth crossing of the Atlantic. On board, and no doubt helping Paynter celebrate this historic event, was Frederick Delius, making the first of two trips to America, en route to claiming ownership of some orange groves in Solano Grove, Florida.

A similar passage into the American wilderness had been accomplished a half century earlier by a famous compatriot of the fledgling composer, the actress Fanny Kemble. In her *Journal of a Residence on a Georgia Plantation* (1838–1839) she struck a prophetic note when she described the singing of the Negro slaves: "The high voices, all in unison, and the admirable time and true accent with which their responses are made, always make me wish that some great musical composer could hear these semi-savage performances. With a little skillful adaptation and instrumentation, I think one or two barbaric chants and choruses might be evoked from them that would make a fortune of an opera."

By 1896, Delius had left his semitropical paradise and was back in England. The orange trees had rotted, but the impact of those "semi-savage performances" had endured. Casting about for a vehicle to contain the full measure of that impact, Delius hit upon a popular novel of the time, *The Grandissimes*, by the American, George Cable. The section on the rebel slave, Bras-Coupé, seemed an ideal subject for an opera. Being a staunch Wagnerite, not to mention a confirmed hedonist, Delius was not to be content, however, "with a little skillful adaptation." England at the time was the home of such worthies as James Barrie and Rudyard Kipling, and was playing host to the stage-struck Henry James and even to Cable himself. Either from lack of acquaintance or literary taste, Delius eschewed their presence and prevailed upon Charles Francis Keary (1848–1917) to fashion a suitable libretto for him. Unfamiliar with American mores (black or white) or Cable's novel, Keary, a literary jack-of-all-trades, went about setting to verse the outlines of the plot as given him by Delius.

The operatic version of *Bras-Coupé*, ("Maimed Arm" in rough translation) was retitled *Koanga* (the original French name in Congolese). Its première in Elberfeld, Germany, in 1904, started a precedent that would become procedure. (*A Village Romeo and Juliet*, 1900–1901, and Delius's final masterpiece, *Fennimore and Gerda*, 1908–1910, first saw the light of the day in German opera houses). *Koanga*'s debut performance sported a Russian as the mulatto Palmyra and an American, Charles Whitehall, as Koanga, in leopard skin and blackface. The opera was not to receive its first London performance until 1935, a year after the composer's death. On that occasion it was conducted by Sir Thomas Beecham at Covent Garden in a revised version by Beecham and Edward Agate. Again Koanga was a white man in blackface (John Brownlee). Lacking full pictorial evidence, I cannot guarantee the leopard skin had been entirely discarded. Both premières elicited identical response: Keary's libretto was denigrated and Delius's music highly praised. Yet alack, alas, and sad to say, Miss Kemble's "fortune of an opera" was not to be. In fact, *Koanga* was not to be again until its American première in 1970, where Keary's gaucheries (revised from a revision) still abounded, while Delius, Wagner-*cum*-spiritual, utterly captivated. More than a decade after *Koanga*'s initial performance, the American Negro composer Scott Joplin (1868–1917) was to create a sister companion to *Koanga* with his *Treemonisha*, wherein Handelian anthems nestle with "semi-savage choruses." In their special ways, both works are transcendental views of racial tensions and aspirations.

"Transcendental" is a key word toward understanding the overwhelming success of *Koanga* at its Washington, D.C., première. *Koanga* is typically Delian. Filled with traditional operatic forms, it is, however, more tone poem than opera. Delius's pantheism is as strong a dramatis persona as any of the opera's characters. Perhaps time has been charitable to this composer, for the new media techniques employed in *Koanga*'s behalf were successful in abrogating the canvas lakes and forests of standard operatic procedures and allowed the virtues of the work to shine in a new perspective.

The Washington Opera Society production was, in its inception, as freakish as anything in the opera's history. Forced to cancel the local première of Virgil Thompson's *Four Saints in Three Acts*, the Society was left to fill a vacuum stuffed with contractual obligations to black artists. When consulted by Mr. Hobart Spalding (then president of the Society), I suggested *Koanga* as a suitable, even inspired, replacement. I assured the perplexed Mr. Spalding that *Koanga* was indeed an opera and not the name of a boy's camp in the Adirondacks.

A play-through of the score created instant euphoria, and plans were immediately initiated for its production. Enter Ronald Chase. He also was one of the artists involved with the defunct Thompson project. A brilliant sculptor and film designer, he was among the first to use media devices effectively. I had admired his *Turn of the Screw* a year earlier (also a Washington Opera Society offering). Chase's solution for Britten's opera seemed to have come right out of my own head—he had been an interloper in my thoughts and I didn't even know the man. Here we finally were, thrown together on our transient shores, and for a while he would still remain unknown to me. Chase, based in San Francisco, and I in New York began our plans for *Koanga* via the telephone. For the next few months we managed a hefty telephone bill between us that the Opera Society willingly paid. The entire production was created courtesy of A.T.&T. Chase and I were actually to meet face to face for the first time on the cutting room floor. We had three months to prepare for the première in December 1970.

THE STORY OF *KOANGA*

Simon Perez, the tyrannical slave overseer on the plantation of Don José Martinez, has been forcing his attentions upon Palmyra, the mulatto slave-girl who serves Clotilda, mistress of the plantation and wife of Don José. Don José announces that he has purchased a new slave, Koanga, who is an African prince and voodoo priest. Koanga, while refusing to submit to the white man's rule, is, however, captivated by the charms and beauty of Palmyra. Palmyra in turn feels an unexplained attraction to Koanga, because of his personal magnetism, and, more important, because he has stirred within her a long-buried pride in her native race. Don José offers Palmyra as Koanga's bride if he will submit to slavery. He agrees and renounces his voodoo oath never to be a slave to those who bought him. Clotilda tells Perez that the marriage must not take place because Palmyra is in fact the illegitimate daughter of Clotilda's own father and a black slave. Because of this Palmyra must not marry a slave. Perez agrees to plot Palmyra's abduction and prevent the marriage, thus saving Palmyra for himself. During the wedding celebration Perez abducts Palmyra and the half-crazed Koanga calls upon his voodoo gods for vengeance. He flees to the hills with a band of fellow slaves. He finds Perez attempting to seduce Palmyra and, in a bitter duel, he slays Perez. Perez's followers in turn slay Koanga. In desperation, Palmyra, mourning her lost lover, stabs herself. The entire story is told as a flashback by a conjureman.

In order to accurately re-create *Koanga*'s Creole atmosphere of the late eighteenth century, Chase was dispatched to Louisiana in September, where he scouted a number of New Orleans

mansions for possible location shooting. The estate Parlange
(recently declared a national monument) was chosen to evoke
the Grandissimes' mansion in the opera. Slave quarters were
discovered in fine preservation on a run-down estate outside
New Orleans. In two and a half weeks, Chase, armed with Nik-
kormat camera, took over five hundred still photographs (of
which two hundred were used) and with a Bolex 16-mm. camera (hand-held and on tripod) shot over thirty minutes of film (of
which twenty minutes were utilized). The media effects were
the result of such techniques as superimposition and a process
called bipacking, whereby films are placed one atop the other
through an optical machine in order to get opaque darknesses
and multiple-color schemes. This process enabled us to create
the occultish landscapes surrounding Koanga's flight from his
white masters, and the ensuing voodoo rites. As in the later *Village Romeo,* three scrims—front, rear, and middle-distance—
served as projection surfaces that could be used interchange-
ably. The film images would be in constant play during the
course of the opera, thereby creating a unique time-space di-
mensional reality. A chorus of forty was kept offstage throughout, their voices emanating from speakers strategically placed in
the auditorium. A suggestion of great distance was obtained and
controlled electronically. Minimal set and props were in evidence: a platform representing the slave block and several cane
chairs were the sole stage properties. Later, in *Romeo,* we
would cover the orchestra pit with scrim so that the orchestra
lights would not interfere with visual effectiveness. The Bay-
reuth-like absence of music stands would increase the poetic
illusion.

Three performances of *Koanga* were given at the Lisner Auditorium on the campus of George Washington University in
Washington, D.C.—the last on my birthday. It was a huge
goodie and for once I didn't feel slighted or forgotten in the
holiday rush. Those responsible for *Koanga's* success were: the
media team of Ronald Chase, who designed both the film and
stage settings; Nananne Porcher, lighting designer; Skip Palmer, media operator representing Staging Techniques (and its
battery of sixteen slide projectors and three 16-mm. movie projectors); costume designer Joseph Bella; and choreographer

Doris Jones. Heading the cast of superb soloists were Eugene Holmes and Claudia Lindsey, both black artists—at last! The Washington Opera Society chorus and orchestra were under the leadership of Paul Callaway.

John Coveney, Director, Artist Relations at Angel Records and an ardent Delian himself, described the fruits of the collaboration: ". . . it was beautiful in an unearthly sort of way, but at the same time totally real. The spell of the Delius music was heightened to an extraordinary degree by the warm, glowing colors in the changing imagery of multimedia, as the singers wandered among lush beauties of nature. . . . "

While *Koanga* may not make a fortune for the Delius estate, this production, along with *Makropoulos* and those to follow, was to help create a form of visual poetry that has helped forge a new theater metaphysics in America. Its methods stretched the horizons of total theater and, most important, a springboard was found to activate dormant musical masterworks of the recent past.

Shortly after *Koanga*'s American debut, I received an inquiry from Sadler's Wells in London regarding my interest in mounting the work for their company. I naturally assumed our media team would be hired for the venture, but English ardor cooled at such a prospect and we were left dangling our heels. The London revival did take place with the Washington leads, Eugene Holmes and Claudia Lindsay spearheading the cast. Charles Groves, a not always ideal Delian, would conduct idiomatically, however, and Keary's text, revised for the umpteenth time by Douglas Craig and Andrew Page, finally made sense out of nonsense. The physical production was realistically conceived, and a visible chorus of white singers donned blackface. The critical reception was less than mixed in its praise. A witness at one of the performances reported spotting patches of white gleaming through the slapdash make-up of the chorus, adding a note of hilarity to the occasion. *Koanga* had lacked size and punch for the British public, while it had received a roaring welcome in America.

Can a production of any given musical work really make or break it? A moot point, certainly—yet the success of *The Makropoulos Affair*, and the ensuing bouquet of *Koanga, A Village*

Romeo, and *Tote Stadt* in a media context had made a huge difference in encouraging audience interest and their continued patronage of these problematic masterworks. *Makropoulos* had appeared in over four seasons of repertory since 1970 at the New York City Opera. *A Village Romeo* spanned three seasons since 1971, and *Tote Stadt,* a recent addition, played the winter of '75 and spring of '76. All three will be revived in the near future, and they constitute the largest single aggregate of mixed media stagings by any opera company in the world.

Collectively these works share a common problem: the composer's uncommon vision or bias that places him outside the mainstream of operatic currency. *Trovatore* can manage under any given circumstance—it is a substantial pasta with a bottle of Bardolino. But *A Village Romeo* is a special herbal brew. Given a realistic staging, it inevitably comes up heady but awkward, for its greatest effects are made in the orchestral interludes, while the curtain is down. The pantheism espoused in *Koanga* is *Romeo's* operating center—its modus vivendi. The opera's tragic dénouement is defined in this ambience and no expenditures on constructed scenery could ever do justice to its evanescence.

"Poetry without rhetoric, sound without uproar, reticence instead of exaggeration. Delius is the last great champion of romance in the twentieth century." These remarks by Sir Thomas Beecham characterize both the composer and, most specifically, his *Village Romeo and Juliet.* Beecham might just as well have been describing Debussy's *Pelléas and Mélisande.* Both works have a mutual aural affinity; Delius's opera was published in 1901, while Debussy's was completed a year later. *Village Romeo* is Delius at the peak of inspiration and, along with his *Mass of Life,* his chef-d'oeuvre.

Romeo is Delius's fourth opera, based on a novella by Gottfried Keller. It is not a rural paraphrase of Shakespeare's play, although several of its features are reminiscent of it. Instead of a feuding aristocracy, we have a pair of farmers fighting ownership over a strip of land. The opera was originally composed to a German text arranged by Delius's wife, Jelka. It was given its première at Berlin's Komische Oper in 1907. Three years later, the English première took place at Covent Garden under the baton of that *echt* Delian, Sir Thomas Beecham. Jelka's English adaptation of the German suffered considerably in the Channel crossing, a situation that has lasted to this day. Although *Romeo*, of Delius's six operas, is the most often performed, it has maintained a "festival" status wherever it has surfaced. Like some precious family heirloom, it is gingerly but lovingly brought into the light of day and just as quickly consigned to the trunk for safekeeping. I had been peddling the work to managements for literally over two years and had been on the threshold of production so often, I was practically slaphappy by the time the Washington Opera Society took it on. *Koanga's* triumph had paved the way for its musical peer.

Koanga's team was again at the helm, with one difference; Theoni Aldredge would design the costumes. Instead of the dear old inadequate Lisner Auditorium, we would produce *Romeo* in the plush opera house at the recently completed Kennedy Center.

THE STORY OF
A VILLAGE ROMEO AND JULIET

Act I, Scene 1

Manz and Marti, rivals for a strip of wild land that lies between their fields, are both plowing. When the other is not looking, each takes an extra furrow from the waste land. Sali and Vreli bring their parents' midday meals and later rejoin the two fathers as they eat together. The Dark Fiddler is heard in the distance. Marti recognizes him as the true owner of the wild land, but, being illegitimate, the Fiddler has no legal right to it. The discussion about the sale of the land erupts into a quarrel, and the two fathers furiously forbid their children to play together.

Act I, Scene 2

Sali approaches Vreli's house, which has fallen into disrepair during the six years since he last saw it. Both his and Vreli's parents have been involved in bitter lawsuits over the ownership of the wild land. As Vreli comes toward the house Sali stops her and they talk dejectedly about the situation. Sali hopes that all may yet end well if only they do not lose each other, and they plan to meet that evening in the wild land.

Act I, Scene 3

Sali and Vreli are enjoying each other's company when they hear the playing of the Dark Fiddler. He reminds them that they have played on his land and suggests, now that they are all beggars, that they come with him and share his vagabond existence. They refuse, and talk happily of their childhood days. Marti discovers the lovers and is dragging Vreli away when Sali fells him with a blow.

Act I, Scene 4

Sali's blow has damaged Marti's mind and he is taken away to a sanitarium. Now Vreli sits alone with her few remaining possessions. As Sali comes to say good-by, Vreli tells him that she too must leave, for the house has been sold. They sit together in front of the fire and fall asleep in each other's arms. They dream they are being married, but as dawn breaks they awake. Together they leave the house to share one day of happiness.

Act II, Scene 1

Sali and Vreli join in the gaiety of the fair until they are recognized. They buy everything that attracts them but suddenly notice they are being watched curiously by the crowd. Self-consciously they leave the fair and set out for the Paradise Garden, a country house near the river now used as an inn.

Act II, Scene 2

The Dark Fiddler and his friends, the vagabonds, sit around a table in the Paradise Garden. The Fiddler is telling them of the origin of the strife between Marti and Manz. As he is finishing, Vreli and Sali enter. The Fiddler urges them again to join him and his friends and take to the open road. The two lovers decide that their only way out is to drift down the river like the bargemen whose voices they hear, except that they can never return. They get into the boat.

Characters

Manz		Baritone
rich farmers		
Marti		Baritone

Sali, son of Manz

as a child	Soprano
as a man	Tenor

Vreli, daughter of Marti .... Soprano
The Dark Fiddler, rightful heir to the wood .... Baritone
Two Peasants .... Baritones
Three Women .... Sopranos and Mezzo-Soprano
Gingerbread Woman .... Soprano
Wheel-of-Fortune Woman .... Soprano
Cheap-Jewelry Woman .... Mezzo-Soprano
Showman .... Tenor
Merry-go-Round Man .... Baritone
The Slim Girl .... Soprano
The Wild Girl .... Mezzo-Soprano
The Poor Horn-Player .... Tenor
The Hunch-backed Bass Fiddler .... Bass

Time: Mid-nineteenth century. Six years elapse between the first and second scenes

Place: Seldwyla, Switzerland

Delius's Sali and Vreli are really embodiments of Adam and Eve who wander back to the Paradise Garden from which they were expelled. The heart of this bucolic tragedy lies in the lovers' choice to return to a state of grace by drowning. Unable to cope with life's corruptions, they prefer to meld with the incorruptible force of nature and therein seek a blissful and continued revival. A terrible beauty, all this—and a perfect media subject.

This time the production would claim 402 color slides and 4,000 feet of 16-mm. color film—of which every bit was used. Four film projectors were employed, and, as in *Koanga,* 16 slide projectors. The interaction between slides and film was continuous from curtain rise to finish. Three stationary scrims were used—front, center, and rear—and all film materials were front and rear projected. The slides were arranged in pairs and programmed on tape. A master console was controlled by a crew of three to four men. On specified musical cues, any combination of slides could be projected by the pressing of a single button. The film, operated manually, interlaced these projections. The only prerequisite was the necessity of maintaining two projections side by side at any and all times, in order to properly fill the expanse of the front scrim. The edges of the individual images were kept hazy to help achieve continuity. At the moment

of changeover, one could see sets of double images overlapping
one another, adding greater density and texture to the overall
scene. All images were photographic shots of actual places and
landscapes. Their combinations and superimpositions produced
an almost phantasmagoric illusion, rivaling, while simulating,
nature caught in the very processes of change. The singers
moved in and out of this evocative ambience—vulnerable and
transitory pieces of nature's immensity. Nan Porcher's artful
lighting accentuated this symbiotic relationship between man
and environment. The orchestra pit was totally covered with
black scrim, which allowed sound to pass through while blan-
keting out orchestral lights, thus linking the audience even
more totally with the stage.

The acting style required an even greater naturalness, the
scrim and special lighting creating closer focus on the actors'
reality.

Ron Chase and I had prepared *A Village Romeo* for over a
year prior to the first day of shooting. The film scenario was
relatively simple: a matter of catching nature in her varied
moods and the brief glimpses of the lovers suspended in them.
Naturally, the location for all this was of paramount importance.
My suggestion that the films be shot in Appalachia, U.S.A., met
with resistance on Ron's part. The terrain seemed too rugged
for Keller's delicate tale. The original locale is Switzerland of
1856. Ron took off to have a look and discovered Switzerland
1970—antenna-laden and worldly. The Switzerland of Delius's
fancy was discovered to exist in the Moselle Valley of Germany,
with its mixture of French and German influences. In two
months' time Ron shot churches, fields of poppies, houses, forests and lakes, and skies, skies, such unbelievable skies! An actual country fair popped up out of a children's fairy-tale book.
In every detail it seemed divinely dispatched to represent our
village fair of Act II. This "happening" became one of the high-
lights of the production, of which there were three more:

a) The Dream Sequence in Act I: Sali and Vreli fall asleep
and dream of their wedding day. This is as much as Delius tells
us of this episode. It is one of the interludes left for the orchestra to paint with curtain lowered. We imagined it as a combination wedding and funeral (clearly the intent of Delius's

scoring). Against overgrown paths and whirling gravestones, the lovers, dressed in pristine white, are joined in marriage. Yet the spectral presence of the Dark Fiddler and his cohorts suggests the even darker resolution to come. The children Sali and Vreli appear beside the pair, and even their fathers effect a reconciliation denied them in life. Nature for once is overwhelmed by the stained-glass glory of the local cathedral. These images of religious splendor are transformed into a predawn sky reflected in water—the one constant motif throughout the opera.

b) Another musical interlude, known as The Walk to the Paradise Garden, was written by Delius to cover a scene shift in the second act. It is one of the most famous pieces of its kind in musical history and practically a staple in the symphonic repertoire. It is a ten-minute idyll that functions like *Tristan and Isolde's Liebesnacht* music. This walk back to Eden was the inevitable pièce de résistance of the evening. The singers, John Stewart and Patricia Wells, the very embodiment of young love, leave the village fair and enter the woods. During the length of the interlude, they appear and disappear both in the flesh and in their filmic counterparts. They seem to penetrate deeper and deeper into the very heart of their own and nature's mysteries. They frolic, swim, meditate in the sylvan wonders that embrace them. Finally they emerge into the sunlight, thoughtfully moving toward their destiny in the Paradise Garden. As the walk was shot in Marin County in northern California, two actors other than Stewart and Wells, who were busy elsewhere, were chosen locally to represent the stage action. All facial close-ups were avoided to keep verisimilitude between the two pairs of lovers. The costumes prepared by Theoni Aldredge were identical to the ones employed in the actual production.

c) The opera's finale found the two wanderers setting themselves adrift on a hay barge. The lovers lie down on the straw as the barge is caught up in the stream's current. The stage darkens, and although the boat moves imperceptibly, the play of light suggests a long journey downstream. With the aid of the film and slides, we have the sensation of actually seeing the tiny craft sinking out of sight. The water continues its almost phosphorescent rippling, gradually fading to nothingness.

15

Lulu

Dear Mr. Gockley,

I intended to call you directly regarding last night's performance of *Lulu* but I have not sufficiently calmed down about it to make good sense. I suppose one must give your company points for attempting such an enterprise, but I, for one, want little to do with it in future. Whatever else it may represent, besides plain filth, frankly eludes me.

My husband and I are new members of the community and we have considered our subscription to the opera an important part of its cultural life. We are sufficiently angered and shocked by this affront, that nothing short of canceling our subscription can represent the true measure of our response.

We enclose tickets for the remaining portion of the season for you to dispose of as you choose.

Yours sincerely,

The time is March 1975. The place: Jones Hall for the Performing Arts in Houston, Texas. The above is one of several hundred letters received by the management of the Houston Opera in the weeks following our multimedia version of Alban Berg's *Lulu*. On the whole, eight out of ten letters received were abusive, and four out of ten canceled subscriptions. On opening night the audience response was divided. The negative faction soon took courage and began a barrage of boos and catcalls—a typical Corsaro opening night. Opera audiences are perhaps the trigger-happiest group in all the performing arts. They rival those of political rallies and sports events in the intensity of their approbation and/or vilification. In Paris, several years ago, when Maria Callas canceled her appearance as Norma in mid-performance, she was forced to escape by foot through back alleys to throw a pursuing mob off her scent.

The brunt of Houston's attack was not aimed at anyone behind the footlights. It was directed toward the unseen presence of the long-dead composer, Alban Berg; the object of its fulminations, an acknowledged operatic masterpiece.

Premièred in Zurich in 1937, *Lulu* has made the rounds of the world's stages and its ability to shock and dismay at this late date seems undiminshed, much to one's surprise. When our production was announced for presentation by the Opera Society in Washington the following spring, the local hue and cry against its importation discouraged the Washington, D.C., management from following through. *Lulu* continues to be strictly a connoisseur's delight, and most probably will never attain wide acceptance by American audiences.

Alban Berg (1885–1935) showed aristocratic tastes in his choice of libretti. The first fruit of his genius, *Wozzeck*, was based on Georg Büchner's pathbreaking play of the same name. *Lulu* (left unfinished at the time of Berg's death) derived from two plays by Frank Wedekind, *Earth Spirit* and *Pandora's Box*.

THE STORY OF THE OPERA

Prologue: An animal-tamer, accompanied by the clown from his circus, steps in front of the curtain and introduces his troupe, amongst whom is Lulu dressed in Pierrot's costume.

Act I

Lulu, since the age of thirteen the mistress of Dr. Schön, was married by him to an elderly medical specialist, Dr. Goll. While sitting for her portrait, being done by a little-known artist whom her husband has known, she talks to Dr. Schön and his son, Alwa. After father and son leave, the young artist, fascinated by Lulu's beauty, tries to approach her. Returning to the studio, Dr. Goll, enraged by the locked door, breaks it open. In his jealous fury, he suffers a stroke and dies.

Lulu marries the artist through the machinations of Dr. Schön, although she still remains his mistress. Schön secures important commissions for the artist, who believes they are evidence of his personal success. Lulu, meanwhile, is visited by Schigolch, an old panderer with whom she spent her childhood. He comes begging for money but slips away when Dr. Schön arrives. Dr. Schön wishes to terminate his relationship with Lulu because he is engaged to a young aristocratic socialite. In the heated words that follow, the artist comes into the room and Lulu leaves. Schön tells the artist of Lulu's past and discloses his relationship with her. In his despair, the artist commits suicide.

Alwa, who has written a revue in which Lulu is the featured dancer, sits in her dressing room while she prepares for the performance. During her dance, Lulu sees Dr. Schön in the audience with his fiancée and pretends to faint. When Dr. Schön hurries backstage, Lulu threatens to leave him and go to Africa with the Prince, one of her admirers. Realizing he may never see her again, Dr. Schön agrees to send a farewell letter to his fiancée, dictated by Lulu.

Act II

Lulu and Dr. Schön are now married. Their relationship is reaching a crisis. With and without the knowledge of Dr. Schön, strange persons meet at the house: the Countess Geschwitz, a woman deeply in love with Lulu; Schigolch, Lulu's old friend; his questionable companion, Rodrigo, an acrobat; and a young student entranced at the idea of his first meeting with Lulu. Dr. Schön, almost insane with suspicion, hides in the room. Under his eyes, his son Alwa declares his love for Lulu. In a rage of madness, Schön gives Lulu a revolver with which to kill herself. Instead, she fires five shots into his body.

Lulu, now sentenced to ten years in prison for Dr. Schön's murder, has contracted cholera. Geschwitz, Alwa, and Rodrigo discuss a plan to rescue her from the prison hospital: Geschwitz will take her place and Lulu will escape and flee. When the plan succeeds, Rodrigo is disgusted by Lulu's appearance as she returns home, and he leaves, threatening to expose them all to the police. Alwa, more fascinated than ever, decides to flee the country with her.

Lulu now lives in the slums of London with Geschwitz. The two barely manage to keep alive on Lulu's earnings as a streetwalker. The last of Lulu's customers is a sexual assassin who murders her. As he escapes he also kills Geschwitz, the witness.

Characters

Lulu	High Soprano
Countess Geschwitz	Mezzo-Soprano
A Wardrobe mistress	Contralto
A Schoolboy	Contralto
The Doctor	Speaking part
The Artist	Lyric Tenor
Dr. Schön	Baritone
Alwa, Dr. Schön's son, a writer	Tenor
An Animal Tamer	Bass
Rodrigo, an athlete	Bass
Schigolch, an old man	High Bass
The Prince, a traveler in Africa	Tenor
The Theater Director	Buffo Bass

Time: Last quarter of the nineteenth century
Place: A German city

In my multimedia production of *Lulu,* I tried to capture the genius-loci of the character. Lulu is a genius, albeit a sensual one, and very much the female extension of Don Giovanni. She lives wholly in an atmosphere of self-gratification—the eternal child who can satisfy all its appetites, knowing she can do so without malice while totally unaware of inflicting harm on anyone else. Hers is the energy of the polymorphous-perverse personality—direct, positive, and balanced within the scale of her psychosis. She is never calculating, which would make her dangerous. If she were a whore, one could deal with her, but with this overwhelming child it is another thing altogether. I think that is what most fascinated Berg and Wedekind—innocence seen as the triumph of sensual reality. Not sexual, but sensual. Such innocence belongs to a fabulous and rapacious jungle beast... and you lock up such beasts, you do not let such creatures loose. Lulu the invincible ultimately dies at the hands of Jack the Ripper, a beast of another stripe, at a time when she has degraded herself into prostitution and poverty. Like Giovanni, her male self, her destruction is signaled by a specific act of homicide. Both victims, the Commendatore in *Giovanni* and Dr. Schön in *Lulu,* are parent figures and represent the essential oedipal struggle in their respective dramas, which in Berg's opera is played against the confines of a repressive Prussian society in the Germany of 1885. Lulu's plight is a curious kind of *via crucis*—with the flesh as the cross. It is the opera's idée fixe. Unable to unshackle herself from its demands, Lulu must pursue it to its final extreme. Her punishment becomes the moral element of the tale.

Lulu and *Giovanni* remain exceedingly disturbing subjects for contemplation and analysis. Their "implications" cannot be entirely tamed by the mandates of law and order. While Lulu's and Giovanni's proposition of sensual liberty is hardly to be condoned, sublimation of such drives has been achieved within our society through the pursuit of power through money (sexual reality made manageable: a Freudian cliché) and thus another Eden ($) is substituted for the legendary one—itself vicariously poised over the secrets shared between apples.

Lulu and Giovanni remain anarchic but ever-beckoning figures of temptation and they must be controlled in order to keep the flow of blood in the streets down to a minimum. Accordingly we keep inventing new checks and balances against them rather than gaining new perspectives on their sexual imperative. As we expand our sexual horizons we may eventually loosen the hard knot of taboos—and even render passé the very notion of sexual anarchy in any form. Am I talking about a Space Age sensuality?

Flesh as the idée fixe is central to the production devised by Ronald Chase and me. The stage becomes more a state of mind than a piece of actual reality. Strange, terrifying and exotic, Lulu's world of drawing rooms and dressing rooms is a series of cages changing in a landscape of filmic flesh. One of the first images is Lulu regarding herself in a mirror as she adjusts the stays of her corset. The period itself is dramatized in this symbol of repression. Working within the same framework as *Village Romeo*, the combination of film and slide pictures created a limbo world of alienation, stacked with details of the period and its environment. The filmic backgrounds were shot in an empty elephant cage in the San Francisco zoo. With its imposing doors and enormous slabs of stone, it was formidably Greeklike. Pieces of realistic sets were placed within this context. Stray bales of hay were added to each scene, their quantity increasing as the drama progressed.* Wedekind envisioned his plays enacted in a circus atmosphere to best describe Lulu's bestiality and amorality. The "world as a circus" notion has been done to death by now—and ours seemed a fresh metaphor. Each scene on stage is surrounded by very sensual slides, enormous yet detached close-ups of breasts, buttocks, pelvises, and legs. Fragmented and isolated in their individual parts, they make marvelous abstract design. Only through their repetition is one made aware of what they really are. In their varied geometric dispositions around the stage they become the special prison for our big cat.

The motion-picture material attempts to handle its sensual subjects directly—the only possible option open to its producers. To do less would be to negate the work itself and vitiate its strengths.

The orchestral interludes binding the scenes are dramatized filmicly; they attempt to create episodes in Lulu's life and career alluded to in the text. The most poetic yet chilling segment follows on the death of Lulu's second husband, the artist. On film we see Lulu wandering through her husband's abandoned studio, full of gigantic, untouched canvases. The setting is pristine. Lulu pauses before one of the canvases, disrobes, and stretches out naked on the ground before its overwhelming whiteness. The final death scene in a London garret is the only instance of simultaneity between stage and screen action. A squalid pallet lies tucked away at a far distance upstage. A flimsy clothesline separates Lulu's bed from Geschwitz's quarters. The love scene between Lulu and Jack the Ripper is magnified on the front scrim on film. The effect is hallucinatory, all the vividness of its details are a harrowing, yet clinical, documentation of Lulu's rape and murder.

The old media team of *Koanga* and *Village Romeo* were again on hand; the singing-acting cast was superb, with Patricia Brooks's uncanny Lulu straight out of Pandora's box.

The news of the recent death of Alban Berg's widow is now

---

* A detail we were unable to effect in Houston—but that will be added to the next revival of this production.

about to open a new chapter in *Lulu*'s travels. It has been
known for years since the composer's death that the last act exists in manuscript form and, but for large patches of unfinished
orchestration, it can be performed intact. The widow had kept
jealous vigil over this material, never permitting it the light of
day, and meanwhile turning away most of the world's great
composers and conductors who offered their services in behalf
of the incomplete orchestration. The ritual of refusal was always
somewhat the same, it seems: Frau Berg, who kept her husband's effects alive down to shirts and the petrol to fill the tank
of his unused car in the garage, would welcome the distin-
guished guest and, apprised of his intention, she would promise
to consult Alban for the desired permission to complete the
work. Next morning the pilgrim would return to the shrine.
Frau Berg would punctiliously descend the stairs and inform
the humble supplicant, "Alban said no!" And that was that! The
widow became a teutonic Turandot, with no one able to pose
the riddle to open the lock. Since her death, Pierre Boulez has
become the lucky winner in the *Lulu* sweepstakes. His realization of the third act will be premièred sometime in 1978–79
under his baton at the Paris Opera. It is hoped that our production of *Lulu* will incorporate this missing act, and perhaps then
make the rounds of American opera houses.

16

Die Tote Stadt

The day following the Houston opening of *Lulu*, Ron Chase, Nan Porcher, Skip Palmer, and I caught an early-morning flight to New York. We were due for our first technical rehearsal of *Die Tote Stadt* at Lincoln Center within an hour of landing.

Scheduling problems in the operatic field often create preposterous snags. It seems every company in the world wants one's services at the same time. It's possible to find yourself rehearsing two brand-new productions concurrently, while applying Band-Aids to the hoary heads of repertory items. In 1974 I lived an Alice in Wonderland existence for several months. Implacably committed by conscience and contract, I was obliged to direct Cherubini's *Medea* for the City Opera and Pasatieri's *Sea Gull* for Houston side by side. I had staged *Medea* for the Caramoor festival the previous summer so it was assumed I could scramble it together in no time, despite a preponderantly new cast, chorus, and conductor. Mornings and afternoons were devoted to *Medea*, and evenings to *Sea Gull*. Both operas were rehearsed in their preliminary stagings in New York. This situation could hardly exist in the theater, which is a full-time occupation, but in opera, where the staying power of the larynx is of considerably shorter duration, such practices are normal. *Medea* would open in New York two nights after *The Sea Gull's* debut in Houston. When not preoccupied with Chekhov in Houston, I was on the long-distance phone to the State Theater in New York. In this instance long-distance reassurances were but long-distance lullabies—if a production is to convey a point of view, even in its trillionth revival, the director's presence is mandatory. Pasatieri prospered, while *Medea* succumbed in the crunch.

Die Tote Stadt by Erich Wolfgang Korngold was known to me for years as the darling of the underground set—which included purveyors of pirated recordings (in all their garden varieties), bibliophiles, and champions of the cult of E. W. Korngold—he who had committed minor heresy by defecting to Hollywood and the tainted dollar. The only available recording of the entire work was a vocally muddy and sonically dim tape of a performance made somewhere in outer Silesia; there were also sprinklings of Marietta's *Lied* in collections made by sundry divas.

By chance, at a party one night, I met Korngold's son. If you're ever in need of a fanatic proselytizer for special causes, meet George Korngold. I left that night with a Care package containing the score and a special tape of the opera. I played it the next day and was immediately impressed with the quality of the music and its theatrical possibilities. The New York City Opera is a little bit of Austria transplanted to Lincoln Center anyway, and so the *Kugel* and *Kirschwasser* flowed instantly at the prospect of recultivating this tender blossom of memory.

The Korngold revival was being sparked by RCA's recent release of the composer's film scores, as part of a wave of a country-wide nostalgia that is still gathering momentum. Visions of Errol Flynn brandishing his cutlass and Olivia de Havilland thrilling demurely to his mustachioed bravado were awakened. I can't recall how many knishes and Milky Ways had been downed and sometimes chucked up to Korngold in the darkened movie houses of my youth. For a while the Korngold mystique flooded the market—quintets, sonatas, concerti, songs, and even a symphony—music of quality written by a master in the genre, apostate or not.

Erich Korngold (1897–1957) was born in Janáček's home town, Brno, in Czechoslovakia. In contrast to Janáček, whose talents evolved gradually, Korngold's took instant flight. By the age of nine he was already a *Wunderkind,* and would remain the last of his species in pre-Hitler Europe. The delicious cartoon of the period (see page 179) tells the story completely.

The son of a powerful music critic and publisher, Julius Korngold, the young Erich was given every possible advantage and encouragement to develop his astonishing natural gifts. Proclaimed a genius at fourteen by Gustav Mahler, the arbiter of musical taste in Vienna at the time, the stripling was dispatched to the composer Alexander von Zemlinsky for instruction in harmony and counterpoint. Thereafter the boy's career took off like a brush fire. At eighteen, he produced his first effort: two one-act operas, *Violanta* and *The Ring of Polycrates*. By the time *Die Tote Stadt* was completed three years later, over twenty opera houses were vying to produce it. The première took place on December 4, 1920, in the two major opera houses in Hamburg and Cologne. Opera was a way of life then, with all the cachet and glamour associated with the modern film. Multiple premières were often de rigueur for the master practitioners of the day. I believe Mascagni holds the record, with seven simultaneous opening nights for his opera *Le Maschere* (The Masks). Korngold's work became the rage of Europe, and was the first German-speaking opera to be heard at the Metropolitan after World War I.

THE STORY OF THE OPERA

The atmosphere of Bruges (the dead city)—the mystic peace of its churches, cloisters, and bells, its weather-worn Gothic façades, its stagnant waterways and abandoned canals—permeates the thoughts of the living with remembrances of the past.

Act I

Paul, whose cherished wife Marie has been dead for many years, devotes his life to her memory, sorrowfully worshiping at the shrine to her that he has created. Here, surrounded by relics that include her portrait and locks of her long hair, he loses himself in the past. He tells his friend Frank about a woman he has met who resembles Marie in every detail. Marietta, a dancer with an itinerant opera troupe, enters. Paul begins to believe she is a reincarnation of his dead wife and soon transfers to her the emotions he feels for Marie. Marietta's seductive dancing attracts him but he becomes repelled by her behavior when he thinks of the purity of Marie. He asks her to leave. In a daze, he now hears Marie's voice urging him to be aware of and to understand what is happening. Two men appear to escort him on a journey through Bruges.

Act II

It is night; Paul, torn with jealousy, waits for Marietta. When Brigitta passes by with a group of nuns on the way to the cathedral, he discovers that his faithful housekeeper has deserted him because of Marietta. Paul argues with Frank, who has become one of Marietta's lovers. Horrified and angered by the sacrilegious revelry of Marietta and her companions, which mocks his belief in the resurrection of the dead, Paul bitterly reveals that he loved in her only her resemblance to his beloved Marie. Her vanity wounded, Marietta challenges the dead woman's hold on Paul, passionately seducing him once again. To make her triumph complete, she insists they spend this night at his house—Marie's home.

Act III

After their night of love, Marietta roams through Paul's house. Paul returns, to discover her in Marie's shrine room. He angrily rebukes her and orders her to go. Marietta ridicules Paul's false piety and remorse and attempts to distract him from the sounds of a religious procession passing by. She denounces his hypocrisy and superstition when Paul defends his belief in love and faith. Paul imagines the procession advancing upon him, threatening him. When Marietta rejects his efforts to remake her into his idea of purity, Paul curses her. She defiantly takes Marie's hair and begins to dance. Enraged, Paul seizes her and strangles her with these same strands of hair. Paul awakens with a start as Marietta actually returns for the parasol she had forgotten when she left—just moments before. Paul ignores her hint that she may stay and, with a shrug, she leaves. He too will leave Bruges, the dead city, and all that it represents.

Characters

Paul	Tenor
Marietta/Marie	Soprano
Frank	Baritone
Brigitta	Mezzo-Soprano

LA TRAVIATA, Act III. The fête galante in Moorish style at Flora's estate. The space includes an area for the entertainers to perform while the guests are at supper beneath the tent and in other parts of the house. This scene usually takes place indoors, with the emphasis on the main salon. (*Courtesy New York City Opera*)

MADAMA BUTTERFLY, Act I. The love duet. Cio-Cio-San (Francesca Roberto) entertains Pinkerton (Placido Domingo) in geisha style on her wedding night. (*Photo by Fred Fehl*)

FAUST, Act I, Scene 2. Marguerite (Beverly Sills), chaperoned by Marthe Schwerlein (Muriel Costa-Greenspon), encounters Faust (Michele Molese) at the kermesse, with the brooding figure of Christ in the background. (*Copyright © by Beth Bergman*)

(ABOVE) THE MAKROPOULOS AFFAIR, Act II. Emilia Marty (Maralin Niska) becomes the Eugenia Montez of the past. Film portrayal of her former life is played against the present. (*Photo by Henry Grossman*)

(RIGHT) THE MAKROPOULOS AFFAIR, Act I. Emilia Marty (Maralin Niska) reveals herself as the ancient 342-year-old woman. (*Photo by Henry Grossman*)

PELLÉAS AND MÉLISANDE, Act II, Scene 1. The fountain in the
park. In most productions there is merely a well on which the lovers
perch precariously. In this production the singers are André Jobin and

LULU, Act II. Returning from prison, Lulu (Patricia Brooks) makes love to Alwa (John Alexander), the son of the husband she murdered. (*Courtesy Houston Grand Opera*)

DIE TOTE STADT, Act III. Marietta (Carol Neblett) torments the obsessed Paul (John Alexander) with his dead wife's tresses while leering Ensor masks heighten her tirade. (*Courtesy New York City Opera*)

POPPEA, Act I. Poppea (Noelle Rogers) pleads with Nero (Alan Titus) to remain with her after a night of love. (*Photo by John Brooks*)

A VILLAGE ROMEO AND JULIET, Act I. Sali's and Vreli's dream of their wedding day in the village church. The music's ominous funereal overtones to the occasion are expressed in a visual counterpart. (*Copyright © Beth Bergman*)

TREEMONISHA, Act II. The voodoo conjure-men torment Treemonisha with their masks and animal cries. (*Photo by Grethe Holby*)

```
Victorin ........................................... Tenor
Count Albert ...................................... Tenor
Juliette .......................................... Soprano
Lucienne ............................... Mezzo-Soprano
Fritz ............................................ Baritone
Gaston ........................................... Dancer
```

Time: Turn of the century
Place: Bruges, Belgium

To peruse the libretto of *Die Tote Stadt* one would hardly suspect Korngold of being the affectionate optimist he was. What drew him to the subject is difficult to determine. Georges Rodenbach's novel, *Bruges La Morte*, from which the opera was adapted, is steeped in the lurk and murk of the symbolist movement, a bastard bloom off the French impressionist bush. The symbolists' god was Maurice Maeterlinck, and its holy ghost, Edgar Allan Poe. Death was the password, and tolling bells the characteristic sound. Debussy or Puccini (both aware of the novel) would have been ideal composers for this miasmic romance, but perhaps the weight of so much melancholy pressed too mightily on their own predispositions. The subject was left to be tackled by a rosy-cheeked *Jüngling* and his enterprising papa. Both would collaborate on the libretto under the pseudonym Paul Schott (the first name of the male protagonist of the opera, coupled with that of the original publisher of the score). What they produced was not exactly a laugh riot—their optimism notwithstanding—but they did manage to lift the leading characters from their shrouds and reinstate them as beings of flesh and blood. The medieval city of Bruges, which dominates Rodenbach's novel, took a back seat to the gusty contest between those symbols of the life and death forces, Paul and Marietta. There are enough falling leaves in Korngold's opera to satisfy any necrophile, but the librettists' shift of emphasis made for a more accessible arena of interest and involvement. The ending alone was a dramatic overlay by the two Korngolds. The novel concludes with Marietta's death, and the whole tale slips away into decay and despair. Instead, *père* and *fils* constructed a cunning coda. Paul awakens as from an opium dream and, about to commit himself to action that might turn nightmare into reality, alters his course and renounces worship of the ghostly Marie and the symbiotic Marietta. Free of their influence, he opts for a new way of life "out there." Thus the bulk of the novel becomes a play within a play, and the expiatory ending is an affecting, if sentimental, resolution.

Ron Chase and I approached this tale of male suttee entirely as a dream play. Reality and fantasy resembled each other, although demarcation points were sufficiently established to create the necessary dramatic tension. We again duplicated our format for *Village Romeo* and *Lulu*. A simple structure resembling the altar to Marie's memory, two window frames, and a small couch were our points of departure into Paul's leap into his dream state. The real city of Bruges, with its unending canals and deserted streets, was photographed at the actual sites during a rainy ten-day period in late November '74. There were exactly three days of fitful sunshine to alleviate the general dank. The procession of the Holy Blood, an annual event recreated by the Church fathers, occurred during one of these breaks in the weather. Still, television antennas and the one-time-only aspect of the parade forced shooting on the spot from particularly unsatisfying angles. The filmic realization of the *Robert le Diable* sequence in the opera was the only other material shot besides Paul's entrance into the heart of Bruges. The view of Marietta as the entrapped nun of Meyerbeer's opera accompanied the third-act prelude on the screen. A group of nonsinging English actors had been hired in London for much the same arrangement as was used in *Makropoulos Affair.* To emphasize the unreality of these filmic sections, we resorted to the paintings of James Ensor, Belgium's national adornment and contemporary of Rodenbach. Ensor's devil masks and Bosch-like figurines helped define the Walpurgis-night side of the opera. The combination of slides and film thus created our most hallucinatory environment to date. The final production was a photographic amalgam and synthesis of the Belgian symbolist painters, James Ensor and Léon Spilliaert, crossed with the moonstruck vistas of Giorgio di Chirico and Puvis de Chavannes. Quite a rarified collection of *artistes fumés!* Yet all sensually apropos and suffocatingly right. It was like contemplating a lily at twilight, equally malevolent to behold and intoxicating to the senses. This production employed twice the footage of film and half the number of slides employed in *Village Romeo* and *Lulu*.

John Alexander as Paul and Carol Neblett as the two Maries were perfect collaborators, sustaining the music's fiendish *tessitura* and acting its serpentine drama with great authority and finesse.

The critical reaction to the production was generally affirmative, but Korngold's sumptuous score was severely criticized. The old shibboleths were hung out to dry again. The reviews created an imbalance in the general public's appreciation of the work that, I hope, will be rectified in its future revivals. Although not an imperishable masterpiece, *Die Tote Stadt* is a distinctive achievement by a composer of genius, and its musical traceries illuminate a corner of the late romantic sensibility that is both singular and attractive. It is of further interest to note that the opera's revival in this country was sparked by the interest both artistic and financial of that most enterprising and free-wheeling European impresario, Gert von Gontard. This participation augurs well for the future of international artistic relationships, not to mention the general health of opera itself.

SIEGFRIED WAGNER   MAX REGER   ERICH W. KORNGOLD   ARTHUR NIKISCH   RICHARD STRAUSS   EUGEN D'ALBERT

(Courtesy of Herman Lowen)

17

Stylization
in Opera

The use of stylizing techniques in opera can almost be considered an academic issue—for the impression created by most operatic productions is that all opera is stylized. In performance, the singer's behavior in *Don Giovanni* can cross-pollinate his activities in *La Bohème*. There are the same formal movements, the same all-purpose hieratic gestures. These represent both the personal shortcomings and, conversely, the preferences of the performer—their acquired bags of tricks to help create commanding stage presences while simulating apposite emotional states. Such posturings can almost pass muster in the works below the Mason-Dixon Line of opera—those composed during and prior to the eighteenth century, where gods and goddesses ruled the roost. One cannot escape the realization, however, that most operatic stylization is an anodyne for real stage behavior—locked muscle tension masquerading as grace rather than a true projection of the requisite reality. The accepted convention of opera as a larger-than-life art form can create multiple confusion. All art is larger than life, to repeat a bromide, but as in most abstract forms (painting, for instance) each stroke made on a canvas is a very real stroke, with a specific color, shape, and dimension. It is the combination and arrangement of these strokes that creates the abstraction.

Up to and including Mozart's *Idomeneo*, opera was virtually run by one long string of deus ex mechanics—man caught in the vises of heaven. The gods had the last word, and their descent on familial lawns could be accomplished only by the use of heraldic gestures—hence the development of stylization techniques. These have even washed over into modern drama (for example, *Waiting for Godot*), wherein God is figuratively dead and man is seen gripped by unknown forces—a field of unguided energy formerly filled by the heavenly pantheon. Thus superterrestrial forces, named and unnamed, have cornered the market on stylization in dramatic literature, musical and otherwise.

The following two productions demonstrate the extreme ends of the polarities of stylization: the dramatic and the decorative.

Claudio Monteverdi's *L'Incoronazione di Poppea* and George Frederick Handel's *Rinaldo* occupy opposite ends of the musical rainbow. *Rinaldo* was Handel's first opera, while *Poppea* proved to be Monteverdi's last. *Poppea* wrote finis to a century of musical discovery, while *Rinaldo* threw Handel into the arena of that exotic entertainment called Italian opera that flourished in London in the early eighteenth century.

Monteverdi, the "Oracle of Music," as he was called, composed *Poppea* in 1642. He was then seventy-five years old. A year later, much traveled, feted, and exhausted, he returned to Venice "like a swan that, feeling the fatal hour near, approaches the water, and in it . . . passes on to another life singing with suaver harmony than ever, so Claudio in great haste returned . . . " Within days of his arrival, he fell ill and died. "With truly royal pomp a catafalque was erected [in the church of Santa Maria dei Frari] surrounded by so many candles that the church looked like a night sky luminous with stars." *

With Monteverdi's passing, music as drama came to a complete standstill. Not until Gluck's reforms was opera to return to this principle. When *Poppea* itself was ultimately rediscovered, late in the nineteenth century, it automatically took its place beside the greatest masterpieces created in the genre.

Monteverdi's setting of this, the very first historical drama in music, was based on a libretto by Giovanni Francesco Busenello (1598–1659), the least well known of the master librettists of history. Add these up: Quinault, Metastasio, Goldoni, Scribe,

---

* Matteo Caberloh: "Laconissino delle Alte Qualita di Claudio Monteverdi," in *Fiore Poetici—1644*

Da Ponte, Boito, and Hofmannsthal—and it is possible to hand the laurel to Busenello—certainly as far as *Poppea* is concerned.

Busenello was a lawyer by profession and, it appears, only a Sunday scrivener. His oeuvres do not exceed five or six libretti, most of them set to music by Francesco Cavalli. *Poppea* was the third in his output, followed by the second historical drama in existence, the intriguingly titled *La Prosperita Infelice di Giulio Cesare, Dittatore* (1646) or *The Declining Fortunes of Julius Caesar, Dictator*. This libretto still exists, unfortunately without a musical setting. While *Poppea* is rife with the accouterments favored in baroque opera (such as heavenly appearances, comic-relief interludes, disguises, et cetera), it is Busenello's penetrating sense of character and psychologic reality one finds both astonishing and confounding: *Poppea* is undoubtedly the most shocking and amoral tale ever set to music. The triumph of Nero and Poppea over all adversities in the name of love constitutes a view of mankind so cynical, so abhorrent as to be almost insufferable. Nero and Poppea are the regal forebears of Bonnie and Clyde. Monteverdi's wonderment that such creatures could "so get the start of the majestic world and bear the palm alone" places the work among the great cautionary tales of musical drama. *Poppea* throws a searchlight on the past and the ways of man but it condemns the abuses of power by insinuation. Nowhere in this sultry piece is Monteverdi's own voice heard in protest. He was undoubtedly attracted by these complex, modern characters despite their amorality and it is enough that he fully exposes their disorder in the unbalanced scheme of things. *Poppea* is both realistic opera and opera of the absurd at its most profound level.

THE STORY OF *POPPEA*

Prologue:

The Dispute: Fortune, Virtue, and Love dispute their power over man. Love humbles the other two and predicts her supremacy.

Act I

Ottone, the former lover of Poppea, discovers the soldiers of Nero at Poppea's door and realizes that Nero is Poppea's new lover.

The soldiers awake, curse their lot under Nero, and are frightened at his approach.

Poppea begs Nero not to leave; the Emperor promises he will repudiate his wife Ottavia, marry Poppea, and crown her Empress. Poppea sings her happiness. Her nurse Arnalta warns Poppea of the dangers of such a relationship.

The Empress Ottavia laments her misfortune but asks the famous teacher Seneca to intercede for her with the Senate and the people. Her page Valetto mistrusts Seneca and threatens him.

Pallade foretells Seneca's death.

Nero tells his teacher Seneca of his decision to divorce Ottavia and marry Poppea; Seneca tries to dissuade him.

Poppea reminds Nero of the pleasures of the previous night and denounces Seneca as her enemy and a traitor. Nero orders Seneca to kill himself.

Ottone complains to Poppea about her infidelity, and she spurns him.

Drusilla loves Ottone, and laments his feeling for Poppea; Ottone now declares his love for Drusilla and pretends to disown Poppea.

In the solitude of his villa, Seneca receives the messenger of death; his friends gather and meditate on life and death.

Act II

After Seneca's death, Nero and his friend Lucano celebrate the beauty of Poppea and the death of Seneca.

Ottavia orders Ottone to kill Poppea.

Ottone confides in Drusilla and asks for her cloak as a disguise to enter Poppea's house.

Poppea learns of Seneca's death, and asks Love's help. Arnalta soothes Poppea to sleep; Ottone enters half ready to kill Poppea, but is frightened away by Love and the watchful nurse, who calls the alarm.

Drusilla sings her joy, anticipating her rival's death. Nero orders the torture of Drusilla to force her confession. She confesses to save Ottone, but Ottone also confesses that he attempted the murder by order of Ottavia. Ottone and Drusilla are exiled, as is Ottavia.

Nero swears to Poppea that today she will become Empress. They celebrate the removal of their enemies.

Ottavia bids farewell to Rome.

Arnalta boasts of her triumph in now being the confidante of an Empress, instead of a servant.

Poppea is crowned.

Characters

Goddess of Fortune .... Soprano
Goddess of Virtue .... Soprano
Goddess of Love .... Soprano
Ottone, Poppea's former lover .... Baritone
   (originally male soprano)
Two soldiers of the Emperor's Bodyguard .... Tenors
Poppea .... Soprano
Nero, Emperor of Rome .... Tenor
   (originally male soprano)
Arnalta, Poppea's old nurse .... Contralto
   (perhaps, originally, tenor)
Ottavia, Empress of Rome .... Mezzo-Soprano
Drusilla, Ottavia's lady-in-waiting .... Soprano
Seneca, philosopher, Nero's former tutor .... Bass
Valletto, a young attendant to Ottavia .... Tenor
   (originally male soprano)
Damigella, a maid in Ottavia's service .... Soprano
Liberto, Captain of the Guard .... Baritone
Pallade, Goddess of Wisdom .... Soprano
Lucano, Nero's friend .... Tenor
Lictor .... Bass
Mercury .... Bass
   (originally high tenor)

Time: At the time of Nero
Place: Rome

My production of the work was mounted for the Opera Society of Washington (1972) in a new orchestration they had commissioned from Nikolaus Harnoncourt. The stage images were inspired by a combination of Fellini's *Satyricon* and the paintings of Gustav Klimnt. The production was stylized throughout, both in its setting and acting styles. The former consisted of a single thrust platform covering part of the orchestra pit with a huge column dominating the upstage area. The colors were a melding of blood red and gold—the combination that literally jumps from the score.

As with *Pelléas*, the basic approach to the acting problems was realistic, and then transformed into the requisite level of reality called stylization. One example will suffice to illustrate this process.

In the first act, Nero and Poppea are about to part after a night of love-making. It is dawn, and the separation is reluctant. The actors were first encouraged to explore the scene naturalistically—to move and touch each other as contemporary beings. Once this was accomplished, the stylization process began. In essence stylization is an intensification, a heightening of reality. Its purpose is to create the declensions of passions (amorous or otherwise) raveling and unraveling themselves. The various steps toward a climactic stance are physically defined (fixed), with the moment of climax being the highest level of tensity and, therefore, intensity. Although its inner properties partake of naturalism, the physical movement employed to demonstrate said states is perforce nonnaturalistic and usually derived from painting and sculptural models.

Slow motion, acrobatic positions, classical ballet, processionals are other examples of stylization in action.

Alan Titus and Noelle Rogers—the Nero and Poppea—after their naturalistic explorations, were instructed to slow down their amorous interplay. The slow rhythm of the music became the guiding pulse of their game of love. Both Nero and Poppea being arch narcissists, our goal was to arrive at self-adoring tableaux. It was like watching oneself making love in a room full of mirrors—every move and ripple was self-consciously explored and helped create an overripe, hothouse sensuality. Without the living substructure, this game of theirs might be nothing more than a series of decorative poses—the raison d'être and bane of most stylization. We have become drearily used to these "off-the-vase" effects in the theater—games of living statues without living tissue. The charm is not just in duplicating the sacerdotal poses in art but in arriving at their true necessity: the passion those frozen attitudes attempt to define. This close-up of intense life is the sum and substance of stylization.

Each scene was examined in this light—reality explored, then placed in the metrically prescribed envelope.

The superb original cast included, besides Titus and Rogers, John Ferrante, the brilliant countertenor as an overrouged Amor in drag, Maureen Forrester as the blowzy nurse Arnalta, my own wife Bonnie as a ravishing Ottavia, and Tom Paul as the stoic yet warmhearted Seneca. All executed the stylized staging with an acute relish of its special province. The result was a vibrant projection of this, undoubtedly one of the great works in the entire operatic literature.

Rinaldo was my first encounter with *opera seria* —a form that evolved after the death of Monteverdi and extended as far as Rossini. In effect, *opera seria* consisted of song recitals in costume and with elaborate scenery. The stories dealt with mythological or classical subjects and were usually quite inaccurate historically. The plots were both complicated and stilted and the action extremely formalized. The total lack of believability was emphasized by women singing the leading male roles, and *castrati* singing either/or.

Rinaldo saved the bejeweled neck of *opera seria,* for it was in its last perfumed gasp when Handel appeared on the London scene. An insane craze at best: it was devilishly expensive to produce and did not meet the approval of the cognoscenti. Its chief attraction was that new rage, the *castrato.* A gaggle of them had been imported from Italian choir lofts and opera houses, and their novel appearance on English shores met with unbounded enthusiasm on the part of a scandalized and thrill-seeking public. Many of this rare species were consummate musicians and so more than made up for the garish nature of their publicity.

The other star on the horizon was the stage designer—the creator of the fantastic flying apparatus and other mechanical marvels the baroque theater specialized in. In many instances, these masters of the crank and pulley received top billing over the composer and singers, and they outdid one another in their spectacular effects. Bernini, the great sculptor, for a time created some of Italy's most daring stage feats. One seems so amazing as to be unbelievable! In some forgotten opera Bernini arranged for an angry flood to gather upstage. At its height, it was precipitated toward the audience. At the last possible moment, a wall rose up at the lip of the proscenium, thus stemming the tide and gaining the gratitude and titillated plaudits of the audience. Stage action ceased awhile for the ministration of smelling salts.

Rinaldo could boast no such trump card, but it had another adornment: the genius of George Frederick Handel. *Rinaldo's* story is the classic encounter between the Christian crusader Rinaldo and the Witch of the East, Armida. It is opera seria's own Samson and Delilah, with sorcery instead of shears as the chief weapon. It is full of martial splendor and peopled with fantastic beings of land, sea, and air.

THE STORY OF *RINALDO*

Act I

The Christian crusaders are camped outside the gates of Jerusalem on the eve of the battle against the Saracen foe. King Goffredo and his chief general, Rinaldo, anticipate vanquishing the enemy. Goffredo promises Rinaldo his daughter Almirena's hand in marriage to celebrate the victory. Argante, chief general of the Saracens, appears and, in his Queen's name, requests that the battle be postponed. Goffredo grants this amnesty, confident of the eventual outcome. Argante reports back to Queen Armida, who is his lover. Surrounded by her fiendish minions, Armida promises to wreak havoc over the Christian forces. Meanwhile, Almirena awaits Rinaldo's arrival in an enchanted garden. The lovers are united and affirm their vows. Suddenly Armida and her forces appear and kidnap Almirena. Rinaldo swears vengeance.

Act II

A ship lies anchored in the bay and the song of a siren fills the night. Rinaldo and Goffredo arrive and, encouraged by the blandishments of the siren, Rinaldo makes off in the galley in pursuit of his betrothed. Almirena is being held captive in Armida's secret retreat. Argante confesses his growing passion for the hapless girl and promises to help her. Armida arrives and accuses Argante of treachery and infidelity. Rinaldo is brought before the Queen and the warrior challenges Armida to yield up Almirena. Armida is much taken with the Christian and loses no time in protesting her passion for him. In an effort to woo Rinaldo, Armida resorts to sorcery. She causes the illusion of Almirena to appear while attempting to take her place at the moment of embrace. But Rinaldo rejects Armida and is left to lament Almirena's absence.

Act III

Rinaldo wanders through Armida's kingdom in search of Almirena. Goffredo, pursuing Rinaldo's path, learns from a wizard of the whereabouts of Armida's fortress. Armida bemoans the rejection by Rinaldo, but soon joins Argante once she recognizes the mutual folly of their infatuations. They proceed to torture Almirena. Rinaldo appears and, backed up by Goffredo and his approaching forces, effects Almirena's rescue while the enemy escape. Outside the fortress, the Christian and Saracen champions do battle. The Christians, led by Rinaldo, defeat the Saracens, destroying their fortress. With Armida and Argante prisoners, the Christian forces, led by Goffredo and Rinaldo, enter Jerusalem victoriously.

Characters

Goffredo	Tenor
Rinaldo	Mezzo
Almirena	Soprano
A Herald	Baritone
Argante	Bass
Armida	Soprano
A Siren	Mezzo
A Wizard	Baritone

Time: The Crusades
Place: Palestine

Rinaldo's American stage première took place in Houston, Texas, in 1975. While practitioners of the great flying machines flooded the market in Handel's day, we could find nary a one to undertake such an assignment in ours. An English designer was finally located, but the basic cost of such an endeavor appeared prohibitive. The grand clincher came with the discovery that the design could only be accommodated to the theater prescribed for. A completely new set of levers and catapults would have to be devised for future engagements elsewhere. We gave up on this Haymarket folly and settled for a more modest spectacle. Designed by Franco Colavecchia, who perpetrated similar delights for *Treemonisha,* our *Rinaldo* had more than a fair share of flying tents, chariots, beasties of every shape and variety, war machines, monstrous bird cages, and enough fog, mist, and sulphurous emanations to satisfy the heart of any baroquier.

Our trump card was Marilyn Horne—that astonishing singer who donned Rinaldo's plumes and armor to tread on grounds untrodden since the palmy days of the great *castrati* Picolin, Cafarelli, and the mythic Farinelli.

The style of acting in this fantastic allegory tended to emphasize the decorative element of stylization. The glamourous stage picture, the conceit of the artful pose, and the hypnotic delights of the static tableaux were uppermost in my mind. In the rare moments of introspection, as in Rinaldo's final aria in Act II, "*Cara sposa,*" we blended the external with more internal elements. The sheer ability to execute the score's formidable vocal difficulties insured a built-in excitement of its own.

The most dynamic event was the conception and execution of the final battle scene. Two war machines occupied extreme ends of the stage. The rival forces were represented by no more than fifteen warriors. Rinaldo posed on the jutting arm of one of the catapults, placing him mid-stage suspended over the heads of the warriors below. These consisted of a group of gymnasts, interspersed with some dancers. Modern calisthenic exercises were mixed with formalized dance patterns. Every movement was choreographed. Bodies tossed in mid-air, while some flipped in attitudes of victory or defeat. Others rolled, dived, and executed complicated aerial twists to heighten the idea of actual battle. At each of Rinaldo's vocal apostrophes, with their incredible flights of *fioritura,* all action on the field of battle froze in mid-thrust, to be resumed again with the orchestral music. It was a child's heaven of sword play and caught the spirit of the baroque spectacle in a fresh and vivid manner.

In essence, lacking the wherewithal to re-create the mechanized splendors of the baroque, and unwilling to fall victim to its "camp" derivatives (gods descending on swaying clouds, papier-mâché boats and waves, all the stillborn devices vilifying the style), I was forced to reinvent the baroque in my own terms. This I tried to accomplish by finding imaginative equivalents in modern art forms as they reflected the ancient order of things. In so doing I suddenly realized that our own times are historically the nearest thing to the baroque. Sporting even higher platform shoes than ever, we strain as mightily to lift ourselves out of the torpor of multiple confusions and spiritual ennui. We have placed our faith in the sovereignty of the "image." Our gods, however, are the superstars of the media, who dominate and influence our daily movements as surely as did the heavenly hosts of yore.

Rinaldo's splendors were conceived accordingly, and the mixture of innocent ferocity underlying its spectacle brought it close to the world of the Brothers Grimm.

18

Treemonisha

Scott Joplin's *Treemonisha* is many things, but primarily it is a sweet sermon on goodness. Its heroine is a combination savior and forerunner of women's lib. The music is a mixed grab bag of Handel, Weber, and some Negro folk material, all stitched together with a show-biz savvy circa 1910. The people speak in the down-home accent of a backwoods black community of the 1880s. Whatever the work's profile, at first sight it hardly seems the stuff of grand opera. Further, its basic theme of salvation through education is neither typically operatic nor original. However, Joplin's insistence on his character's spiritual dignity and charity, seen from the perspective of some sixty-five years' distance, is a remarkable revelation. The opera emerges as a sort of *Magic Flute,* American style. Both works are spiritual "vaudevilles," whose pranks shine with a special incandescence.

My initial reaction on playing through the score was stupefaction and disbelief. I was as dumfounded as any member of its first audience, which gathered in a Harlem studio where Joplin supervised its first read-through over fifty years ago. That scene is redolent of the old Warner Brothers film biographies of yesteryear: a dismal hole in the wall with an upright piano; a well-heeled but hard-nosed crowd from downtown; perplexed and underrehearsed black artists; music publishers grown fat on rag profits and all thirsting for the next Joplin hit; an anxious, doubting, yet hopeful wife, her frazzled composer-husband already in the throes of a terminal disease. The former entertainer at bordello and saloon was writing an opera, of all things! An uppity, uptown bit of grandstanding—and all about an ignorant bunch of blacks to boot!

I found myself embarrassed by its archetypical details.

Mammy-ism seemed to be having a riotous field day. A semi-classical watermelon festival was hardly in keeping with our aspirations. By the time I had reached the finale I suddenly realized I was face to face with the original—the nexus of the black experience itself, confounded and made the stuff of parody by succeeding generations. *Treemonisha* was innocent of all our guff and she had bided her time.

I approached directing the opera as a tightrope walker might measure his task ahead. How to preserve *Treemonisha*'s innocence and pass over the conventions and abuses of chauvinism, past and present?

Treemonisha's decision to lead her people out of ignorance and superstition forms the climax of the opera. Historically, this would seem to be a bit of social realism, were it not for Joplin's vision of the peaceable kingdom to come. To produce the opera realistically would be to abrogate the poetic intensity of that vision. Taken literally, the events are so humdrum that they seem incapable of filling the requirements of a one-acter. Seen symbolically—even ritualistically—all is inevitable.

The dramatic issue in the opera is the conflict between good and evil, with the community representing good and the voodoo conjurers as nemesis. The central action revolves around the abduction and rescue of Treemonisha from the conjurers' den. This action is played within the environs of woods and village, and a lovely pantheism radiates from the work's orchestral interludes and distant choruses. At the point of rescue, Treemonisha is about to be punished for her affront to the voodoo brotherhood by being thrown onto a hornet's nest. This device seems simplistic, until one realizes that the object of this ingenuous torture is death. We are again traveling in the domain of the Grimm fairy tale, and therein lies Joplin's power to charm and horrify. The production was shaped around this image. The hornet's nest became symbolic—a huge affair over twelve feet high, shaped into a voodoo mask. Its surface crawled with deadly hornets and, its wide mouth agape, it hungered for its young victim.

On opening night in 1975 at Houston's outdoor Miller Theatre, a howling of dogs was heard at the first appearance of this evil nest onstage. Members of the local canine community, free to wander under the stars along with the spectators, were simply expressing a primal reaction to its presence among them. The audience laughed at the baying, but it was the thrilling laughter of collusion.

Similarly, the magic tree of the opening scene, under whose branches Treemonisha was sheltered at birth, was rendered as a series of hand-held sculptured forms to create a dreamlike mosaic. Every fence, bush, rooftop—down to our final rainbow— was hand operated and manipulated. The players created and lived within this shifting floating ambience. Herein bears, alligators, heron birds, and giant moths disported themselves, safe in a child's dream of Paradise before the Fall. The costumes were not denims of convention, but a colorful amalgam of myth and fantasy—poverty seen as a clean and vibrant simplicity. Only the practical objects of the workaday world (the wash, cotton sacks, corn bushels, chains on a surviving slave block) were realistically fashioned. In short, a heaven was attempted and created. This seemed mandatory in framing Joplin's message of good will—a message that speaks of and to the essence in man, wherein faith and wonderment perpetuate themselves eternally.

Treemonisha, once it was Broadway bound, was also caught up in the Broadway bind: to the show-biz mentality the word "opera" is anathema! Hours were spent in trying to subvert the work into a more "acceptable" category. What to call it? How to advertise it? One of its main co-producers had never seen the work until its final week in Washington. He had expected a sequel to *The Wiz*; instead, there were all those arias!

The show opened in New York after a delay of several weeks because of a strike. It was well received, but the insistence on calling it other than what it was perverted the advertising and created confusion in the audiences' otherwise enthusiastic endorsement of the piece. The limited-run engagement was extended but, still fearing the curse of "opera," the producers curtailed the run in favor of an incoming musical starring Yul Brynner that lasted all of one performance. What strange karma follows *Treemonisha* is not for us to know. A gentle masterpiece has been bedeviled from its origins until this day. Perhaps the tide will turn and a favorable balance restored to this work, which has in it all of Joplin's soul as well as his hopes of recognition as a "serious" composer.

19

Opera, Opera Singers, and the Performing Arts

I think just about every actor I've ever met has wanted to sing, while not every singer has wanted to act. Intimidated by academicians and vocal coaches, the opera singer has remained the backwoodsman among thespians. Instead of melding these arts, he has been encouraged to place the vocal cart before the theatrical horse in the belief that if one possesses a voice nothing else matters. Inevitably the stage director has inherited the results and finds himself in the hapless role of Svengali.

The assumption made by the musical experts is that all a singer's problems and needs are answered in the music. Here we skirt the edge of the San Andreas fault. We all know that just to sing the notes and scrupulously attend each fluctuation in a score is primary, but it does not awaken the spirit of a composition. The answer is not to be found in the musician, but in the human being housing him. Poor *Doppelgänger*—all too willing to be left in the vestibules of world conservatories along with his galoshes. We must concede, at least in opera and song, that music represents a crucible of human experience. One is inconceivable without the other. It is the old chicken and egg routine that must produce life at one end or the other in order to sustain itself. If a singer's vocal resources are not plugged into his emotional life, he is only half a singer. The combination creates individuality and the assertion of that personal self onstage. This concept has become contentious in musical circles. It raises the usual bugaboo concerning the conflicts between a composer's intention as against the private idiosyncrasies of the performer.

The history of famous singers offers interesting ground for speculation. Open any anthology devoted to the *casta divas* of yore and one comes across some startling facts. Chief among these is the realization that over half of the great singers mentioned were not vocal paragons. Their ability to translate emotional states into song constituted the cementing factor of immortality. Such singers obviously followed the dictates of their hearts, willing to risk and forgo the pearly tone and let an abrasive sound suggest the moment of experience. Inconsistent vocal production is a minor sacrifice to pay in the shaping of great art. Somehow our overall view of the singer is not in sympathy with this. We have been brainwashed into believing that the "true" singer is the one with the azure-clad voice—one odd or coarse sound constituting a fall from grace. It's part of the Norman Rockwell syndrome, where art and artists, like all winter days, are valentines. On the contrary, the Melbas and Tetrazzinis are the rarer birds of passage. I am not suggesting one must have faulty vocal equipment to enter Valhalla, but I am certain that without the added dimension of private involvement many in the category of greats would not have attained that height. The pity is that while the Malibrans, Gardens, and Pastas were creating new standards, they never tabulated the implications of their techniques. If there were anything comparable in this department, say, to the Garcia *Manual of Vocal Training*, what a different perspective one would have of the singer's profession. Instead, we have countless handbooks with close-ups of tonsils and laryngeal valves—and shelves of memoirs interspersing remembered triumphs with the paprika of backstage skulduggery. A pity that a Stanislavski did not surface along the way to do as proper a job in this area as has been accomplished for the merely spoken word. Thus, while I blanch, I am still not surprised when I receive letters and calls from opera singers asking to be taught the value of "expression." "How do I use my hands?" "How do I walk on and off stage?" "How do I simply stand?" Such are the effluvia of ancient malpractices, characterized by the work of such innovators as Delsarte (the master of mime) and Dalcroze (the master of eurythmics). From about the late 1800s on, opera singers have latched onto their findings, and latter-day camp has had its field day. Such practices are immortalized by old photos of maidens grouped together on a lawn, their arms and knees bent in dithyrambic bliss—votives of Isadora and Raymond Duncan. You laugh at this dainty recollection? Here am I, in the seventies, and the following questions have been asked of me over the past ten years.

Horror, How to show it! Should one use one's hand? One hand or two? And how does one drop the pose after the imprecation?

Exaltation, Vengeance, Malediction, Rage, Despair! Should one throw one's head back, use fingers, fist, or how? In bravura passages, should the singer suggest the bravura aspect in some graceful physical way? And how?

Invitation and/or Allurement, as in *Carmen.* Should one's hip be thrown to the right or left when in sexual repose? What are masculine stage attitudes (as for princes, kings, high priests, and such) and what are not masculine attitudes? How do you drag yourself along onstage if, say, you're Aida on the verge of supplication?

I will not go into the department of eye movements, or the subtle declensions of listening, suffering, and other ridiculous pace-setters. Critics still speak in their reviews of this one's face, arms, legs, as if these features were separate from the total being's expression of self. "There are more things in heaven and earth, Horatio, than are dreamt of in your philosophy." I'm sure Hamlet was anticipating, among other things, the arrival of the players.

From Talma to David Garrick, Voltaire, Stanislavski, and Lee Strasberg, the actor's art has been speculated on and elucidated. The fact that such important findings are relevant to its sister art in music is only now beginning to have some currency again. The moment has come for the singer to 'fess up to his unclaimed heritage. The property of the great singers of the past should now become a household word in the present. It is true that the nonsinging actor creates his own time and space, which is remarkably fluid and flexible. Such is not yet the case in music, and most certainly not in opera. There the individual is infinitely more regimented. The chain of command influencing him is far more complex, and in that assembly line musical considerations dominate the dramatic. The true balance is one that gives equal stress to both the music and the drama. This implies a whole new avenue of investigation and even training in various departments—from the conductor on up or down. And finally, how in the light of all that's humanly possible does one begin to grasp the impulse trapped in the musical page?

Giacomo Puccini's publisher, Ricordi, at the time of *Bohème*'s publication, wrote to him: "There are all kinds of possible and impossible indications [in the score]. It is a forest of *p-pp-pppp* or *f-ff-fff-ffff*, of slowing up and going ahead—so that the conductors will lose their heads. . . ." Puccini replied: "As for the *pp*'s and the *ff*'s of the score, if I have overdone them it is because, as Verdi says, when one needs piano, one must put *ppp*." At the point of Mimi's death, the B minor chord that signals it is marked *pppppppp*.

Puccini's paranoia is universal, for his seven pianos are an appeal to the imagination, which is placed in a secondary position in the musical scheme of things, where "correctness" reigns.

In the theater such concerns are academic. One hardly bats an eye at the Edwardian Olivier-Miller production for *The Merchant of Venice*, say, but let an opera director try such tricks (as was the case of Patrice Chéreau in his recent mounting of *The Ring* at Bayreuth) and he is called to the strictest accounting. Music is a plentiful feast, but the young artist—and this includes instrumentalists as well as singers and directors—has not been encouraged as a musical pup to feed at such tables. Too early and too soon he finds himself at the end of the line. Personal considerations of feeling and judgment—the very elements that drove him to music in the first place—are overlooked and even dismissed. This affects professionals and amateurs on all levels. The top professional learns to throttle his private aspirations in the service of "professional" demands—demands being made by other professionals similarly afflicted. The "big time," after all, is hardly the place to experiment with the idiosyncracies of one's soul—the very core of the performer tried and untried. The question of responsibility in the organic training of such aspirants is of the utmost importance in constructing our operatic future.

In 1918, with the support of the State Theatre Management and Arts Council of the Bolshoi Theatre, Stanislavski was commissioned to open an opera studio devoted to the re-examination of opera traditions and to raise the cultural level of the actor-singer. In essence, a working ensemble was created. The results were phenomenal. The ensemble was the fusion of highly trained professional singing-actors that is the very life blood of the opera house. A dream come true that lasted from its inception until 1933.

Stanislavski's productions of Tchaikovsky's *Eugene Onegin* and *Pique Dame*, Rimsky-Korsakov's *The Tsar's Bride* and *May Night*, Puccini's *La Bohème* and Moussorgsky's *Boris Godounov* proved it was possible to attain and maintain high standards of performance in the pursuit of a continuing and unifying aesthetic viewpoint. This artistic revolution was eclipsed by the political crisis in Russia, and only gradually were the extraordinary results of that foment within the grand ferment made public.

Stanislavski's Opera Studio Theatre was also responsible for creating the archetype of the twentieth-century opera director: combination teacher, visionary, and practical man of the theater. At the instant of this writing, such goals seem far from the patterns governing the American cultural scene. Art itself, in all manifestations, remains low man on the list of national priorities, and the complexity of forces required to maintain an opera house is a compounding obstacle. Opera's best intentions concerning ensemble are further being aggravated by the American's curious antipathy to the idea. His preference is for *who* is in it, rather than for *what* it is, and the very word "ensemble" suggests anonymity—a definite no-no in our go-go society.

Most Americans still regard opera as caviar for the general anyway—a Beluga no cultural center should be without, but foreign stuff nonetheless. So the airlines keep busy piloting our best American artists hither and yon, with no musical home to really call their own. They feed on theatrical scraps while pursuing the gorgon success, suffering frightful jet lag between Manon in Chile and Lucia the next night in Helsinki.

Yes, America's investment in the arts seems, at present, far from the desired and deserved norm. The word "seems" is an intentional qualification. I cannot help feeling, or at least hoping, that, like inflation, the situation will alter or even reverse itself. Who knows? The notion of the ensemble may even become fashionable again, for in essence it lies at the very heart of the democratic ideal.

But, caviar or not, investment good or bad, a future subsidized or no, opera continues to be the extraordinary in the ordinary of my life. For me it is a commitment, a compelling necessity not far removed from an inborn need to perform good works in the name of all the gods at once—even if proof of their benevolent auspices still stubbornly hangs in the balance. No single art form better encapsulates this aspiration of the human toward the divine. At flame heat, the operatic experience gives us all wings. Such aspirations, such flights, surely, one way or another, make mavericks of us all.

THREE
FINISHED
PRODUCTIONS
IN DETAIL

All translations in the ensuing
chapters are not literal. They are
meant only to convey the idea.

20

La Traviata

Characters

Alfredo Germont, lover of Violetta .... Tenor
Giorgio Germont, his father .... Baritone
Gastone de Letorieres,
    a young man about town .... Tenor
Baron Douphol, a rival of Alfredo .... Baritone
Marquis d'Obigny .... Bass
Doctor Grenvil .... Bass
Giuseppe, servant to Violetta .... Tenor
Violetta Valery, a courtesan .... Soprano
Flora Bervoix, her friend .... Mezzo-Soprano
Annina, Violetta's confidante and maid .... Soprano
        Ladies and Gentlemen; Servants and Masks;
                Dancers and Guests.

Time: 1850 *
Place: Paris and vicinity

ACT I
(The living room in the house of Violetta Valery)

The curtain rises directly after the prelude. The room is overflowing with people, some lounging, most milling about. The Baron Douphol is seated by the window, watching Violetta, who is kneeling on a stool before him. She is playing with a necklace he has just offered her and examines it greedily; she is obviously contemptuous of its donor. She casts glances at a group that includes Dr. Grenvil. To their vast amusement she shows off the jewel with sarcastic play of lips

* The original libretto indicates the year 1700, the time of the hoopskirt, which we felt was a restricting factor.

and shoulders. She pretends to consider accepting the necklace but suddenly hands it back to the chagrined Douphol, who catches her wrist as she starts to leave him. She pulls away from the Baron, flipping her fan in his face to express her disgust. Violetta joins Grenvil and his friends (including the actress Rachel),* who have also enjoyed Douphol's public humiliation. Immediately following this, Flora and three gentlemen (among them the Marquis) enter. Flora is quite drunk and is smoking a cigarillo. Her dress is gaudy and this side of bad taste (true of everything she does, in fact). She is laughing hysterically at some off-color remark made by the Marquis, thus gaining the attention of the entire room. Posing preposterously, she extends her hand to several young soldiers who are attending the party, along with their quite inebriated commanding officer. Momentarily they leave their girls (four or five grisettes gathered around the ever-watchful eyes of their madame duenna, seated by the fireplace). One or two of the girls already have their shoes off, although they have remained playfully cool to the propositions of the young men. The soldiers, with mocking gallantry, kiss Flora's proffered hand as some guests sing the opening phrase, *"Dell'invito trascorsa è già l'ora"* (You're late. What kept you?). Violetta leaves her group after making a slurring remark about Flora's dress and approaches Flora directly. The two women, with little love but much affected camaraderie, kiss the air on each side of their respective cheeks. Violetta indicates Flora's dress is really stunning, looking back to Grenvil's group with a malicious smile as Flora preens. Gastone, carrying a white angora cat, and Alfredo, holding a small box of flowers, enter through a group gathered round the doorway, precisely at the first chorus entrance, *"Sì, la vita s'addoppia al gioir"* (Life is made for pleasure). During this response, Violetta sees Gastone, opens her arms to her favorite gossip, and pets his cat. She is completely oblivious of Alfredo's presence until Gastone introduces him. In this production Gastone is a rich and bored degenerate, in no way related to the rather touching character in Dumas's play. This decision was made to help characterize the hopeless demimonde surround-

* The famous French actress whom I included among other personages to give tone to the soiree.

ing Violetta. Therefore, as his actual presence in the opera is negligible, each stroke had to be bold and telling. After the introduction Gastone indicates to the rather tense Alfredo that he step forward. He does, taking Violetta's limp hand. The Marquis, having retired with Flora (who has paid her respects to the madame, her girls, and a female guest in man's clothing), now comes forward and puts his hand on Alfredo's shoulder. Alfredo is surprised and relieved to see a familiar face. During all this, Gastone waves to friends. A servant enters to inform Violetta that all is in readiness for the next phase of the party. Violetta sings, *"Miei cari, sedete"* (Sit down, my dear friends) and, during the answering chorus, they all do so. Alfredo deposits his gift on the settee and sits there at Gastone's left as Violetta returns to her guests. During the ensuing orchestral interlude, Violetta is joined by Annina (her maid and companion, played in this production as a much older woman than usual—a sort of mother to the ailing girl). Annina shoos the guests out of the way as Violetta claps her hands, signaling the entrance of a large float. From its camouflage it is not clear of what the float consists. Violetta teasingly plays with the drapery covering it, which further piques the guests' curiosity. Violetta quickly removes the covering to reveal a plastic statue of the goddess Hebe, surrounded by clusters of grapes and countless bottles of champagne. The chorus applauds the sight; *"E al convito che s'apre ogni cor"* (That's enough to warm anybody's heart). Three footmen simultaneously enter with trays of champagne that they distribute among the guests. Violetta, during the next interlude, goes to the dowager madame, who congratulates her pupil on the splendid surprise. The other girls corroborate by giggling. The madame wants to know who the late arrival is. Could he be Gastone's latest lover? —but that doesn't seem likely, as the dear man has not taken his eyes off Violetta since arriving. "Go tend him," she winks at her former pupil. Violetta takes two champagne glasses off a nearby tray and approaches the seated Alfredo, who rises. She hands him a glass and sidles by him. Gastone insists that *"Sempre Alfredo a voi pensa"* (Alfredo never stops thinking of you). Violetta laughs frivolously throughout their exchange. Gastone secretly enjoys this toying with the bumpkin Alfredo. Only when Violetta sings *"Le mie*

grazie vi rendo" (Thank you very much) does she barely hint
that somehow she is touched by Alfredo's devotion. She quickly
stifles the impulse by turning it into a biting reminder to Douphol of his own tiresome attentions. Douphol, still smarting
from his rejection, is no match for her. Flora warns Douphol to
keep cool. Gastone rubs a bit of salt in the wound by proposing
that the Baron offer a toast. Douphol refuses. Violetta nods toward Alfredo, and the excited young man agrees with alacrity.
During the musical introduction to his toast, he seats Violetta
on the stool near Douphol on the settee and moves about the
room, saluting the various guests, now very much a part of the
festivities. He addresses the throng, who indicate their satisfaction with him. Gastone is positively delighted that Alfredo has
not proved to be a total dud after all. At the conclusion of his
toast, Alfredo turns to Violetta directly. Douphol, in an effort to
reingratiate himself, comes close to Violetta, but she moves
abruptly away from his proffered glass and rises, singing her
brindisi. On the words *"È un fior che nasce a muore"* (a flower
that buds and fades), she taps Flora on the head with her fan
and swings saucily by her. Gastone laughs under his breath.
Flora kicks him. There is general amusement at this catty dou-
ble-entendre. Violetta continues her aria, joining the soldiers,
who leave their annoyed grisettes. Violetta empties the rest of
her champagne into their glasses; then, supported by them on
either side, waltzes backward to the float. This is accomplished
during the chorus singing *"ah godiamo la tazza* (let's drink).
Alfredo, during this same chorus, approaches Violetta, and willingly waltzes her around the room. This allows their exchange
to have an intimate quality while still being part of the ensemble. Douphol finally loses his composure. Enjoying the spectacle of the rattled older man, Violetta takes Alfredo's arm and
places it suggestively around her waist as she faces Douphol
directly. Her interest is only in using Alfredo as a foil to torment
Douphol and as a final excuse to break off her relations with
him. During the chorus, Douphol, incensed beyond reason,
starts to approach the pair, but soon realizes he has become a
spectacle; in great anger and embarrassment, he leaves the
room just before the climax of the drinking chorus.

As the sound of music is heard from the next room, Violetta

takes a bottle of champagne from the float and, urging the others
to do so, invites them to dance. She is about to precede them
when a dizzy spell overcomes her. She hands her bottle to a
guest, making light of the incident, and insists they leave her
momentarily. The guests, much used to these seizures and considering them bids for attention, romp off. Only Alfredo holds
back. Thinking she is alone, Violetta gives in to her dizziness.
She makes her way toward a small table in front of a huge Oriental screen and finds a bottle of smelling salts. Recovering her
balance, she regards herself in the mirror above the fireplace.
"Oh, qual pallor!" (I'm so pale). As she says this, Alfredo steps
forward and Violetta sees him in the mirror. In the background
couples are seen dancing in the hallway. Violetta, again dissem-
bling, comes forward to meet him: *"Sto meglio"* (I'm better).
But no sooner are the words spoken than her dizziness returns.
Alfredo catches her, *"Ah, in cotal guisa v' ucciderete!"* (You'll
kill yourself living like this!). But Violetta has no time for death
and is impatient with these reminders of it. She grasps Alfredo's
hand and turns his pitying gesture into an invitation to dance
with her. Alfredo backs away, appalled at her lightheadedness.
As the conversation continues, Violetta waltzes around the
chaise longue by herself. Another dizzy spell forces her to stop
her play-acting. Alfredo, angered by her self-destructive behavior, declares *"Perchè nessuno al mondo v'ama"* (Because there
is no one who really loves you). *"Nessun?"* (No one?) she
flashes back, on the attack. *"Tranne sol io"* (No one but I), he
answers. Violetta proceeds to belittle him. Her answers snap
the air. She sinks into the chaise, laughing raucously at the confused young man. *"Ah si, da un anno"* (I've loved you for a
year), Alfredo cries and, kneeling at her feet, deposits his gift
before her. There is a long pause. The music ends while the
still-laughing Violetta opens the gift box and, looking at the
white camellias, looks at Alfredo with a puzzled expression.
Only after that look does Alfredo confess: *"Un dì felice"* (One
day I saw you), and the orchestra gently picks up the threads of
his pounding heart. As he sings, Violetta takes the flowers out of
the box and, with Alfredo's *"Di quell' amor, quell' amor ch' è
palpito"* (I fell in love with you the moment I saw you), she
places the flowers against her cheek in a sudden rush of long-

ing. This and the earlier *"Le mie grazie vi rendo"* (I thank you very much), when she brought Alfredo and Gastone their champagne, are Violetta's only soft moments to this point in the action. They have stolen upon her unawares. But immediately she is her former self. *"Ah, so ciò è ver"* (If what you say is true), she laughs, and continues, *"Solo amistade io v'offro"* (I can only offer you friendship), trailing a line with the camellia from Alfredo's shoulder to thigh. He turns away from the gesture and her laughter reaches its peak. *"Amar non so"* (Love doesn't interest me). All the ensuing triplets in the score are laughter, (part song, part speech). Violetta retires behind the chaise and deposits the flowers in a vase on the small table where earlier she had sought the smelling salts. She proceeds to join her guests as Alfredo turns to her, *"Oh amore."* Violetta sighs and kneels on a small stool. Alfredo touches her arm tenderly but Violetta hits it playfully with her fan and practically bounds away to the other side of the settee. Again she warns, *"dimenticarmi"* (forget me, if it's love you're after). She starts to leave through the arch but Alfredo persists, and her second *"dimenticarmi allor"* is a cry of exasperation. She sits on the settee, trapped by his persistence. Violetta resigns herself. Alfredo takes her unwilling hand and the duet concludes.

Gastone, entering the living room with a young cavalry officer, who is cradling Gastone's cat, cries out, *"che diavol fate?"* (what are you two doing?). Violetta answers, "It's none of your affair," and Gastone exits in pursuit of the officer. Violetta, with an eye toward the departing Gastone, admonishes Alfredo, *"Amor, dunque, non più"* (implying, There's love for you). Alfredo understands all too clearly and starts to leave. As a departing tease, Violetta suggests that Alfredo may call again. Alfredo's *"Perchè?"* (But why?) is desultory. She offers him a camellia and intimates that he may return when the flower has faded. Alfredo is beside himself with joy. She toys with the bloom, but Alfredo snaps it out of her hand and says, *"Domani?"* (May I come tomorrow?). "So you still think you love me," Violetta laughs. They are again almost kneeling side by side on the small ottoman. More waltzing couples pour through the arch. They are now completely drunk and watch Violetta and Alfredo, who are oblivious of their presence. It is cat and mouse between the couple. She is both coy and cool: *"D'amarmi?"* (You love me, you say?), and, mocking, *"Partite?"* (Don't tell me you're leaving?). Violetta opens her fan and offers a formal *"Addio,"* but Alfredo takes her chin in his hand and turns her face toward his own for the second breathless *"Addio."* He kisses her lightly on the lips and leaves. Violetta remains immobile, lost in her thoughts, as the dancing couples careen about the room. They are all now quite disorderly. The almost marauding quality of their behavior suggests Flora has probably invited everybody to her house for more fun and games. The gentlemen start fitting the ladies with their discarded shoes. One couple falls shamelessly on the settee. Flora puts on her wrap and is the first to approach Violetta, who has remained absolutely lost in reverie all during the entrance of the chorus. Flora's *"Si ridesta in ciel l'aurora"* (It's time to go now), sung with the chorus, signals Violetta's reawakening. Again the false kissing between the two ladies. The madame duenna is next. Then the lady in trousers and her companions come forward and bid Violetta adieu. Violetta waves farewell to the rest. Precisely at the forte outburst of *"Ah! si ritempri"* (We thank you), one of the disheveled grisettes runs in, shoeless, with a young officer in pursuit. He is sodden with drink, his tunic unbuttoned. As the grisette circles the settee, she grabs Violetta's hand and swings her around with her. Violetta pulls away and retires, breathless and gasping from the precipitous action. The grisette falls into the arms of the officer, who twirls her around. She jumps out of his grasp and runs off. The officer is given a last drink by one of the other male guests, who grabs him by the shoulders and shoves him in the direction of the disappearing grisette. This particular action is accentuated by the eighth-note rising violin scale before the final choral tutti. Violetta's back is to her guests. She waves her hand in a final effort to appear cheerful and the guests exit, laughing raucously. The commanding officer is seen in back being led out through the arch by three grisettes; one grisette has his sword, another is pulling him forward by his belt buckle, the third is pushing him from the rear. The couple gamboling on the settee exit, the lady simulating a matador, and her man, the horned bull. The last to leave is the shoeless grisette now astride the waist of her young officer.

There is a long pause after the *fermata*. The only sound is the gradually diminishing laughter of the chorus offstage, during which Annina enters with Violetta's shawl and orders the two footmen to remove the candelabra. She helps Violetta sit on the chaise by the fire and exits with the footmen. Violetta, cold and shivering, seeks the fire's warmth, her thoughts elsewhere. This pause before Violetta speaks is crucial to the division in the first act. Here is the hidden Violetta, alone, exhausted, sick and despairing, party mask discarded. The drain on her energies leaves her powerless to continue immediately. The chorus laughter fades completely; silence reigns. This pause should never be less than half a minute in length. Violetta, huddled by the fire, draws her shawl tighter around her shoulders, amazed at her own thoughts. Alfredo has awakened a long-suppressed desire and a doubt. Could she ever be capable of real love? She leans back, serious now for the first time, *"Ah, fors' è lui"* (Could it be he). *"A quell' amor quell' amor"* (Yes, love is the most important thing in life). As she recognizes this truth, she reaches out to the fire as if she could draw love to her by her gesture. She puts her feet up on the chaise, leans back against the headrest, *"Croce, croce e delizia"* (Oh, sweet burden) and remains in this position, dreaming away. Again the shadow falls, *"Follie!—follie!"* (Folly, madness!). She rises and paces the floor, dramatizing her plight—the actress on her own stage. *"Sola, abbandonata"* (Alone and abandoned). Mocking herself, she removes her shawl—her comforter, almost—and describes a wanton figure with it. Wrapping it round her bare shoulders, she sings, à la Carmen, *"Gioire. Di voluttà"* (I'll revel in pleasure). On *"Gioire"* (revel), she removes the shawl and, seeing Alfredo's flowers, swings at them playfully, dropping the shawl on the chaise at the end of her coloratura. At the Allegro introduction she rushes across the room and picks up several champagne glasses, emptying the remains into one glass. She toasts herself, *"Sempre libera"* (Always free). She dances, twirling about during the first part of the aria; but, being now quite tipsy, she is forced to sit on the settee before Alfredo's voice is heard offstage. He is serenading her from the street below (contrary to popular convention—and a strange one it is in context to the rest of the opera—that would have us believe Alfredo's voice is completely imagined by Violetta). She sits there and drinks, looks up startled, then rises and strides to the window. She raises her glass and salutes mockingly, *"Oh amore!"* (Here's to love) and drinks. As Alfredo continues, she lowers her now empty glass, shakes it several times, and is about to get more champagne when the weight of her despair suddenly overwhelms her. She looks about this now empty, gaudy room, drops her glass, which smashes on the floor, and sinks to the ground, her head buried in her arms on the small stool. She remains in this position all during the latter half of Alfredo's serenade. Then she raises her head and suddenly cries out *"Follie!"* again. She tries to recapture her former mood, but the two repeated *"gioirs"* (to enjoy) are agonized in feeling, completely contradicting the literal meaning of the word. She rises to her self-imposed mood and fiercely declares herself *"sempre libera."* She attempts to dance but the spirit is no longer willing. *"Dee volare"* (Just keep going) finds her waving away her imaginary guests in revulsion, and the screw is turned even tighter. Alfredo's voice now actually frightens her. She sits on the chaise, covering her ears in an effort to block it out. Cradling herself, she moves to center stage, still insisting that her choice to remain free is the only possible one. In the final bars Alfredo suddenly appears in the doorway, rushes down to the startled Violetta, and falls at her feet, his arms around her waist. Violetta, shaken in her conviction, sinks to the ground in complete surrender.

The curtain falls.

ACT II

(The living room of a country house near Paris. It is late afternoon. Summer is gently slipping into autumn.)

The curtain rises immediately on the first bar of music. Through the French windows Alfredo rushes in, holding a small bunch of field flowers. Slightly breathless, he pauses to look back for a moment through the garden. Seeing Violetta in pursuit, he enters the room and hides behind the screen as she rushes by. During the last two bars of the introduction, Alfredo, having eluded Violetta, sneaks from his hiding place, glances through the French windows and turns back into the room. He is smiling, content, and full of boyish mischief. Violetta is off searching for him, and Alfredo has won this round in their game of hide-and-seek. He awaits discovery, for it is certain she will eventually return to the house. This entire act derives from the idea of games on a summer day (See chapter on rehearsal with Placido Domingo). Violetta herself never appears at the opening. Alone, Alfredo calmly assesses his good fortune. At *"Ed or contenta"* (And in these peaceful surroundings), Alfredo places his batch of posies in a vase on a table behind the chaise and roams about. At the end of his recitative, Violetta is heard offstage calling "Alfredo" twice in playful exasperation. Alfredo, at the sound of her voice, goes to the doorway and shuts it quietly. He stands with his back against it as he begins his *"De' miei bollenti spiriti"* (I've never felt so alive). He concludes the aria reclining on the chaise, pressing a small pillow to his chest. After a brief pause following the aria, Alfredo rises and, hearing the sound of approaching footsteps, returns to his original hiding place behind the screen. Annina enters through the French doors and moves toward the chaise. Alfredo, thinking it is Violetta, springs out and grabs the startled servant. His line *"Annina! donde vieni?"* (Annina, where did you come from?) expresses his surprise and good humor. The startled lady loses her bonnet in the encounter. Alfredo seats her on the chaise and pats her back. When she informs Alfredo that Violetta had sent her to Paris to dispose of her belongings at auction in order to support their present mode of living, Alfredo (contrary to convention) is not struck by remorse but, sustaining his antic manner, suggests he will manage the required sum himself. He instructs her not to divulge this to Violetta, but to keep it a secret. He exits. The *"Oh, mio rimorso"* (Oh, my remorse) aria is gratuitous. As noted earlier, it has become currently fashionable, based on the drawing power of the tenor, to reinstate it. It is a diversion and tends to add nothing to the action—except misleading musical fireworks. It is interesting that despite Verdi's need to "explain" his hero, this cabaletta has not taken hold of the public. This "traditional" cut in *Traviata* permitted me to develop a clearer line of action. Violetta enters, calling Alfredo. Informed by Annina of his departure, Violetta accepts a letter from Giuseppe, a workman who now enters. As Giuseppe is deaf, Violetta raps out her instructions to him. She opens the letter and, smelling the scent rising from the invitation within, sits on the chaise next to Annina. The perfume is undeniably Flora's, and the invitation a gaudy, red card. Giuseppe, hovering in the doorway, informs Violetta that a gentleman has just arrived.

Thinking it is none other than an expected caller on business matters, Violetta remains seated. Annina rises and hustles Giuseppe out. As the two servants exit, the elder Germont appears at the doorway with walking stick and gloves. (Contrary to convention, he will not retain them throughout the ensuing colloquy; he will set them aside at his entrance. He speaks from the doorway.) Violetta is still seated with the invitation and rises only when Germont identifies himself. Instinctively she rushes to him and takes his arm in welcome but Germont draws back. Her arm drops and with dignity and control she says, "You're in my house, sir, talking to a lady." She starts to leave him. Germont's *"Quai modi"* (What gentility) is not delivered as an aside, but as a natural response. Violetta retraces her steps, her dander up. *"Tratto in error voi foste"* (You're laboring under a delusion). She crosses in front of him to a large cabinet and, taking a bill of sale from one of its shelves, hands it to Germont. As he examines it, Annina enters with a tea cart. Expecting Violetta's lawyer, she had prepared a late tea. Violetta tells Annina sotto voce who the visitor is. Annina exits, greatly upset at Germont's presence. Violetta takes back the document on *"Più non esiste"* (My past life is dead). She beckons the visibly shaken Germont to join her at tea. He crosses and sits at the side of the table during *"Nobili sensi invero!"* (Noble sentiments indeed!). In the next few lines, Violetta, sitting on his right, pours tea for Germont, just before the introduction to the aria *"Pura siccome un angelo"* (Pure as an angel). This effort at domesticity is made doubly poignant by the fact that it is not socially expected from a woman of Violetta's calling—certainly as a Germont might envision it. It is in reality a most ordinary habit in her new life. Amid the tension of the present meeting this late tea underlines a multitude of ironies. Dramatically its details serve to stress the ordinary

movements of life at moments of impending tragedy. During his
aria, Germont removes a locket from a watch chain and shows
Violetta a small daguerreotype of his daughter, whose imminent
marriage is threatened by the liaison between Violetta and his
son. Violetta puts down her cup to examine the picture. After
doing so, she places it on the table between herself and Germont, but he does not replace it on his chain. Violetta resumes
drinking, assuming he implies that she and Alfredo should separate until after the marrige takes place. Germont rises, holding
his cup in a quite steady hand. He informs her he requires
much more than that. Violetta, refusing to accept the idea of
complete separation, rises from her chair and moves away from
him. There is a long pause during which Violetta paces back
and forth. She is frantic with fury and pain, but she attempts to
control herself. By the time she reaches *"Ah, il supplizio"* (I
can't do it) she has lost that control. Her final *"morir"* (I'd rather
die) is hurled as a challenge in Germont's face. The latter has
tried to interrupt her, but to no avail. He sets down his cup and
attempts to calm her. He touches her shoulder on *"ma pur tran-
quilla uditemi"* (try listening calmly). She brusquely moves
away from his touch and firmly stands her ground. She continues holding her own during, *"Ah più non dite"* (Don't go on),
but the chill in the air is affecting her. During the agitated triplets in the orchestra and Germont's plea, Violetta shuts the
French windows. Her *"Gran Dio!"* is an agonized outcry as she
stands framed in the autumnal sun. In the short pause following, she moves haltingly to the burning stove, seeking its
warmth. From this moment on, the leaves, which have fallen
with romantic effect, suddenly take on a more sinister meaning.
Germont moves toward his prey with a swagger, each note of
"Un dì, quando le veneri" (Someday you'll regard this episode
quite differently) is almost buoyant. His arrival beside Violetta,
"Pensate" (Think things over), signals her next move away from
the stove toward the chaise. Germont continues closing in on
Violetta. Her first *"È vero!"* (What you say is true) finds her still
trying to resist the force of his logic. Her second *"È vero!"* is
broken, as she sits disconsolately. Germont, now convinced he
has her where he wants, sits beside her, offering her a crumb of
sympathy. *"Ah dunque, dunque sperdasi"* (Then don't torment

yourself with dreaming). *"Siate di mia famiglia l'angel consola-
tore"* (Be my family's angel of mercy). Violetta, repelled by this
new ploy, moves away from him. Germont, having been caught
at his own game, loses composure and berates her, *"Violetta,
deh pensateci"* (Think what you're doing) and, instead of a conventionally mellifluous *"È Dio che ispira, o giovine,"* he in-
vokes the name of the deity as his ally.

This does the trick, for Violetta, under her veneer, is still
very much the superstitious girl from the provinces. As Violetta
turns away in defeat, Germont attempts to regain his equanimity. He finally regards his victim coolly, for he can now afford to
be generous and sympathetic, despite her direct allusion to him
as *"l'uomo implacabil"* (unforgiving man). Moving restlessly
about, her eyes suddenly light on the tiny daguerreotype on the
table and she picks it up. After a slight pause she sings: *"Ah,"*
holding the note as long as possible, imbuing it with a deep
sense of resignation and loss. *"Dite alla giovine"* (Tell the
young girl not to worry) and she sits dejectedly at the table. On
the word *"vittima"* (victim), Germont moves to the French windows rather guiltily. Violetta sits almost in shock. This is the
turning point in the opera and her death can be reckoned from
this moment on. The falling leaves and Germont's rigid back
complement the scene. As Violetta's tears flow, the older man
turns and fatuously encourages her, *"Piangi, piangi"* (Cry, don't
be afraid). Violetta, refusing to make a further display of herself,
holds back her sorrow and extends the locket to Germont as she
repeats *"Dite alla giovine."* During this reprise Germont takes
the memento and places it back on his watch chain, grumbling
his ineffectual homilies. Unable to restrain herself any longer,
Violetta rises, walks a short way across the room, and almost
immediately collapses beside the chaise. Germont sits next to
her, a picture of apparent sympathy, as the duet concludes. Violetta rises wearily as they discuss the ways and means of dealing with Alfredo in the break that is to come. Even Germont
seems lost for a moment. Violetta, reassuring Germont that she
will find a way to restore Alfredo to his family, moves to the
cabinet and takes writing paper and quill. Germont, beside
himself with victory, magnanimously ventures, *"Generosa"*
(How generous you are). Violetta turns suddenly and shrieks

"*Morrò*" (I will die), and the writing paper falls to the floor. Germont, misconstruing this to mean she may kill herself, is thunderstruck and admonishes her, "*No, generosa, vivere*" (No, you will live). He moves to her and, as she bends to pick up the writing paper, he anticipates her gesture. They stand together and, calmed by her own outburst, Violetta comforts herself, "*Conosca il sacrifizio*" (He must be told of my sacrifice). Grateful for a more reasonable estimate of her plight, Germont corroborates her new sobriety, "*Premiato il sacrifizio*" (I honor your sacrifice) and an odd moment of mutual sympathy occurs between them. They are companions within the cages of their own mores. They touch for the first time. Pretending she hears a noise outside, Violetta asks Germont to leave. He hurriedly retrieves his hat, gloves, and cane, and is about to depart when Violetta repeats "*Conosca il sacrifizio*." Germont pauses at the door and answers respectfully. He looks at his watch, however, at his second "*si*," wanting to get this interview over. They repeat their "*Addio!*" from these positions and Germont exits. A long pause—at least twenty seconds—as Violetta crosses to the table. She rings for Annina immediately, scribbling the single word, "*Ritorno*" (I'm coming back) on a sheet addressed to Douphol. She is almost brutal to Annina, in order to allay her own fears. Annina leaves with the message. Violetta sits at the table, trying not to cry, as she next ponders her note to Alfredo. Alfredo himself appears in the garden as the clarinet solo begins. He cannot see Violetta's face from where he stands and, having last left her in a jocund mood, he cautiously enters, tiptoeing toward Violetta, now applying sand to paper. As she rises, he places his hands over her eyes and asks, "*Che fai?*" (What are you doing?). Violetta, surprised and confused, stammers; sensing his playful mood, she quickly imitates it. Alfredo scoops her up in his arms and carries her across the room, placing her on the chaise as on a pedestal, kneeling in front of her in tender worship. His buoyant spirits cannot be dampened, even though he now tells Violetta of his father's imminent arrival. (In most productions a conventional pall is usually thrown over the proceedings by this fact.) Violetta, mastering her fears, continues the jocund mood of the opening scene; "*Ai piedi suoi mi getterò*" (I'll throw myself at your father's feet when he comes), she declares melodramatically. "Everything will go well because you love me, isn't that so?" *"Oh quanto!"* Alfredo answers in similar playful style. Suddenly she leans her head back and expresses her anguish. But she lies, claiming her tears are those of joy. Alfredo lowers her from the chaise and they sit down beside each other. "There, I'm calm, you see," and she places the note she has written on the couch beside her. Alfredo picks it up, but Violetta grabs it coquettishly. *"Sarò là, tra quei fior"* (I'll be outside in the garden. Soon you can come find me), she says, and starts to go. She freezes momentarily, for this may be the last time she will ever see Alfredo. She turns, and with great feeling (but no despair) says *"Amami, Alfredo"* (Love me, Alfredo). Slowly she approaches his outstretched arms and presses herself against him. As he is seated and cannot see her face, she can allow the final *"Addio"* a full measure of its real meaning. She holds the *"addio"* for as long as possible. She quickly turns and runs out through the French doors.

Twilight has fallen. Alfredo rises and, remarking that his father is late for their meeting, crosses to the cabinet. He takes a book out of it (Prévost's *Manon Lescaut*) and sits at the table, awaiting the elder Germont. Giuseppe arrives and informs Alfredo of Violetta's departure, meanwhile giving him Violetta's letter. It is redolent of her special scent and does not (as is the wont of convention) throw Alfredo into an immediate paroxysm of fear. As if he were an actor in his own game of love, he toys with the note, affecting a variety of romantic stances suitable to the stage lover. These are not overprojected, but rather savored for his own titillation. The message of her departure is grasped midreading and comes as a thunderbolt. The elder Germont, appearing as Alfredo starts reading the letter, stands beside the young man while the first wave of shock settles. Still hoping the letter is part of some game, Alfredo rushes out, thinking he will find Violetta enjoying the success of her latest prank. He returns, walking slowly back into the room, the letter still in his hand. He moves dazedly, rereading it in disbelief. Germont, helpless to do anything else, comforts him as he sings his well-known aria, *"Di Provenza il mar"* (In Provence, you will find peace). Even before the affair with Violetta, father and son had been estranged. Alfredo's restlessness had driven him away from the family seat and, seeking a new way of life in Paris, this alliance with a courtesan has only led him to compound the felony of his taking off. At the conclusion of the first half of the aria, Alfredo, having dropped Violetta's note (one more falling leaf), looks at his father but can find no comfort in his as yet stern visage. Alfredo thinks, "What can this comfortably set-up burger know about what is happening in the world around him—least of all the passions now tearing me apart?" With a slight, disdainful shake of his head, Alfredo sits forlornly at the table, staring numbly into the void. (Conventionally, at this point Alfredo falls into his father's arms like a helpless child.) Germont permits a moment of sticky sentiment to break through his reserve, "*Ah, il tuo vecchio genitor tu non sai quanto soffrì*" (You have no idea how I've suffered these past months). He approaches Alfredo and stands behind him, almost gushing his paternal concern. It is genuinely felt, for there once had been great rapport between them. Toward the end of Germont's aria, Alfredo has begun to fidget under these bromides and inadvertently picks up Flora's invitation, which Violetta had left lying on the table. This triggers his worst presentiments; rising, he flings the invitation to the ground disdainfully. He exits through the French doors as Germont, after his "*Ah! ferma!*" (Don't go!), picks up the crumpled invitation and starts in pursuit of his enraged son.

The curtain falls.

ACT III

(A pavilion in Flora's country home outside Paris)

When the curtain rises (on the first notes of the introduction) Flora is giving a *fête champêtre* and the guests are all in party costume and mask. Some are roaming out toward the gardens offstage. Two men, one dressed in an ape costume, the other as a pasha, wave at the Marquis and Dr. Grenvil, who are dressed as sultans with golden masks. They are seated at a small cabaret table. To their right is a slightly raised platform with a Moorish canopy and inner curtain—the entrance for the entertainers. Behind them is a long, open tent running upstage from left to right

and continuing thereon offstage. This area is crowded with tables and chairs for the supper to be served; lanterns illuminate
it. Flora, dressed as an Alice in Wonderland Queen (replete
with a fan of white ostrich feathers), is talking to three matrons
and a gentleman dressed as an American Indian, naked except
for a loincloth. Behind them is another small table and two
chairs. At the moment one chair is occupied by an elderly matron standing on it dropping sweetmeats into the mouth of a
young cavalry officer who attended Violetta's party in Act I. He
dances up and down on his haunches, jumping to catch the fa-
vors as they fall from the lady's ancient hand. Another guest
enters the pavilion from the house. She is dressed as a *bergère*
and carries a crook. Eying the Indian with Flora's group, she
crosses toward him languidly, extending her crook, which he
takes, and, nodding to the ladies, allows himself to be led offstage, a prisoner of love! Flora, having made some off-color remark, asks the other ladies to rejoin their escorts. She then
moves and peeks through the curtains in the entertainers' area.
The preceding pantomime occupies the full length of the opening Allegro brillante. Flora comes toward the Marquis and
Grenvil with her first line concerning Alfredo's and Violetta's
anticipated arrival. Other guests enter. There has been a continuous traffic of people throughout the opening and only at
Gastone's appearance through the Moorish curtains do they
gather as a unit to contribute to and watch the entertainment.
Gastone's entrance signals applause from the guests as he gestures for silence. A group of gypsy girls, led by a fortuneteller,
move in quickly and surround him. The guests sing their part of
the entertainment, *"Noi siamo zingarelle"* (We are little gypsy
girls), as Gastone executes a series of campy mystical passes.
Just before *"Vediamo!"* (Let's look!), Flora, who has joined the
Marquis and Grenvil (seated on either side of her), offers her
palm to the fortuneteller. Coming to Flora, the fortuneteller
starts to read her hand. The rest of the chorus moves in and
surrounds her. When informed that *"Voi, signora, rivali
alquante avete"* (You have many rivals in love), Flora peremptorily seizes the Marquis's hand and tends it toward the fortuneteller for her examination. Registering a mock gesture of con-
sternation and disapproval, the fortuneteller looks away as the

chorus volunteers, "*Marchese, voi non siete model di fedeltà*" (Marquis, you're not exactly a model of fidelity). Flora, taking this antic turn seriously, hits the Marquis with her fan and rises from the table. Anticipating another of her childish tantrums, Grenvil proffers a handkerchief as Flora bursts into tears. She moves away from the table and sulks. The Marquis, protesting he is innocent, tries to placate Flora, but she will have none of it. The rest of the scene consists of the attempts made by the fortuneteller and the dancers to effect a reconciliation. The chorus behind them laughs maliciously. This scene is a parody, enacted by two emotionally bankrupt people, of what will later be serious business between Violetta and Alfredo. Needless to say, the fortuneteller's efforts to join the hands of the mock lovers elicit the desired result, particularly after the Marquis stuffs a wad of money down Flora's bosom. The pair fall into each other's arms at the conclusion of the gypsy dance. The matador part of the entertainment finds the chorus divided into two parts, the men on one side and the women on the other. Gastone, having joined the ladies during the preceding foolishness, removes his cape, which a servant takes, revealing himself in a matador costume. Four male and female dancers in Spanish dress pose alongside him during the musical introduction. Gastone, *dilettente suprême*, soaks in the applause of his friends and then moves toward the Moorish curtain and heralds the dramatic appearance of the chief matador dancer. At the climax of the dance Gastone presents a red rose to the matador's bride, and the troop exits.

Alfredo enters from the house dressed in formal attire and appears perfectly relaxed, with Olympia (a famous beauty of the period) in tow. (In most productions Alfredo usually attends the soirée alone. Participation of Olympia has been borrowed from Dumas). Flora steps forward and cattily asks after Violetta, to which Alfredo responds with a cold "*Non ne so*" (I don't know where she is). It is game time at the Marquis's table and Alfredo is invited to join. Alfredo sits at the table between Gastone and Grenvil. Alfredo's lady for the evening drapes herself decorously behind him. A group of fifteen people remain watching the game, while the rest wander off on the grounds. As Alfredo and the rest stake money, Violetta, wearing vivid red, enters accompanied by the Baron Douphol. She seems composed, but she moves in a trance-like manner, her eyes downcast. Flora leaves the gaming table and comes forward to meet them, smelling a perfect set-up for a brewing scandal. Then she returns to the table, pokes the Marquis, and pulls him aside for a moment, warning him there might be fireworks to come. A simultaneous break in the group around the table reveals Alfredo's presence to Douphol. But Alfredo, aware of Violetta's entrance, pretends not to notice and continues his game. Douphol warns Violetta not to speak to Alfredo, and joins his hostess as Violetta, now startled out of her somnolence, bemoans *"Perchè venni, incauta!"* (Oh, why did I come here tonight!). Flora leaves Douphol with the Marquis as she hurries to Violetta, *"Meco t'assidi"* (Sit here beside me and tell me everything). As Violetta moves to sit at the table, her eyes meet Alfredo's momentarily. Alfredo's card is suspended in midaction by this glance. Violetta turns her back to him and sits. Alfredo now clearly intends that Violetta hear his slurring remarks aimed at her. Flora, still seated with Violetta, cannot resist inquiring about Alfredo, *"Solo?"* (Will you be returning to the country alone?). Violetta hits Flora's hand reprovingly; Alfredo's slurs continue as Douphol, having heard them, moves to face Alfredo. Violetta grabs Douphol's arm, warning him she will leave if he makes a scene. Alfredo nonchalantly invites the Baron to try his luck at the gaming table. Douphol accepts and takes Grenvil's place at the table. Violetta, feeling dizzy, looks away: *"Che fia? morir mi sento!"* (I wish I could die now!). Flora leaves Violetta to herself and avidly watches the proceedings at the gaming table. Alfredo's gambler's luck is still on his side as a footman enters from the house announcing dinner. Flora, ever ready where food is concerned, bids her guests take their places at the various assigned tables. She exits to entertain a small group, which is to include Douphol and Violetta in the offstage dining area.

Douphol angrily rises: *"Per ora nol possiamo"* (We'll continue later). Alfredo stands to face Douphol. Violetta, following her repeated *"Che fia? morir mi sento!"*, beckons the nearby footman. She gives him a red rose that has been pinned to her dress and indicates he is to give it to Alfredo after she has gone inside, with a message asking Alfredo to meet her here shortly. Gastone, Alfredo, and Olympia sit at a dining table while Douphol takes Violetta's hand and escorts her offstage.

The footman crosses over to Alfredo with the message. Drink and food are being served as the lights are lowered to indicate a passage of time. This is the section arousing my greatest animadversion in the entire opera. Conventionally, in or out of doors, the stage would be completely empty in preparation for the coming quarrel and the chorus stampede that climaxes it. Instead, the lowering of lights and the presence of the chorus and Alfredo at supper create a credible "ordinary" for the unexpected events to come. After the brief pause Violetta, in great agitation, enters with Flora; thus accompanied, Violetta could leave the Baron's side with impunity. Violetta addresses her *"Invitato a qui seguirmi"* (I told him I'd see him here) to the flustered Flora. Conventionally, Violetta's recitative is sung in monologue. It makes good sense addressed to Flora, intent on getting Violetta back to the dining table so she herself can attend to her other guests. Alfredo, seeing Violetta, leaves his table and comes to her as she insists *"Questi luoghi abbandonate"* (You must leave here instantly). Hoping vainly that Alfredo will capitulate, Violetta starts for her table. Alfredo, enjoying her plight and spoiling for a fight, sits at the empty gaming table. *"Ah comprendo! Basta, basta"* (I get the picture). Violetta turns back and tells Alfredo she is afraid of what the Baron might do. She sits at the opposite table in an effort not to be seen too directly with him. The other guests at dinner begin to notice the quarrelsome pair. Flora, meantime, walks to Gastone, who is still eating, and begs him to intervene if the going should get rough. When Violetta implies that the Baron may even kill him, Alfredo flushes in anger, *"La mia morte!"* (Would you care?). Gastone comes down and places his hand on Alfredo's shoulder to forestall an open fight; Alfredo shrugs him away. Gastone goes back to Flora, who is now consulting Grenvil at his table. When Violetta demands that Alfredo leave, he rises and approaches her, declaring passionately, *"Partirò, ma giura innante"* (I'll leave if you'll come with me). Violetta quickly refuses his request. Misunderstanding her abrupt reply, Alfredo persists in twisting the knife. Flora, meanwhile, moves toward the pair but, unable to intervene, looks off in the Baron's direction. Then, as Alfredo proceeds *"A chi dillo?"* (Whom have you promised?), Flora tries to make light of the situation by reassuring several of the perturbed guests that all will be over soon. Alfredo and Violetta, now completely unmindful of their surroundings, reach the climax of their quarrel: *"Fu Douphol?"* "Did you promise Douphol?" he asks. "Yes." *"Dunque l'ami?"* (Then you love him?). "All right, yes, I do," Violetta lies. Grabbing her wrist, Alfredo pulls her across the stage and places her on the platform intended for the entertainers. He shouts, *"Or tutti a me!"* (Listen, everybody!). This precipitates that moment described earlier when the entire chorus appears, avalanche-like, in a matter of four bars. In this version, the guests under the tent, already aware of the conflict, merely leave their tables and step forward easily within the four-bar span. The Baron has been alerted by the shouts from the pavilion and is the only one who enters briskly, accompanied by the Marquis and one or two other guests. Violetta, seeing the Baron's entrance, tries to move away, but Alfredo forces her to remain on the little stage. The irony is compounded, for Alfredo is about to achieve a kind of poetic justice, considering Violetta's own earlier humiliation of the Baron in Act I. Alfredo's flair for the theatrical conceives even this as part of the evening's entertainment. He raises Violetta's hand aloft, as if she were a piece of merchandise. *"Questa donna conoscete?"* (You all know this lady?). Then he flings her arm down with abhorrence. *"Che facesse non sapete?"* (Would you like to know a little something about her?). He proceeds to remove his gloves, which he flings onto the gambling table, and approaches the Baron, Flora, and the Marquis. *"Ogni suo aver,"* he lashes out at them. (She spent all her money on me and now I want to pay back the debt I owe her.) He approaches the trembling Violetta and, removing a large handful of winnings from his inside coat pocket, flings them in her face. They fall like heavy leaves about her feet. As the chorus thunders its disapproval, Violetta, trying to compose herself, descends the platform and starts to move toward Flora. She staggers at midpoint, and, in complete contrast to his attack on her, Alfredo rushes to prevent her collapse. With the energy of a wronged woman in desperate straits,

Violetta violently pushes Alfredo away and falls into Flora's arms. Flora seats her at the gambling table, meanwhile ordering the footman to get some smelling salts. Alfredo tries to leave the premises, but is confronted by Gastone and a group of other men who challenge him. Flora turns to get the smelling salts and encounters the elder Germont, who has witnessed Alfredo's attack on Violetta. Flora stares at him, but the footman's return with the smelling salts brings her back to Violetta. Alfredo, unable to contend with the aroused guests, decides to leave in the opposite direction. As he dashes across the stage, Germont seizes him by the arm and throws him backward. Now at fighting pitch, Alfredo is about to retaliate when he recognizes his adversary. The recognition takes place in the long pause immediately after the chorus has stopped singing. *"Di sprezzo degno?"* (How dare you do this?) challenges Germont, and Alfredo looks down in sudden shame and remorse. (Usually the tenor is instructed to literally take five giant steps across the length of the stage, look up, freeze, and Hello—there is Papa!) Violetta is seated at the gambling table, surrounded by Grenvil and Flora, the Baron and the Marquis behind her. Germont and Alfredo are at opposite ends of the stage. The other guests are in the background. An early autumn moon has risen. As Germont continues his harangue, the beaten Alfredo slowly begins his *"Ah si! che feci!"* (What have I done!). During this self-chastisement Germont walks over to Violetta, kisses her hand, and makes her recall her promise. Turning, he sees the Baron and bows to him. At the beginning of the ensuing ensemble, Gastone moves to Violetta's table and joins the group there. When Violetta regains composure, she calls weakly but tenderly *"Alfredo, Alfredo"* (Alfredo, if I could only tell you), which signals the Baron to move away, followed by the Marquis. The insulted Baron moves directly behind Alfredo, singing *"A questa donna l'atroce insulto"* (I will pay him back for this insult). The Marquis follows him, trying to prevent further mayhem. They remain there until Douphol, still muttering threats, is persuaded by the Marquis to leave well enough alone. As Violetta and Flora sing, Violetta first, *"T'amerò"* (I'll always love you) and Flora *"Ah! fa cor"* (Have courage), the Baron decides to leave and starts for the main exit. He stops and looks back at Violetta and suddenly removes his gloves. As the ensemble ends, the Baron shrugs off the Marquis and advances on Alfredo. He strikes him twice across the chest with his gloves and throws them to the ground at Alfredo's feet.* This gesture brings Alfredo to his senses and, realizing the situation in a flash, he picks up the gloves and stands there glowering at the Baron. Violetta rises feebly from her chair, gesturing helplessly toward the men.

The curtain falls.

ACT IV

(Violetta's bedroom—now stripped bare of all decoration)

The curtain rises slowly during the final three-bar trill in the prelude. The room is in almost total darkness. Annina sits on the chaise, her head nodding but her body still alert. Violetta can hardly be seen in the huge bed. There is a long pause before Violetta calls to Annina, who goes to the bedside and, helping to prop Violetta, pours her a glass of water. Then she moves to the window and draws the curtains, admitting the pale, wintry sunshine. Informing Violetta that Dr. Grenvil has just entered below, she moves to support Violetta, who has started out of bed. Annina would keep her there, but Violetta's vanity demands that she receive the doctor standing, as if to belie the seriousness of her condition. Annina helps her to the chaise, during the short orchestral interlude following, *"Alzar mi vo—m'aita."* (I want to get up—help me.) The doctor enters and stands in the doorway at the conclusion of the interlude, just prior to *"Quanta bontà!"* (How kind you are!). Grenvil sees a ravaged beauty in the throes of her last illness, dressed in a gray, almost shroudlike nightgown, holding onto her companion's arm and smiling a bewitching smile. He crosses to her, *"Come vi sentite?"* (How do you feel?) and proceeds with the

---

* The challenge to a duel is accomplished earlier in most productions, approximately during the card game, when Alfredo says, *"La disfida accetto"* (I accept the challenge). This seems a weak device and is certainly anticlimactic. Without a strong climax one is forced to ring down the curtain at the end of the concertante, leaving everyone caught with a bit of egg on his elegant face.

ordinary of those days. He seats her on the chaise and, as they
converse, Annina goes to the medicine table to prepare a mixture. Grenvil crosses around the table and raises Violetta's feet
onto the chaise, allowing her to rest more comfortably. He sits
beside her and places the back of his fingers on Violetta's forehead. *"E questa notte?"* (Did you sleep well?). Annina brings
the medicine glass to Grenvil, which he hands to Violetta. She
barely sips it during his *"Coraggio adunque"* (Have courage).
Grenvil hands the glass back to Annina, who returns it to the
table as he starts out. *"Non mi scordate"* (Don't forget me), Violetta demands coyly and he smiles warmly. The preceding
routine is perfunctory. Grenvil can do nothing for her. She
should have died long before, but her tenacity is unfathomable.
His visits are made to break the awesome loneliness that have
descended on this house since she fell out of fortune. Now in
the doorway, allowing Annina to help him with his cape, he
must repeat again that it's almost over for Violetta. He departs.
Annina, having heard the worst time and again, cannot but still
react strongly. She averts her face from Violetta who, lost in a
reverie, has not heard a word of the last exchange. *"Giorno di
festa è questo?"* (It's a holiday, isn't it?), Violetta asks. Annina
confirms that it is carnival time and Paris has gone mad. She
moves to stand beside the fireplace, still not daring to look at
her mistress for fear of what Violetta may read in her eyes.
"How much money have we left?" Violetta dreamily asks.
"Twenty louis," Annina replies after gazing at the contents in
the drawer of the table next to Violetta. "Give half of it to the
needy," Violetta continues. Annina protests, but Violetta persists and then asks that Annina now check the mail. Naturally
there are no longer any letters or messages, but the ordinary
must be maintained. This little ritual signals the real purpose of
sending Annina out. Crumpled in her hand, forever with her
even in sleep, is the last letter from Germont. As Annina exits
on her pointless mission, Violetta unfolds the letter and reads it
aloud. Halfway through, she puts the letter down and speaks
the familiar words from memory. The reading of the letter,
while it must be metrically correct, should still be simple and
natural, the Gregorian chant of most performances avoided.
Suddenly, with harsh and savage accents, Violetta cries out, *"È*

tardi!" (It's too late!) and throws the letter to the floor. But rather than truly thinking it is the end, she tries to believe her condition is a punishment before her reconciliation with Alfredo. She persists in this all-too-human delusion until the very last moment. After discarding the letter, she picks up the hand mirror from the table beside her and looks at herself. She keeps the mirror next to her on the chaise as she begins *"Addio del passato"* (It is over). She takes another look at her sunken cheeks during *"le rose del volto"* (The roses in my cheeks have vanished). Putting down the mirror, she sees the letter on the floor and, bending over, picks it up. During *"l'amore d'Alfredo"* (if Alfredo would only come), she smooths out the almost shredded paper and folds it neatly again. Oh, how many times has she repeated this ceremony! She rises and totters over to the priedieu: *"Conforto, sostegno"* (Comfort, help me) she says, kneeling. For the first time we realize that a thin rosary has been wrapped around her wrist. She unwinds it as she prays, pleading to God for another chance. She becomes momentarily short of breath as a result of her exertions, and her *"Ah! tutto"* (It's all finished) is sung in the sudden panic of fear. Yes, she is really ill! She bows her head at the end of her lament and the rosary hangs over the edge of the priedieu.

The carnival passes by. Violetta looks up and, just as suddenly as she had been plunged in the depths of despair, she recalls the gay times. When Annina enters, she finds Violetta still at the priedieu, her head cradled in her arms, lost in the past. Annina stands near Violetta as she attempts to tell her the unexpected good news. At first Violetta answers almost indifferently. Only when Annina announces *"Una gioia improvvisa"* does Violetta come to life. Knowing who the visitor may be, Violetta tries to rise. She succeeds and falls against Annina in a frenzy of anticipation—Is her hair all right, does she need rouge, her eyes?—but all too late. Alfredo is standing in the doorway, holding a small box of flowers. They address each other from across the room in duet. At its conclusion, Alfredo places his flowers on the bed and rushes to Violetta. They embrace and whisper endearments as Annina, herself now in tears, exits. Violetta can hardly believe Alfredo is actually there. She touches his face, his hair, his clothes, and finally they kiss passionately. *"Parigi, o cara"* (We'll leave Paris, my beloved), Alfredo sings as he picks Violetta up in his arms and cradles her. A small sigh of childish delight escapes her. Standing and rocking her in his arms, Alfredo continues the *"Parigi, o cara"*. The action stresses the lullaby quality of this famous love song, and as originally performed by Placido Domingo and Patricia Brooks it was a deeply moving moment. Unfortunately, it has not been duplicated, since the action was conceived for both these particular artists. Other tenors who have succeeded Domingo have had neither his physique nor stamina. More's the pity! Violetta's reprise was sung with her face buried in his chest. It seemed a childlike echo of Alfredo's wish. Alfredo takes Violetta over to the chaise and seats her tenderly. He sits beside her and leans her back against his shoulder. With his resumption of *"Parigi, o cara"* he rises, crosses to the bed, and returns, kneeling at Violetta's feet with the white camellias he had brought her.

She accepts them with a pang. In the short pause after *"de' corsi affanni"* (we'll always be together) they kiss briefly, then conclude the duet. Alfredo then rises and begins to kiss her cheek and the back of her neck passionately. *"Ah, non più!* (Don't go on, please), she remonstrates, feeling the rise of a passion she cannot consummate. Her already overexcited senses betray her, and she sways. *"Tu impallidisci"* (You've gone pale), Alfredo fusses, kneeling in front of her. Annina enters in time to see Violetta's second seizure, which follows immediately after the first. *"Gran Dio! Violetta!"* Alfredo cries out in alarm. He, too, poor lad, never believed that death was imminent. He has even managed to erase the evidence of his own eyes and can see only the woman he first loved. Violetta, rising to the occasion, dissents in the old manner, *"È il mio malore"* (It's only my time of month). Continuing this fatal game, she rises shakily, *"Ora son forte"* (I'm all right now). The trill should be dangerously shaky as she moves toward the dumfounded Annina, handing her the flowers. Alfredo watches Annina as she places them in a vase. What he sees on her face elicits his *"Ahi, cruda sorte!"* (It's unfair!). Violetta claps her hands imperiously, ordering Annina to *"Dammi a vestire"* (Help me dress). Violetta, before the stunned eyes of Alfredo and Annina, grabs a party dress out of the trunk and tries to put it on. Its sleeves are inside out and she struggles with it, *"Voglio uscire"* (I want to go out), but her strength leaves her. *"Gran Dio! non posso!"* (My God! I can't!). The dress falls about her feet as Alfredo rushes to prevent her collapse. Annina picks up the garment and exits. Leaning against Alfredo, Violetta looks at her rosary: *"Ma se tornando no m'hai salvato"* (What does it all mean if his coming back can't save me). And in a sudden rage she flings the rosary to the ground, falling to her knees and accusing God of stealing her youth: *"Ah! gran Dio! Morir si giovine."* (Ah, God, to die so young.)

Alfredo gets up and looks out the doorway, foolishly hoping the doctor will materialize then and there. He returns and kneels by Violettta at her words *"dunque fu delirio"* (it was an illusion) and remains thus, close but helpless. As Alfredo sings *"Oh mio sospiro"* (My very breath, my life), Violetta reaches over and, picking up her rosary, kisses it guiltily, pressing it to her breast. Alfredo lifts her from the ground on *"ma più che mai"* (our love will change everything) and, supporting her, leads her to the chaise. Alfredo seats her before Germont enters. The latter rushes over to Violetta and kneels. Alfredo moves away, annoyed by the old man's interference. Annina and Grenvil enter after Alfredo crosses to the fireplace. Alfredo, seeing the doctor, rushes to him, begging him to do something. All he can do is make Violetta more comfortable by forcing her to lie back. He whispers to Annina to fetch a priest. She exits after Germont's *"O cielo! è ver!"* (Oh God, it's true!). Germont joins Alfredo, who has remained rooted in dumb fear. Violetta, opening her eyes, asks Grenvil to give her the locket from the drawer and calls *"Più a me t'appressa"* (Come closer to me, Alfredo). Germont nods for him to do so, as Alfredo seems unable to function. He moves toward the chaise following her summons, encounters Grenvil, and searches his face for a sign of hope. Grenvil shakes his head, dispelling the idea forever. Alfredo stands by Violetta's side as she begins, *"Prendi, quest' è l'immagine"* (Take this locket). Grenvil crosses slowly and encounters Germont. One look between the men is sufficient. Grenvil goes to the door, anticipating the priest's arrival. Germont moves slowly toward the window and turns there to gaze at the lovers. Alfredo refuses to take the locket, as if it sealed Violetta's death, and the trio begins. At the conclusion Alfredo sinks to the ground, burying his head in Violetta's lap. Germont sees his shredded letter at the priedieu and picks it up wonderingly. Annina enters as Violetta sings *"Se una pudica vergine"* (Someday you'll marry) and, sitting exhaustedly on the trunk, Annina begins to cry. Grenvil goes to comfort her. During *"Le porgi quest' effigie"* (Give her this small portrait), Violetta, stroking Alfredo's hair, places the locket in his unwilling hand. She sinks back as the quintet develops. During the quintet, Violetta repeats *"Le porgi quest' effigie"* as in a delirium, her body shaking convulsively in the midst of repetition.

At the quintet's conclusion, Alfredo kneels. Suddenly Violetta sits up. She looks about and sees him. She touches his head tenderly, *"È strano!"* (How strange!), she says, and rises. She takes the camellias out of the vase and approaches Germont cautiously, but with increasing energy. *"Cessarono gli spasimi"* (The pain is leaving me), she says. Smiling and unbelieving, she looks at Grenvil and Annina, who have started to approach her. *"In me renasce"* (I feel reborn), she repeats. She stands center stage, bursting with new-found joy and health. *"Ah! ma io ritorno a viver!"* (I'm going to live!), she says to Germont. Then, turning to Alfredo and opening her arms to him, *"Oh, gioia!"* (Oh, happiness!). Alfredo rushes to her. They embrace and kiss passionately. Suddenly her arms go limp and the camellias fall to the ground, one at a time. Violetta's body crumples against Alfredo, who dazedly holds her. Germont kneels at the priedieu.

The curtain falls.

21

Madama Butterfly

Characters

Cio-Cio-San, Madama Butterfly .... Soprano
Suzuki, her servant .... Mezzo-Soprano
Kate Pinkerton, Pinkerton's American wife .... Mezzo-Soprano
B. F. Pinkerton, Lieutenant, U. S. Navy .... Tenor
Sharpless, U.S. Consul at Nagasaki .... Baritone
Goro, a marriage broker .... Tenor
Prince Yamadori, a rich Japanese .... Baritone
The Bonze, Cio-Cio-San's uncle .... Bass
The Imperial Commissioner .... Bass
The Official Registrar .... Baritone
Trouble, Cio-Cio-San's child
          Cio-Cio-San's relations and friends, servants

Time: Early twentieth century
Place: Nagasaki, Japan

ACT I

(A house and garden on a hillside overlooking Nagasaki)

The curtain rises on the three sustained B-flat trills in the
prelude. Lieutenant B. F. Pinkerton is standing on the middle
of a Japanese bridge, his back to us, taking a last look at the
vista before purchasing the house and grounds adjacent. On the
house level Goro awaits his decision. Three young naval officers are seated at the base of a juniper tree. Two are playing
cards; the third lounges against the trunk of the tree, drinking
from a whiskey bottle. They are in slight disarray, their jackets
opened. After an approving nod to Goro, Pinkerton descends

from the bridge. He counts out some money as he approaches
the marriage broker. Apparently it is not enough and, to his an-
noyance, he must add a bill or two. He hands Goro the money
and leaves him counting it as he himself appraises his new purchase. The two have gone over all the domestic details before,
and after Pinkerton's amused *"all'aperto?"* (in the open?) Goro
reminds Pinkerton how the sliding shoji screens work; "The
house is as frail as a piece of paper," Pinkerton remarks. Goro
demonstrates its durability by pounding on the framework. "It
is as solid as an ancient fortress." Pinkerton moves toward his
buddies and addresses the line *"È una casa a soffietto"* (A
breeze would blow it away) to them. At the fermata, Goro, following Pinkerton, claps his hands three times. Suzuki enters, an
old woman in her sixties (usually played as a young girl), and
behind her, two young servants, one male, one female. Goro
motions for them to come forward. They kneel near the base of
the tree where Pinkerton has joined the card game. Goro introduces the servants who, it appears, come with the house. The
young servants look up curiously from their kneeling positions,
but Goro's abrupt gesture forces them to look down again, *"Son
confusi del grande onore"* (They're beside themselves at the
signal honor). The officer lounging against the tree has passed
the whiskey bottle over to Pinkerton during Goro's recital, and
Pinkerton, handing it back to his friend, whispers something in
his ear. During the orchestral interlude that reintroduces the
opening theme of the opera, the naval officer moves from the
tree to a position above the young servants and playfully shoves
the bottle under their noses. They recoil in confusion, causing
Pinkerton to laugh aloud. Suzuki's *"Sorride Vostro Onore?"*
(Your Excellency is laughing?) is intended as a compliment and
a subtle rebuke. At the conclusion of her first sentence, the officer offers her the bottle. Scandalized, she presses on, *"Schiude
alla perla il guscio"* (Your laughter rivals the pearls in
splendor). During this digression, Goro consults Pinkerton, but
Pinkerton merely shrugs and indicates it is time to get rid of
them. Goro claps his hands again and beckons the trio away
with asperity. The young servants leave hastily. Suzuki lingers
behind, complaining to Goro. She exits by the time Pinkerton
shouts *"A chiacchiere costei"* (Chatter, chatter—it's the same all

over the world with women). All the preceding action should be leisurely and accomplished with pokerfaced humor by the Americans. Playful or not, it is a familiar and ugly little scene.

Goro is looking downhill when Pinkerton asks, "*Che guardi?*" (What are you looking for?). Still looking off, Goro answers, "For the bride." Pinkerton winks at his buddies and indicates that a little more fun is in order. Goro moves toward Pinkerton while the other three men collect the cards and surround the broker. This action should be completed before Goro announces, "*Qui verran*" (The following guests will arrive). All during his speech the men pass the whiskey bottle among themselves. It has become apparent earlier in the scene that Goro would relish a drink himself, but since no offer has been made, he has curbed his desire. He watches the progress of the bottle out of the corner of his eye. By the time he has concluded "*e il matrimonio è fatto*" (the marriage will be official), one of the officers takes a sip and rather ceremoniously hands Goro the bottle. Pinkerton reaches out and grabs it, leaving Goro's hands literally suspended in midaction. "*E son molti i parenti?*" (Will there be many relatives?) Pinkerton asks as he executes this action. Goro, tuned to the ways of the foreign devil, continues his recitation blandly, "*La suocera, la nonna . . .*" (There will be her sister-in-law, her mother . . .). Again the officers execute the whiskey-passing routine absolutely deadpan, and by the time Goro reaches his estimation "*due dozzine*" (about two dozen will show up), the bottle is handed to him as ceremoniously as before. No one moves to take it from his grasp, and, finally included in the amenities, Goro raises the bottle in salute, "*Quanto alla discendenza*" (To your own descendants, may they be many) and proceeds to drink. The bottle is now apparently empty. He shakes it to no avail, and Pinkerton's "You're a pearl of a fellow" does not assuage his frustration. He throws the empty bottle back at the men amid their laughter.

Sharpless appears, crossing the bridge as he sings his opening line. Pinkerton and Goro move to the bridge as the Consul descends. The other men remain on the house level. During the "*Bene arrivato*" (Welcome), Sharpless, wiping his forehead, hands Goro his hat, and Pinkerton interjects, "*Presto, Goro*" (Prepare some drinks). Goro exits behind the house. Sharpless

looks about him, "Nagasaki, the ocean, the harbor. . . ." As Pinkerton concludes *"e una casetta"* (and a house to boot), Sharpless moves to examine the new acquisition, rapidly assessing its
value. The three sailors mooch cigarettes from Pinkerton, who
is about to enjoy a smoke. *"La comperai per novecento"* (I purchased it for nine hundred ninety-nine years). He extends his
cigarette case to Sharpless, who joins the group as he comments, *"E l'uomo esperto ne profitta"* (And you're in a country
where an expert can really exploit the situation). He smiles
ironically and accepts a cigarette. During the statement of the
American national anthem in the orchestra the three officers
strike matches and simultaneously offer to light the Consul's
cigarette. He accepts the nearest. Pinkerton pokes the man to
his left, who lights his. The five men stand there, puffing away.
This tableau is punctuated by Pinkerton's *"Dovunque al
mondo"* (All over the world).

In the brief interlude following, Goro and the two servants
open up the screens of the house, revealing a traveling bar arrangement. *"Milk-Punch, o Wisky?"* Pinkerton asks slyly. Before Sharpless can answer, the three men shout *"wisky"* in
unison. This spoken request is usually made by Sharpless, although it is optional in the score. The three men retire to the
bar area with Goro. They are seen drinking during the first part
of the ensuing scene. Sharpless sits on a wicker chair and, removing a pair of binoculars strapped round his shoulders, puts
them on the ground. Pinkerton continues rhapsodically, *"Af-
fonda l'àncora"* (Wherever the Yankee chooses to anchor). Goro
approaches with a tray and three glasses during the descending
scale before Pinkerton's *"Vinto si tuffa"* (No one can resist us).
Goro offers Sharpless a drink and crosses behind Pinkerton. He is there in time to confirm Pinkerton's *"Per novecento
novantanove anni?"* (For nine hundred and ninety-nine years,
correct?). The officers at the bar leave with their drinks. Pinkerton takes his glass off the tray and raises it in tribute. "America
forever." Sharpless rises. They drink a toast, as does Goro, who
waves a small American flag, much to their amusement. Pinkerton particularly enjoys the participation of the Oriental broker
in this little ceremony. There is something friendly yet patron-
izing about the backslap he gives Goro. Sharpless inquires after

Butterfly, and Goro volunteers to answer his question. A succession of winks and nods from Pinkerton encourages Goro to tease the rather prim, aging Consul with the suggestion that such beauty as Butterfly's is quite available and at nominal prices. Pinkerton pretends to be shocked at this indiscretion; *"Va, conducila, Goro"* (Go, bring her, Goro). He walks away with Goro and whispers some obscenity, provoking Goro's indiscreet laughter. Considering it to be at his expense, Sharpless turns around and stares at the Oriental, who bows in confusion and exits obsequiously under the bridge. Pinkerton wanders over to the tree and sits there smugly sipping his drink. He is now feeling no pain as he proceeds to elucidate the many charms of his bride-to-be. Sharpless rises, hiding his distaste, and informs Pinkerton, *"Ier l'altro"* (Recently she came to see me). Pinkerton, fired by the information and minimizing the Consul's concern, drains his own glass, and asks Sharpless if he wants another drink. Sharpless accepts, and Pinkerton, picking up the Consul's glass, moves to the bar to replenish it. Sharpless joins him and suggests the next toast: "I'll drink to your parents." Pinkerton, instead, chooses to toast his future American bride. He drinks alone. During this exchange Goro has appeared on the bridge. He is padding across it quickly, announcing the arrival of Butterfly and her geisha friends. He claps his hands and the two young servants enter to move the chairs and place them on the upper house level. Sharpless picks up his binoculars and, with Pinkerton, looks off in the direction of the approaching women, whose voices can be heard from afar. Pinkerton takes the binoculars and focuses them on the ladies. As Butterfly is heard singing for the first time, he hands them back to Sharpless, indicating it is Butterfly who has just come into sight.

A group of five geishas appear at the base of the bridge offstage and quickly ascend. *"Quanti fior!"* (Look at the flowers!) they murmur. Butterfly is behind them, *"Anzi del mondo, amiche"* (I'm the happiest girl in the whole world). The geishas move across the bridge as they repeat, *"Quanto cielo! quanti fior!"* (Look at the sky, the flowers!). Butterfly moves to the center of the bridge; *"al richiamo d'amor"* (I heeded the call of love). Behind her, another group of geishas have followed. Three of the older geishas simultaneously pass under the bridge, with Butterfly directly above them. The geishas on the bridge descend to the house level and from this position the ensemble is concluded. One of the geishas then crosses the platform carrying a garland of flowers toward the house. She attaches it to one of the posts supporting the house. Butterfly, having herself descended to the house level, encounters this geisha returning to her group. They bow to each other and Butterfly addresses Pinkerton: *"B.F. Pinkerton. "Giù"* (I make obeisance). As the other geishas echo *"Giù,"* they also bow. They form a tableau as Pinkerton grins a proprietary grin and comes toward Butterfly. Suzuki comes from the house to overhear Butterfly flattering Pinkerton. *"Molto raro complimento"* (That's quite a compliment), he quips rather sarcastically. "I know quite a few more," ventures Butterfly ingenuously yet with humor. *"Dei gioielli!"* (Gems, I'm sure!), Pinkerton answers, kissing his two fingers that he then playfully applies to her cheek. The geishas remaining on the bridge now move across it to start their descent. Pinkerton goes to meet this group of ladies. He greets their most prepossessing leader as one would an old acquaintance. For the first time we see that three of the geishas are separately carrying articles: a samisen (a form of Oriental mandolin), a small chest, and articles of clothing all belonging to Butterfly. Goro re-enters from the house with the three naval officers in tow and looks over the crop of beauties for the picking. Pinkerton leads the ladies down the bridge to the tree. He seats the leading geisha there as Butterfly, confused and annoyed by his attentions to an apparent rival, politely tries to answer the Consul's questions. Sharpless, in an effort at saving the day, has tried to distract Butterfly. Pinkerton remains chatting with the other girls. They are in a twitter of excitement and even seem to enjoy Butterfly's discomfort and jealousy. Butterfly expresses her displeasure through a series of stylized passes employing the use of her fan and the rapid swirling of her flowing sleeves. Pinkerton, grinning sheepishly, excuses himself and circles back behind Butterfly, watching her gyrations. Goro, meanwhile, beckons three geishas to join the American officers, which they do. It is Pinkerton who laughs, not Sharpless (as the printed direction states), eliciting Butterfly's hurt *"Ridete?"* (You're laughing at me?). Pinkerton goes to Sharpless and whis-

pers, *"Con quel fare di bambola"* . . . (She's such a doll, I can
hardly wait). The Consul, staring Pinkerton back to sobriety,
continues his questioning of Butterfly. "And your father?" he
inquires. "He is dead," Butterfly answers, bowing her head.
She moves toward the geishas, who repeat her gesture in com-
miseration. Pinkerton moves swiftly to his Consul and admonishes him to change the subject, while grinning at the older
man's faux pas. When further questioned as to her age, Butterfly
laughs coyly and admits to fifteen years. She looks at her rival,
who, obviously older, snaps angrily at her with her fan. The
other geishas giggle. Sharpless is stunned and becomes furious
at Pinkerton's continued levity, *"e dei confetti"* (she is pure
confection). Goro announces the arrival of the Imperial Commissioner. The latter appears from offstage, moving under the
bridge toward the house. He is accompanied by the Registrar
carrying two white wedding stands. The Commissioner is in a
dress suit and top hat with a colorful flag of all nations hanging
diagonally across his chest. He wears Japanese sandals. The Registrar is in Japanese clothing crowned by a bowler hat. They
bow and, led by Goro, file past Sharpless and Pinkerton and
move into the house. The geishas all bow as the officials exit.
Simultaneously, Cio-Cio-San's relatives appear in their wake,
shyly hanging back. Butterfly's mother and aunt move to greet
the bride-to-be. Six bars after Pinkerton's *"Fate presto"* (Make
it quick) addressed to Goro, the Captain of the *Abraham Lincoln* appears on the bridge with two young women, dressed in
American clothes of the period. They carry parasols and pause
to look at the sight of Nagasaki below. Pinkerton, eyeing the
relatives, who regard him with curiosity and suspicion, remarks
to Sharpless, *"Che burletta"* (What a farce). By the time he has
completed his observation, the American party has crossed over
the bridge. Butterfly is fascinated by the sight of the Americans.
As Pinkerton finishes his part in the ensemble, the American
group arrives at his side. Pinkerton salutes his Captain, then
shakes his hand. He bows to the women, who incline their
heads. Pinkerton seats the women as the Captain exchanges salutes with the other three officers. Butterfly moves toward Pinkerton and whispers to him. Goro suddenly opens one of the
shoji screens and berates the assembled guests, *"Per carità, ta-*

cete un po'." (Keep quiet, for heaven's sake). He goes back into
the house in great fury as Yakuside, a drunken cousin of Butterfly calls out, *"Vino ce n'è?"* (Where's the wine?). Pinkerton asks
if the American ladies would mind standing so that Butterfly
may better see their dresses. The ladies accede with alacrity.
Butterfly entreats them to open their lace parasols, and as they
do so the ladies of the ensemble cry out, *"Ah! hu!"* in admiration. The American women return to their places and Butterfly,
delighted with their courtesy, returns to the geishas. Sharpless,
at the bar, has filled two glasses with milk-punch, which he offers the ladies. Once seated, they look through Sharpless's binoculars at the surrounding countryside. The Captain partici-
pates in this action while carrying on a conversation with
Pinkerton. Two servants have appeared bearing trays full of
small sake cups and begin to distribute them to the relatives
and geishas. After the second appearance of Goro from the
house, again begging for silence, Sharpless begins his *"O amico
fortunato!"* (My fortunate friend!). Concurrently a man carrying
a camera on a tripod appears on the bridge and nonchalantly
crosses it. As he descends he encounters one of the servants
and, taking a cup of sake from her tray, downs the wine in one
gulp. He then crosses the stage to the house and sets up shop.
Butterfly remains with her geisha friends during the rest of the
ensemble; then, moving toward her mother (who carries a small
cane), she leads her forward and, turning back to her relatives,
asks that they all pay their respects to Pinkerton.

After a pause the exquisite Largo begins and Pinkerton
comes to Butterfly. *"Vieni amor mio!"* (Come, my love!) and he
leads her toward the house. Butterfly mounts the few steps as
Pinkerton beamingly inquires, *"Vi piace la casetta?"* (How do
you like it?). Before she answers she embraces Suzuki, who has
been patiently awaiting recognition. Turning back to Pinkerton,
she notices that the three geishas bearing her personal belongings are kneeling in front of the house. *"Perdono,"* Butterfly
interjects, *"Io vorrei pochi oggetti da donna"* (Forgive me,
there are a few personal objects). "Where are they?" Pinkerton
inquires (he has become solicitousness itself since the arrival of
his Captain and the ladies, elegantly playing out the scene of
doting bridegroom. Butterfly is naturally charmed by his minis-

trations). She opens the lid of a small chest held up to her by one of the kneeling geishas, revealing its contents. In the background Butterfly's cousins are taking their siesta. Cio-Cio-San's mother, aunt, and sister-in-law have moved near the bridge. Butterfly continues to display her personal effects to Pinkerton. And at Pinkerton's feigned displeasure with a small jar of makeup, Butterfly throws it away. Pinkerton is about to lift a sheathed dagger out of the chest, but Butterfly anticipates him and removes it. She remains secretive about it, but Goro, who has been watching while matchmaking, pulls Pinkerton aside and sotto voce volunteers, *"È un presente del Mikado a suo padre"* (It was a gift from the Emperor to her father with an order to make use of it). The outcome is graphically described by Goro's gesture of hara-kiri. As silently as he slipped into the conversation, he slides back to the Navy men. Butterfly replaces the dagger and the atmosphere is lightened by the Ottokè, tiny puppet symbols of her ancestors' spirits, which she places on her fingers. Butterfly then discreetly pulls Pinkerton aside after shutting the lid of the chest. The geishas, led by Suzuki, bear the objects into the house. Simultaneously those geishas conversing with Goro and the officers excuse themselves and move across stage to join an inquisitive group of friends. All movement during this entire scene is leisurely and unhurried.

The various groups onstage are individually preoccupied during Butterfly's confession to Pinkerton, *"Ieri son salita"* (Yesterday I went to the mission.). Pinkerton is amazed at her initiative and when she discloses the crucifix hidden in the folds of her kimono, he becomes decidedly perturbed. He had bargained for a complying body, not for a real individual. Butterfly, carried away, mistakes his reaction as some form of compassion and cries out, *"Amore mio!"* (My love!). Goro returns from the house. He has Pinkerton's and Sharpless's hats and hands them to both gentlemen as he calls for the actual wedding ceremony to begin. The Registrar quickly places the two wedding stands for Butterfly and Pinkerton as the Commissioner unfolds the wedding contract. The Japanese gather behind Cio-Cio-San and the Americans behind Pinkerton. Sharpless is next to him. The Captain assists the two ladies to stand on the chairs they have been sitting on. The sharp division of races happens automatically, and has a somewhat disconcerting effect. The Commissioner begins to read his text, *"È concesso al nominato . . ."* (It is conceded that said parties . . .). By the time he has reached *"America del Nord"* (North America) Goro has noticed the flag on the Commissioner's chest is that of Great Britain. He hastily reverses it, revealing the Stars and Stripes. The Commissioner is nonplused but continues the peroration. When the time comes for the bridegroom to sign the document, the Registrar approaches Pinkerton, holding out the stylus for his use. Pinkerton turns to Sharpless, who produces a fountain pen from his inside pocket. Pinkerton signs "Pink" and a hasty dash signifying the rest. Butterfly uses the stylus and signs. *"E tutto è fatto"* (The ceremony is over), Goro concludes. Pinkerton crosses over to Butterfly's side. There is a pause. He puts his arm around her shoulder and indicates that she look in the photographer's direction. The Japanese, startled by the report of flash powder, jabber in confusion. The American ladies now shower the pair with rice they had brought in their handbags for the event. This horrifies the Japanese, who, picking up the grains, cannot comprehend such waste. The young naval officers run to the bride and kiss her cheeks. Pinkerton receives congratulations from the Captain and his companions. Butterfly, besieged by the frisky Americans, frees herself and runs to Sharpless. The Andante mosso theme starts only when Butterfly is safely in Sharpless's arms. The Captain and ladies and young officers move with Pinkerton toward the bridge, on which the younger men line up and salute their senior officer as he passes. The latter turns and nods in Butterfly's direction. She in turn admonishes her relatives to address her as *"Madama B.F. Pinkerton."* She bows to the departing Americans and remains with Suzuki. The Commissioner awaits remuneration and his *"Augurî molti"* (Congratulations) is small talk as Pinkerton figures how much to pay. *"I miei ringraziamenti"* (Many thanks), Pinkerton nods, absently handing him a sizable bill. The Commissioner is delighted. Pinkerton pays the photographer and finally the Registrar. The Commissioner, the Registrar, and the photographer leave, Sharpless behind them. Pinkerton, still handing out money, is about to tip Goro but gestures somewhat obscenely at the marriage broker—enough is enough. On the bridge Sharpless wags a warning finger at Pinkerton: *"Giudizio!"* (Behave honorably!). Waving to Butterfly, who bows, he departs. Goro moves onto the bridge and remains looking down on the concluding amenities.

Pinkerton gestures toward Cio-Cio-San's mother, *"Ed eccoci in famiglia,"* (Well, here we are). This is usually done as an aside, implying that he is anxious to get things over with. However, he is perfectly content now and even enjoying the festivities. There is still plenty of time for romance and all these comings and goings and fussing delight his childish nature. With Cio-Cio-San on his left and her mother on his right, he stands between the two ladies. The chairs that had been placed there for the American guests have been removed by the two servants who entered with Suzuki as the American contingent left. Half the Japanese remain as Pinkerton urges them to drink to their heart's content. The Bonze, a Buddhist priest who is also Butterfly's uncle, is heard approaching. Goro, the first to see him, rushes off the bridge to Pinkerton's side and warns Butterfly. She is obviously disturbed by the angry tone of his voice. The Bonze glares down at the frightened girl. As he descends, the fearsome priest hovers over her. She bows deeply, acknowledging his sacred presence. *"Che hai tu fatto alla Missione?"* he demands. (Why did you go to the American Mission?). Pinkerton, his dander up, is about to attack the priest, but Goro holds him back. *"Son dunque questi i frutti?"* (Is this how you show your loyalty?), the Bonze demands. Impetuously Cio-Cio-San holds her crucifix out protectively. He screams *"Ci ha rinnegato tutti!"* (You have denied your people!), and the scandalized relatives support his accusation. As the Buddhist fulminates, Butterfly turns to the geishas for help, but they, smelling disaster, move quickly onto the bridge. She then turns to Pinkerton, who is in Goro's ironlike grip. She faces her uncle again, suddenly panic-stricken at his words *"Ti rinneghiamo!* (We ostracize you!). She collapses as Pinkerton, freeing himself from Goro, rushes to her side. Goro flees. The priest raises the purple sash of excommunication and hurls it over Butterfly's prostrate form. Having admonished the others to leave with him, they begin to exit. Only Cio-Cio-San's mother and aunt remain behind. Pinkerton, thoroughly incensed, is about to attack the

priest and rushes at him. He thinks better of it and, going back
to Cio-Cio-San, picks up the purple sash. Rushing onto the
bridge, he hurls it after the retreating figure of the Bonze. The
ensemble continues its recriminations from offstage. Cio-Cio-
San starts to cry at her mother's touch. Pinkerton returns and
tactfully asks the old lady to leave him alone with his bride.

It is now twilight. Pinkerton turns and regards the sobbing
Butterfly where she collapsed. *"Bimba, bimba, non piangere"*
(Don't cry, little one), Pinkerton urges, and kneels beside her.
From here on in he is all tenderness and concern. The role of
savior and protector serves his present mood perfectly. To all
intent and purpose he is sincere—this is still part of his "romantic" view of life. And perhaps nothing more could be expected
of this twenty-four-year-old world traveler and Annapolis blue
blood. He raises her up after she promises *"Non piango più"* (I
won't cry any more), and impulsively kisses his hands, explaining she understands this to be considered a mark of respect
among Americans. Suzuki's evening prayer is heard and Pinkerton, anticipating more trouble, rushes to the shoji and slides it
open ready to do further battle. After Butterfly's reassurance,
Pinkerton turns back to look at his bride from the veranda and
in the short interlude their eyes meet. She sees the hunger in
that gaze and turns away, noticing the crucifix still lying on the
ground. Two servants appear with lanterns. *"Viene la sera,"*
Pinkerton murmurs (It's almost evening now). Kneeling with
the cross in her hand, Butterfly is reminded she is *"Sola e rinnegata!"* (An outcast!). But with her second *"rinnegata"* she
turns and beckons to Pinkerton, who rushes to and kneels beside her. She joins their hands around the crucifix, a self-styled
confirmation of vows, and sighs *"e felice"* (I'm happy now).
Pinkerton is embarrassed and dissembles by rising and ordering
the servants to shut the shoji screens. Taking Butterfly's cue
that *"E fuori il mondo"* (We've shut out the world), he fondles
her playfully, *"E il Bonzo furibondo"* (We'll forget the angry
Bonzo too). Butterfly, now safe in his arms, is forced to laugh a
little against her will.

Suzuki now appears at the shoji and Butterfly asks for her
things. (In most productions this scene is played indoors and
refers to Butterfly's toilette. But, pursuing the idea of the ordi-

nary of her life, I thought it becoming to re-create Butterfly's first and only previous encounter with Pinkerton at the geisha house in Nagasaki, the details of which charmed Pinkerton, so unused to this particular kind of female attention.) Suzuki returns, carrying a futon; the two servants are behind her, one bearing the samisen (the musical instrument) and lantern, the other a small tea tray with two cups. Butterfly now seems in charge, all traces of the frightened girl disappear. Suzuki lays down the futon on which Butterfly arranges the samisen, the tea, and the lantern. Pinkerton moves onto the bridge and, lighting a cigarette, watches these nocturnal preparations. After the servants exit, Butterfly asks Suzuki, *"Quest' obi pomposa,"* (Help me take off this obi). The obi removed, Suzuki exits— after Butterfly admits *"ne ho tanto rossor!"* (I'm blushing, I know). As the echo of her recent ordeal is recalled, *"Butterfly rinnegata . . . rinnegata"* (Butterfly is an outcast), Pinkerton stomps out his cigarette precisely on the word "Butterfly" and eagerly moves toward his awaiting child-bride. *"E felice"* (I'm happy), she concludes and indicates for Pinkerton to take his place beside her on the futon. It is now night as Butterfly kneels and Pinkerton lounges by her side. As Butterfly pours the tea, Pinkerton begins his wooing, *"Bimba dagli occhi pieni di malia"* (You're a child with mischievous eyes). During his recitative Butterfly hands him a tiny cup and, lifting her fan, describes the goddess of moonlight descending in her starry heavens. Pinkerton, now cozily ensconced, boyishly demands *"Ma intanto finor non mi hai detto"* (You haven't said you loved me yet). The love game continues as Butterfly protests that the moon goddess knows all the proper words but does not say them, fearing that death can ensue.

Pinkerton rises to his knees and, stealing beside her, slowly folds the fan, revealing the blushing girl's face. *"Stolta paura"* (What foolish ideas you have). As he tries to kiss her she teasingly turns her head away. They are kneeling next to each other. Butterfly looks about her in a sudden resurgence of panic as the orchestra thunders out the theme of ostracism. Pinkerton rises and starts for the bridge to assuage Butterfly's fear. But her outstretched hand brings him back to her. She rests against his leg as he stands behind her reassuringly. *"Siete alto, forte"* (You are tall and strong), she continues, basking in his protective presence. He looks at her as she affirms *"Or son contenta"* (I'm all right now) and again he lies down. This time he places his head in her lap. Butterfly picks up the samisen and starts to tune it. Meanwhile she interjects *"Vogliatemi bene"* (Love me a little). At the conclusion of her third phrase, Pinkerton raises his hand to her cheek and rests it there. Butterfly presses her head against his palm. Slowly during the next *"vogliatemi bene"* Pinkerton lowers his hand back onto his chest. As Butterfly becomes more passionate, *"Profonda come il ciel"* (My love is as boundless as the sky) Pinkerton, now aroused, declares, *"Dammi ch'io baci le tue mani care"* (I want to kiss your hands). He lifts her up gradually and encircles her with his arms at the words *"tenue farfalla"* (you're like a butterfly). Struck suddenly by a thought, Butterfly breaks from his grasp and moves away. She tells him she has heard that beyond the ocean, in America, butterflies are caught, impaled, and then locked in a glass case. She describes her fear by winding and unwinding the pendant sleeves of her kimono, underlining *"Trafitta"* (impaled) with a downward stroke of her fan against her wrist. She backs up against the tree as Pinkerton approaches her in mock menace. Caging her against the trunk with his arms, he smiles and says, *"Io t'ho ghermita"* (I've caught you). Butterfly, with unexpected firmness (as opposed to the conventional melting tone) proclaims, "Yes, I am your wife forever." Pinkerton then kneels and exclaims, "Then come to me." Usually at this point there is nothing but the actual duet to contend with. The story is temporarily suspended as the two singers stand there vocalizing. In this version, rather than falling into Pinkerton's arms, Butterfly, still frightened, rushes across the bridge to escape him, but at his words *"È notte serena"* (Look how serene the night is) Butterfly hesitates. Where is she going? Back home? There is no home any longer. What could she have been thinking? *"Dolce notte!"* (Sweet night!) she answers timorously. *"Quante stelle!"* (All those stars!) And she thinks, I was foolish to panic—I'll be all right—he loves me. Pinkerton moves to the steps of the bridge and encourages her to come to him. Each *"vieni, vieni"* (come to me) is full of amorous promise, yet cajoling as to a child. Slowly, as in a trance of love and hope, Butterfly moves toward Pinkerton. She takes his outstretched hand as she sings *"Ah! quanti occhi fisi attenti!"* (The stars are like so many eyes staring at us!). They descend to the house level and Pinkerton moves behind her toward the house, *"Ti serro palpitante..... Ah vien!"* (I can hear your heart pounding. . . . Come!). They embrace as the orchestra continues. Butterfly moves coyly away from him, then returns to his opened arms, cuddling against his breast. Pinkerton slides the shoji open. Removing the wedding garland on the house post left by the geisha, he kneels, extending it to Butterfly. She takes it uncomprehendingly, cradling it in her arms. Suddenly Pinkerton lifts her off the ground and slowly proceeds to carry her "over the threshold."

The curtain falls.

ACT II

(Three years later. Inside Cio-Cio-San's house consisting of two wings with a connecting passageway. Victorian furniture clashes with Japanese.)

Cio-Cio-San, in American dress, is warming her hands over the fire. Suzuki is praying to a statue of Buddha inside a chest. The curtain rises at the woodwind coupling during the prelude. Butterfly moves up to the tokonoma during the rising scale of the denunciation theme. Her walk is less pronouncedly geisha, but the suggestion is still there. The rain visibly beats against the roof, contributing heavily to Cio-Cio-San's melancholy. The entire first part of this scene prepares for *"Un bel dì"* (One fine day), suggesting the aria is an ordinary outpouring, a sentiment expressed often by Cio-Cio-San, come rain or shine. She stops at the tokonoma, staring out at the rain. Suzuki, kneeling in silent thought, now strikes the tiny bell on top of the chest that will conclude her prayers. Cio-Cio-San, without moving and still staring out, states, *"Pigri ed obesi son gli dei giapponesi"* (The Japanese gods are vain and selfish while the American God is all-understanding and protects one). She kisses her fingers and touches the crucifix in emphasis. Suzuki is scandalized at this bit of sacrilege, but she is tolerant, if disapproving. Shaking her head, Suzuki resumes her labors, the mending of one of the tatami. It is now evident that the mats and screen partitions are full of patches. Glancing at Suzuki's efforts but still lost is reverie, Cio-Cio-San asks, *"È lungi la miseria?"* (How much money do we have left?). Suzuki rises arthritically, crosses to the American bureau, and takes some money out of a drawer. She crosses to Cio-Cio-San and shows her the exact amount. Cio-Cio-San merely glances at it and with a small nod in the direction of the American furniture sighs, *"Oh! Troppe spese!"* (It cost too much!) Suzuki grimly replaces the money and returns to her work, lighting a small pipe and puffing on it as she mends. The two women do not look at each other as they argue for the two-hundredth time. Butterfly, rapt in her role of the perfect Victorian wife, dismisses Suzuki's arguments with lofty disdain and returns to the hibachi to describe the last conversations she had with Pinkerton before his departure. When she tries to force Suzuki to repeat with her, *"Tornerà"* (He'll come back), Suzuki breaks down momentarily and turns away from Cio-Cio-San. Approaching Suzuki, Cio-Cio-San accuses her of lacking faith, and starts *"Un bel dì"* (One fine day) standing next to Suzuki. She remains there: *"Mi metto là sul ciglio del colle e aspetto"* (I'll wait for him at the top of the hill), and quasi-reenacts her fantasy meeting with Pinkerton to come. Suzuki is partly caught up in this figment of Butterfly's imagination, but she lives on an infinitely more realistic plane. She merely sighs, shakes her head, and resumes her labors during the postlude, while Butterfly continues dreaming, warming her hands over the fire.

Sharpless and Goro enter. Sharpless has on a hat and raincoat. Goro carries an umbrella. He peers into the house to ascertain if anyone is at home. *"C'è. Entrate"* (They're home. You can go in). Goro hangs up his umbrella and Sharpless his hat and coat on a stand in the passageway. Sharpless is about to remove his shoes, but Goro indicates he needn't bother. Twice Goro reminds him of this fact before Sharpless knocks, somewhat bewildered. Suzuki rises and opens the partition, admitting the two men. She retires as Butterfly joyfully greets the Consul. She takes his hand and shakes it in the American style. *"Il mio signor Console, signor Console!"* (Welcome, Mr. Consul!). At the sight of her American clothes, Sharpless, dumfounded, looks at Goro, who nods sagely, implying "I told you so." *"Benvenuto in casa americana"* (Welcome to my American home), Cio-Cio-San says. Suzuki has moved to the brazier, where two large pillows lay, and is about to place them in the center of the room for the comfort of the guests, but Butterfly commands otherwise, indicating that chairs are in order. Suzuki, aided by Goro, sets out two Victorian chairs for Sharpless and Butterfly. Butterfly sits at the edge of her chair as any proper lady should. Suzuki as is customary offers Sharpless a pipe, which he refuses. Cio-Cio-San asks if he would prefer an American cigarette. He accepts, somewhat surprised at the offer. Suzuki grudgingly moves to the alcove and returns with a small box. Butterfly removes a cigarette and offers it to the Consul. She then strikes a match and lights it. The Consul nearly chokes. It has been in that box for three years. Suzuki grins in triumph. Goro is warming his hands at the hibachi. Suzuki joins him and together they sit sharing Suzuki's pipe. During the next exchange Sharpless rises and puts out his cigarette in a dish on the bureau. Butterfly explains *"Mio marito m'ha promesso"* (My husband promised he'd be back when the robins nest again). As Sharpless tries to explain that he knows nothing of ornithology, Suzuki pokes Goro and gestures for him to see if Butterfly's potential suitor, Prince Yamadori, is in sight. There obviously is a conspiracy between the two to save Cio-Cio-San from her American folly. Goro laughs to himself as Butterfly wonders whether the habits of the robins are the same in America as in Japan, for they have already nested three times in her country. Goro gestures toward the hillside and Butterfly, with an amused shake of the head, cries out *"Eccolo"* (Here he is again). The first thing we see is a huge green and white Japanese umbrella. Under it is Yamadori, wearing geta (elevated Oriental footwear) and protected from the rain by a small cape. Two men hold the huge umbrella aloft. The third man carries a gift. The men are covered with straw—straw hat, straw jacket, and straw leggings. They move rapidly across the stage during Yamadori's entrance music. Expertly the umbrella is shut as Yamadori enters the passageway, has his cape and shoes removed by the men, and the gift box deposited into the hands of Goro,

who has come to the door to greet him. The three servants retire
and sit by the partition, looking like one huge haystack. Butterfly has moved to receive her wealthy guest. Suzuki bows continuously as Cio-Cio-San puts out her hand to Yamadori, who,
surprised by her gesture, suddenly recoils. Laughingly Butterfly
takes his hand and shakes it American style as she pronounces
his name. Yamadori looks askance at Goro, who merely shrugs.
As Yamadori purrs *"Tra le cose più moleste"* (My thoughts
vainly fly to you each day) Butterfly orders Suzuki to place a
pillow for his pleasure—no chair for this idiot. Yamadori moves
down to it and sits as he sings *"L'ho sposate tutte quante"* (I've
been married several times) as Goro places the gift by
Butterfly's chair and retires to Sharpless. Yamadori is a rather
effete and ineffectual dilettante. He is not overly bright, but he
is a very rich man and a collector of wives (an Oriental Tommy
Manville). Sharpless speaks what is usually an aside to Goro,
"Il messaggio, ho gran paura" (At this rate I'll never deliver the
message). Butterfly urges Sharpless to resume his seat as Goro
excoriates her for her recent behavior toward Yamadori's marriage proposals. Butterfly blithely informs him that as an American wife she is subject to American law. She picks up a small
toy representing a Navy man and, assuming the voice of an accusing judge, harangues the symbolic husband, using a high-
pitched wail of complaint. She manipulates the arms of the toy
to signify the husband's dissatisfaction with his lot. Again the
judge's booming voice is employed as she castigates the recalcitrant husband. She sentences him to prison and drops the toy
into a cricket cage. She gently urges *"Suzuki, il thè"* (tea). Butterfly exits victorious, the abashed Suzuki in tow. The three
men watch in silent astonishment. Yamadori considers his cause
quite lost, but Sharpless assures him of the contrary. Yamadori
moves to Goro for consultation. Perhaps there is a chance after
all. Butterfly comes in quickly and whispers to Sharpless, *"Che
persone moleste!"* (What pests they are!). Goro signals Yamadori
to leave, and the latter approaches Butterfly. *"Addio. Vi lascio il
cuor"* (Good-by for now. I leave you my heart full of love and
still hopeful). Butterfly smiles mischievously. Yamadori looks
back to Goro, who indicates that Yamadori offer her his hand in
a handshake. Yamadori complies in limp fashion. Butterfly picks

up his present and thrusts it in his face. Insulted beyond endur-
ance, Yamadori indicates that Goro take the gift and, angrily
snapping his fan, he leaves, followed by his servants. Goro
grabs the gift from Butterfly. He encounters Suzuki about to enter with a tea tray and tells her not to bother. Grabbing his umbrella, he follows Yamadori's train. Butterfly laughs at the little
farce she has perpetrated. Suzuki, after returning the tea tray to
the kitchen, runs back into the living room; the sight of her
startled expression throws Butterfly into a greater paroxysm of
laughter. Butterfly is at the tokonoma as if sharing this triumph
with Pinkerton. Suzuki looks at Sharpless, who has watched
everything. He moves back to his chair: *"Ora a noi"* (Now, as I
was about to say,) and produces a letter from his inside pocket.
Butterfly takes it, kisses it, and places it over her heart. The
Consul puts on his pince-nez and begins to read, already feeling the pressure of what is to come. Butterfly speaks *"Anche lui
li ha contati!"* (Even he has counted the years!) to Suzuki beside her. Asides, incidentally, are absolutely minimized in this
production; a logical reason is always found to relate most of
these lines to someone in the room. Even the *"Pazienza!"* (Patience!), spoken shortly by Sharpless, is addressed to the apprehensive Suzuki behind Butterfly's back. Suzuki remains in the
passageway. Butterfly, impatient and fantasizing, demands to
know all: *"Presto! presto!"* She runs to the tokonoma, touching
the wedding picture, as Sharpless, unable to contain himself,
moves away, cursing Pinkerton under his breath in what
amounts to the only real aside in the act. Concurrently Goro
appears and leads Suzuki off as he tells her what has transpired
with Yamadori. Butterfly turns to Sharpless, her face beaming at
the good news she anticipates. When she hears the real facts
she is shocked into silence. There is a long pause and the orchestra does not resume until she sits.

When she speaks of the two alternatives left her should
Pinkerton really abandon her (return to the geisha house or
death), Sharpless moves to her, pleading that she accept Yamadori's offer. Rigid in her chair, she coldly admonishes him as he
cries, "Oh God, what's to be done," moving behind her seated
figure, where the sight of the American-styled tokonoma rattles
him even further. Butterfly, collecting herself, rises and with

great dignity calls "Suzuki, Suzuki. The Consul is leaving."
Sharpless chides her momentarily, but Butterfly holds her
ground. She moves to the chair and with *"Oh, mi fate tanto
male"* (You have no idea how much you've hurt me) she has a
sudden attack of dizziness. Sharpless takes her arm but she
withdraws it, *"Niente, niente!"* (It's nothing, nothing at all. It
was just a passing cloud) in a passage redolent of Debussy. She
sits staring ahead for a moment, then cries out fiercely, *"Ah!
m'ha scordata?"* (He has forgotten me?). Butterfly hurries off
through the passageway to the annex section of the house as
Sharpless collapses on the chair in quiet exhaustion.

He remains seated in the room alone, unnerved by Butterfly's reaction. Her cry *"E questo?"* (And what about this?) is
repeated offstage twice. Immediately thereafter the child, Trouble, appears, a little boy dressed in short pants, white socks, and
a colorful American shirt. He moves quickly across the connecting passageway into the house. He pauses and makes a polite
bow to Sharpless, who looks startled. Sharpless rises as Butterfly re-enters the scene, completing *"egli potrà pure scordare?"*
(will he be able to forget this child?). Sharpless kneels; *"Egli è
suo?"* (It's his child then?). Butterfly's description of the boy is
dictated by the appearance of the tenor performing Pinkerton.
The convention of tacking some frightful blond wig onto the
child's head is a grotesque joke still unfortunately adhered to in
many a high and low musical place. *"E Pinkerton lo sa?"* (Does
Pinkerton know about the boy?), Sharpless inquires fearfully.
"No. No," Butterfly responds. During Butterfly's importunate
demand that Sharpless contact Pinkerton regarding his son, the
boy picks up a toy battleship with a tiny American flag on it and
lies down on the ground next to the hibachi, his head cradled in
his mother's lap. Butterfly strokes his forehead as the child
plays with the boat, pretending his chest is the mighty ocean on
which it sails. She starts *"Sai cos' ebbe cuore di pensare quel
signore?"* (Do you know what this gentleman had the heart to
suggest?). Butterfly knows how to plead her case and, having
the opportunity, she nails the hapless Consul to his own cross.
As if to affirm her previously stated alternatives to Pinkerton's
abandonment of her, she rises, leaving the child by the fire, and
confronts Sharpless, *"Morta. . . . Ah! morta!"* (I'd prefer death).

She sheds no tears, as is the usual case; she is a determined mother willing to put her life on the line rather than face the ignominy entailed by a return to her former life. Sharpless, now looking directly at her and sensing her resolution, comments "*Quanta pietà!*" (How sad!). Facing her unflinching gaze, he resolves to help her and suddenly takes his leave. He throws his coat around his shoulders. Butterfly and the boy follow and stand in the passageway bidding him good-by. The boy is holding his toy boat. "*A te, dagli la mano*" (Give him your hand), entreats Butterfly, and the boy complies. Sharpless, in a rush of feeling, picks up the boy and holds him in his arms, asking "*Caro, come ti chiamano*" (And what's your name?). Butterfly, holding her child's boat, asks him to whisper his name. "*Oggi il mio nome . . .*" (Today I'm called Trouble, but tell my father that on the day of his return my name will be changed to Joy), the child whispers in the Consul's ear. Sharpless puts the boy down and with even deeper conviction than he evinced before reassures the lad that "*Tuo padre lo saprà, te lo prometto*" (Your father will know everything. I promise you). With a final pat on the head and a now mutually exchanged handshake with Butterfly, he exits down the path. As the Allegro vivo starts, Butterfly and Trouble are both waving at his receding figure. Eight bars after the start of the new theme, Goro appears, followed by an irate Suzuki brandishing Goro's black umbrella as a weapon, screaming "*Vespa! Rospo maledetto!*" (You damned evil-minded serpent!). In an effort to escape her fury, Goro dashes toward the steps but encounters Butterfly and the boy blocking him. They are both looking at him, having been attracted by Suzuki's cry. Caught between the two angry women, Goro makes a dash through the house. Suzuki anticipates his move and meets him midway in his flight, simultaneously hitting him with the umbrella. Goro falls under the blow, losing his glasses. He remains, poking on the ground for the glasses, while Suzuki stands over him ready to rain further blows on his back. "*Che fu?*" (What's all this?), Butterfly demands. Goro pauses in his hunt and on his knees corrects Suzuki: "*Dicevo solo . . .*" (I merely remarked that in America an orphaned child is frowned upon and can look forward only to a long life of rejection). Butterfly, giving a wild cry, "*Ah tu menti!*" (You're a

liar!) dashes to the Buddha chest, opens it, and seeks the ances-
tral knife. Goro finds his glasses just as Butterfly places the
weapon against his neck. *"No!"* cries Suzuki, who grabs the
boy, trying to shield him from the sight of violence. Butterfly
contains herself and orders Goro to get out. Goro rises gingerly
while putting on his glasses, backs away from Butterfly, and,
aware that Suzuki is hiding the boy in the folds of her kimono,
quickly wrests his umbrella from her hand and rushes out. Suzuki stares at Butterfly who, her anger subsiding, becomes
aware of the dagger in her hand. She replaces it in the Buddha
chest—a signal for Suzuki to release the boy. He rushes to Butterfly's arms as she sings *"Mia pena e mio conforto"* (My pain
and my joy). She promises the boy that *"nella sua terra, lontan
ci porterà"* (your father will take us to his faraway country).
Now that the rain is over, Suzuki is preoccupied opening the
shoji screens. The sound of a cannon shot is heard. The three
figures on stage freeze. There is a pause. Hesitantly but still
hopeful, Butterfly and Trouble make their way hand in hand
into the garden. *"Una nave da guerra"* (It's a warship and it's
flying the Stars and Stripes), she says. Suzuki quickly seeks the
telescope in the alcove. Trouble climbs up the trunk of the juniper tree to a resting point and looks straight out at the ship anchoring in the harbor. *"Reggimi la mano"* (Help me steady my
hand), the trembling Butterfly asks of Suzuki. Not until Suzuki
herself confirms with a look the arrival of the *Abraham Lincoln*
does Trouble get to see the sight himself. *"È giunto! è giunto"*
(He's come back to me!) Butterfly concludes in a burst of happiness and rides Trouble piggyback across the stage. She lowers
the boy as the sobbing Suzuki joins them and the three mutually embrace. It is a short tableau and Butterfly sinks down on
the platform of the house, as does Suzuki. Suzuki is weeping as
she sings *"quel pianto"* (you're weeping) to the ecstatic Butterfly who, if crying, is unaware of her tears. During the exchange
between the two ladies the boy tries to continue the piggyback,
first with Suzuki and then with Butterfly, who, holding his
hands around her neck, asks him to *"Va pei fior"* (Get some
flowers). The business of the gathering of the flowers is usually
Suzuki's province, but the child's participation adds a dimension to the proceedings that contributes vastly to its tender hu-

manity. Butterfly sits on the top step as Suzuki returns the two chairs to their original positions. Trouble reappears with two large chrysanthemums and Suzuki comments, "*A voi, signora*" (Look what he brought you). Butterfly rises and accepts them, asking Suzuki to take the child and "*Cogline ancora*" (Get some more). Suzuki answers "*Soventi a questa siepe . . .*"(How long you've waited). Trouble, anxious to get on with it, tries to pull at Suzuki's left hand during her recitative. By the end of it, he succeeds in getting her off and they go to the garden via the pathway. Butterfly, left by herself, speaks to the photo in the tokonoma as she arranges the flowers beneath it. "*Guinse l'atteso*" (He's coming back) and she rests against the wall as if it were Pinkerton's shoulder. During the interlude, Butterfly moves to the wooden chest and removes a futon with two pillows wrapped inside. She lays down the bedding, opening its folds, finishing as Suzuki and the boy return with more flowers. "*Spoglio è l'orto*" (There are no flowers left), Suzuki says with a smile, for the child's zeal has yielded a small harvest of blooms. Suzuki takes them and goes to the tokonoma for the vase, as Butterfly picks up Trouble's toy boat by the brazier. "*Tutta la primavera*" (We've gathered the springtime in his room), sings Butterfly as she holds the boat aloft for the jumping boy. He reaches the toy and is patted offstage by Butterfly, who remains by the doorway. The two ladies gradually move toward each other until, just before "*Gettiamo a mani piene*" (Let's arrange them together), they are kneeling side by side. Instead of strewing blossoms all over the room as is the tradition, they make a flower arrangement in the vase, which continues throughout the duet. Butterfly strews the petals of a white chrysanthemum over the quilting. She hands the stem to Suzuki: "*Or vienmi ad adornar*" (Now help me dress). As Suzuki goes to throw away the stem, Butterfly changes her mind. "No. Bring the boy first." Suzuki goes for Trouble as Butterfly languorously stretches out in fond remembrance of magic nights. With her head on the pillow she looks up and sings "*Non son più quella*" (I'm not the girl he remembers). She turns sensually and hugs one of the pillows to her, "*e l'occhio riguardò*" (my eyes reflect fatigue from so much gazing in the distance). Suzuki re-enters with the boy. She carries a small white Navy jacket, trousers, and cap. She sets them down as she moves toward the bureau to Butterfly's make-up box. This consists of a tiny doll-like bit of furniture, a replica almost of the Victorian bureau itself. As Suzuki urges Butterfly not to move while she combs her hair, the impatient Trouble demands attention. Butterfly indicates that Suzuki dress him first, while she applies the makeup herself. As she puts on rouge, Suzuki dresses the boy. Her line, *"È fatto"* (It's done) relates to its completion. Butterfly, lost in memory, suddenly asks that Suzuki fetch her old wedding gown. Suzuki is delighted with this request. At last Butterfly will be her old self again and forget her American pretensions. As Suzuki fetches the kimono, Butterfly, almost in confirmation, moves to the tokonoma and regards the photograph. The child stands watching the two ladies. He is now fully dressed in a white Navy uniform, an exact duplication of Pinkerton's first-act costume. Suzuki starts to slip the kimono over Butterfly's dress. Suddenly Butterfly catches herself making the change. Coming out of a dream, she removes the kimono and, indicating she will remain dressed as she is, she says, *"Così"* (He'll see me like this). This is a most important moment in the second act, and it is essential that the orchestra have good horn players, for they must sustain the note F until the moment is properly completed. Suzuki sighs in defeat and returns the garment to its alcove. Butterfly moves to the boy and, kneeling beside him, starts a game. *"Nello shosi farem* (We'll put up the screens).

Suzuki takes a small screen out of the alcove and sets it up. Butterfly fetches the make-up box, returns it to the bureau. She then shuts the screen door and, signaling playfully to Suzuki, joins her behind the screen. After the first pizzicato in the lower strings, Butterfly claps her hands three times. The ladies wait behind the screen breathlessly as Trouble enters from offstage, now wearing his Navy cap and carrying his toy warship. He enters the room as if in quest of someone. He finds no one. Then, turning and seeing the ladies, he steps forward and gallantly removes his cap. He bows. Butterfly and Suzuki practically faint with joy and rush to gather him up in their arms. By the time the brasses in the orchestra intone their chorale, the three figures are behind the screen: Butterfly proceeds to poke holes in the paper shoji so they may best see Pinkerton's entrance. At the *forte-piano* brass Butterfly turns panic-stricken. "He will not come to us," she thinks. Suzuki touches her hand reassuring. Butterfly relaxes. The business is completed by the *ppp* that ushers in the humming chorus. All three remain stock still from here on, their backs to the audience as they peer through the shoji. Little Trouble falls asleep against Suzuki's shoulder midway through the chorus. The stars appear and the moon lights up the room. By the conclusion of the chorus, the three are silhouetted behind the screen. An almost votive light seems to illuminate the tokonoma. All is stillness as the music fades. On this nocturnal vision of hope and expectancy, the curtain falls slowly.

ACT III

(The next morning.
Inside Cio-Cio-San's house. Same as Act II)

The curtain rises five bars before the cries of the sailors are heard. Suzuki and the boy are asleep. Butterfly is kneeling, her back to the audience, her head lowered. In more traditional productions, Butterfly remains standing throughout the vigil and is so discovered at the rise of the curtain. It is a bit of improbable gallantry I felt best to bypass. As the prelude continues, the sun, already risen, spreads its light across the scene. The first rays penetrate the shojis and strike the unused futon. It is full daylight by the time Suzuki awakens with a start. She sees Cio-Cio-San and tentatively calls her. "He'll be here," Butterfly says; she is still motionless, her slumped body giving a lie to her words. Gathering up the boy with Suzuki's help, she moves offstage, hoping to get some rest before Pinkerton's arrival. Suzuki anticipates her exit by opening the screen door. *"Dormi, amor mio"* (Sleep, my love), Butterfly sings as she gradually moves to the passageway. Suzuki shuts the partition behind her and intones, *"Povera Butterfly"* (Poor Butterfly). Butterfly concludes her lament offstage. Suzuki sees the unused bed and repeats her *"Povera Butterfly."* Wearily she begins putting the house back into some order. As she starts to open the back screens Sharpless appears, followed by Pinkerton, now

in a dark blue Navy uniform. Sharpless knocks. Pinkerton fid-
gets with his cap. Suzuki opens the screen and exclaims. The
two men follow her into the room. *"Zitta! zitta!"* (Not so loud!).
Suzuki falls to her knees, grateful for their appearance. As she
jabbers on, she takes Pinkerton's hand and kisses it, which adds
to his discomfort. Sharpless has meanwhile looked outside,
trying to make sure Butterfly is not nearby. Prevented from calling Cio-Cio-San, Suzuki continues her chores as the two men
stand looking at the futon covered with blossoms. She picks up
the now cold hibachi and proceeds to take it to the alcove. Kate
Pinkerton appears in the garden, in an American dress similar
in style to Cio-Cio-San's but of a different color. Suzuki, turning
from the alcove, sees her, and asks, *"Chi c'è là fuori nel giar-
dino? Una donna!"* (Who is that woman in the garden?).Pinker-
ton looks away, sits on the chest, and puts his cap on it. Sharpless is finally forced to answer the frantic old lady. *"È sua
moglie!* (It's his wife!). Suzuki is stunned at the news. Sharpless
indicates to Pinkerton that he attend Kate in the garden as he
tries to calm Suzuki. Pinkerton exchanges a few words with
Kate and asks her to retire to another part of the garden until
they have completed their mission. He tries to kiss her cheek,
but Kate turns away. She has no taste for his shenanigans and
expresses her disapproval over the whole matter. She moves
slowly across the stage as Suzuki moans, *"Che giova, che giova"*
(It's hopeless, hopeless). She reluctantly starts to follow Kate as
Sharpless entreats, *"Io so che alle sue pene"* (I know how painful this must be for you). Suzuki sits dejectedly at the tree trunk
while Sharpless follows her there. Pinkerton, looking at the
house, enters it and, remaining alone in the room, gives vent to
his agitation. He again looks at the flowers on the bed, *"vele-
nosa al cor mi va"* (their smell is poison to me). He crosses
behind the screen to the tokonoma. *"Il mio ritratto!"* he sobs
(It's my picture). Turning away, he notices the children's toys
and goes to them. He picks up the toy battleship and in great
anguish cries, *"Tre anni son passati"* (Three years have gone
by). At the trio's conclusion, Sharpless, having made his point,
begs Suzuki to make peace with Kate and help facilitate the
arrangements for the child. Suzuki goes in search of Kate. Pinkerton, still clutching the toy, seems traumatized and behaves

like a stunned, helpless child. Sharpless then re-enters the house. He is out of humor, having been forced into this humiliating situation. As Pinkerton continues "*Sì, tutto in un istante*" (I understand everything all at once), Sharpless regards the pathetic spectacle of the self-chastizing lieutenant. He walks over to him and places his hand on Pinkerton's shoulder: "*Andate: il triste vero*" (You'd better go before I tell her the news). Sharpless's touch brings Pinkerton back to himself and, seeing the toy in his hand, he replaces it where he found it. There is a short pause as he looks at the room once more. With his back to the audience he starts his "*Addio.*" He turns after the opening phrase and approaches the futon. He kneels just before Sharpless replies, "*Ma or quel cor sincero*" (That poor girl must have some inkling of what's to come). Pinkerton picks up the petals from the quilt and, as he continues in a final burst of self-punishment, "*Non reggo al tuo squallor*" (I'm guilty to the core), the petals slip between his fingers and fall. Sharpless cannot bear to watch this indulgent display of self-pity and moves away again to be confronted by the picture in the tokonoma. He approaches Pinkerton angrily, "*Andate, il triste vero*" (Go, before she gets here). With an impatient and commanding gesture, he orders Pinkerton out of the room. Like an obedient schoolboy, Pinkerton grabs his cap and leaves.

Sharpless kneels beside the futon and as Kate, preceding Suzuki, enters, he picks up the blossoms slowly and regards them. Something of his own loneliness and despair is revealed in this private moment. Kate pauses at the threshold. Suzuki enters and beckons Kate to do likewise. "*Lo terrò come un figlio*" (I'll treat him as if he were my own son), she says, looking about at these strange surroundings. As Suzuki answers, "*Vi credo*" (I believe you), Sharpless, pained by his own memory of lost love, throws down the petals despondently and rises to resume his official duties, his eyes clouded in sorrow. The three are standing there when Butterfly's voice is heard offstage. Suzuki is galvanized into motion. She indicates that Kate and the Consul be careful. She approaches the partition as Sharpless moves to Kate. Kate sees the tokonoma and turns away from the wedding picture. Despite Suzuki's protestations, Butterfly approaches the house proper, "*È qui, è qui*" (He's here. I know it but where is he?). Sharpless opens the partition door. *"Ecco il Console"* (There's the Consul). Butterfly beams joyfully and goes to him. Kate, seeing the toys on the ground, picks up a Japanese geisha doll and steps back against the screen, looking at it in wonderment. Butterfly flies precipitously past the Consul in her search for Pinkerton. Kate is completely obscured from Butterfly's vision by the screen. Butterfly opens a shoji, *"dove? dove?"* (where is he?). Sharpless looks at Suzuki standing near him. As Butterfly turns back to them, she sees the screen Suzuki had set up the night before and imagines that Pinkerton has been hiding there. She playfully rushes to it, anticipating his arms about her. *"Non c'è!"* (He's not here!) she cries, facing Kate. The two women regard each other. In confusion Kate drops the doll and moves away. Sharpless goes to Kate and puts his arms around her protectively. Butterfly, standing rigid, demands, *"Quella donna?"* (What does that woman want?). Sharpless leads Kate down the steps of the house platform where they pause a moment for Kate to regain her composure. Counterpointing this move, Suzuki steps forward from the doorway and sinks to her knees, groaning audibly. Butterfly already has guessed the truth and from this point on speaks in a monotone, her brain racing faster than words can express. She tenderly asks Suzuki, *"Perchè piangete?"* (Why are you crying? No, don't tell me, I might die if you told me). Quickly asking for a simple yes or no answer, "Is Pinkerton alive?" *"Sì,"* Suzuki admits. Butterfly sighs in relief, but then resumes, *"Ma non viene più"* (He's not coming back to me. Is that it?). During the interlude she stares at Suzuki, who looks away. At the first two pizzicati in the low strings, Suzuki attempts to answer. She bows her head at the next similar effect in the strings. Butterfly, still not moving, screams *"Vespa! Voglio che tu risponda"* (Answer when I ask you), and Suzuki tells her the truth. Kate, now in command of herself, awaits Sharpless's next move. He remains by the doorway. Butterfly sees Kate and speaks again in that earlier chantlike manner, *"Ah! quella donna mi fa tanta paura!"* (That woman frightens me!). Sharpless takes this cue and moves slowly down to her, *"È la causa innocente d'ogni vostra sciagura. Perdonatele"* (She is the innocent cause of your grief. Please forgive her). *"Ah! È sua moglie!"* (She's his wife!)

Butterfly answers with surprise and wonderment. *"Tutto è morto per me! tutto è finito! Ah!"* (It's all over for me!) she says in a small voice. Trying to muster up her courage, she moves toward Kate but pauses. "She wants my child, is that right?" Sharpless answers: "So that he may have better opportunities in life." While Butterfly mutters quietly, *"Ah! triste madre!"* (Ah! poor mother!), Sharpless looks beseechingly at Suzuki, who moves away contemptuously.

In traditional productions the preceding scene is a regular blood bath of tears and wringing of hands. It takes a strong and vital actress to curb such demonstrations, which unconsciously only militate against sympathy with a modern audience. Butterfly is a woman in shock. The volcano of self-destruction is accumulating.

Butterfly enters the garden after instructing herself, *"E sia! A lui devo obbedir!"* (Yes, I must obey him in everything). Kate, who has been pacing back and forth impatiently, comes forward at Butterfly's approach and offers her hand: "Can you ever forgive me?" she says. Butterfly looks at Kate. Although they are both similarly dressed in American clothes, Butterfly refuses the proffered hand and bows deeply and then kneels in an abject gesture of submission: *"Sotto il gran ponte del cielo"* (Under the great arch of heaven...). Kate moves to Sharpless. *"Povera piccina!* (Poor thing!) she says. *"È un immensa pietà!"* (It's a great pity!) answers Sharpless. "Will she give me the boy?" Kate asks in a steely tone. Both people are anxious to get this over with and Sharpless looks at his watch. They are now the American landlords who will brook the native's plight only so far. Butterfly, overhearing Kate's question, answers in the affirmative. She rises and looks across at Suzuki. *"Fra mezz'ora ..."* (Be back in half an hour and you can claim him), she says. Kate again offers her hand to conclude the pact, but again Butterfly refuses it, bowing instead. Kate's peremptory withdrawal indicates her displeasure and Sharpless leads her out down the pathway.

There is a pause. Butterfly's back is to the audience. As the orchestra resumes, she begins to shake. She starts toward the steps leading to the passageway, her body now wracked with sobs—the second time in the entire opera that she has broken down. Suzuki rushes across stage to support her. She compares Butterfly to a lost bird caught in a net. Once inside, Butterfly suddenly pulls herself together during the line, *"Troppo luce è di fuor"* (There's too much sunshine in the room. Shut it out). As Suzuki starts to close the partitions, Butterfly, framed by the screen, assumes full composure, her face mask-like. The room darkened, Suzuki next moves the screen back to the alcove; at Cio-Cio-San's rather ceremonial gesture she brings the white wedding kimono and fearfully approaches her with it. Butterfly dons it over her American dress and then removes her shoes. "Where is the child?" she asks. "He is playing. Shall I get him?" "Let him play. Go keep him company." Suzuki, in near despair, protests, "No. I'll stay with you." Butterfly suddenly overlaps the two sides of her kimono, completely hiding the American dress hitherto visible beneath it. "Go. I command you to go." Butterfly is as still and hard as granite. Suzuki exits hastily.

Butterfly turns slowly and regards the tokonoma. She approaches it slowly, her movements now thoroughly Japanese. During the cello solo she lowers a small bamboo screen to the ground, shutting off the offensive sight behind it. She turns and moves as in a trance to the Buddha chest, accelerating her pace as she goes. As the renunciation music is heard she opens the chest and takes out a cloth. In it she discovers three or four strands of her own black hair, cut off after her marriage three years ago and obviously preserved by Suzuki. This was a misguided gesture toward the American style made on her wedding day. In the seven bars before the knife theme is heard, Butterfly tries vainly to reattach the strands to her head: once— twice—three times she makes her fruitless effort. Her eyes maddened by despair, she holds the last strand against her head as the Imperial Theme fortissimo sounds in the orchestra. She releases the hair and sees the dagger in the folds of cloth in the chest. She picks it up and reads, "He shall die with honor who cannot live with honor." She proceeds to raise the knife as Suzuki enters with the child still dressed in the white uniform. Suzuki pushes him into the room and rushes down the pathway in search of Sharpless. The boy moves to his toys. Butterfly sees him out of the corner of her eye and in a sudden wild impulse raises the knife in his direction, *"Tu? tu?"* (You? you?). But it is not the father, it is the son, and she drops the dagger before her. *"Piccolo iddio! Amore, amore mio"* (My little god, my love). She raises her arms, but the boy has been frightened by her threatening gesture and regards her with staring eyes. Assured of her love and that perhaps it was only some game, he rushes into her arms. He remains a little white figure against his mother's white ceremonial dress as she pours out her anguish and love. She presses him to her, *"Amore, addio"* (good-by, my love) and the two whites meld, so that mother and son are one. At the conclusion of the aria she rises, taking the boy by the hand. "Come, let's play," she says and picks up the toy warship. She admonishes him to turn his back and shut his eyes as she hides the toy somewhere outside in the garden. She exits, and returns shortly. She taps the boy's shoulder and indicates that he find the toy. He runs out. Sure that he is safely preoccupied, she looks at the dagger and moves steadily toward the futon beside the Buddha chest. She opens her kimono and kneels, turning her back to the audience. Slowly she raises the dagger and plunges it into her vitals as the percussion crashes. She doubles over. The boy, having discovered the toy, rushes back in and goes to his mother to show her his discovery. He cannot understand why she won't look at him. Sharpless enters and, seeing Butterfly, picks up the lad and retires with him. Suzuki collapses in the passageway. After the final offstage *"Butterfly!"* Pinkerton runs in, sees her, and kneels beside her. He touches her delicately. Then and only then does she fall sideways on to the ground—her wedding bed, her grave. The horrified Pinkerton backs away quickly. Sharpless places the boy on the ground; Trouble then moves to Pinkerton and, standing in front of him, offers him his toy boat. Pinkerton looks at the boy a moment and in a sudden rush of pity and love lifts him up.

The curtain falls.

22

Faust

Characters

Faust, a learned doctor .... Tenor
Méphistophélès .... Bass
Marguerite .... Soprano
Valentin, a soldier,
    brother to Marguerite .... Baritone
Siebel, a village youth,
    in love with Marguerite .... Mezzo-Soprano
Wagner, a student .... Baritone
Marthe Schwerlein,
    neighbor to Marguerite .... Mezzo-Soprano
                Students, Soldiers, Villagers,

Time: Sixteenth century
Place: Germany

PROLOGUE

(Faust's laboratory)

The curtain rises at the very end of the orchestral prelude—during the last three bars marked Largo. Faust is dressed in a long dusty gown. He is bearded, wears glasses and a cap. His back to us, he inspects the contents of a test tube held above the flame of a burner. There is a short pause. Three knocks are heard before the orchestra continues with the Moderato. During the long introduction the following pantomime is enacted. Upon hearing the knocks, Faust sets down the test tube, walks rather lamely to the desk, and picks up a candle and a small coin bag. Holding the candle aloft, he goes out. Another brief pause, and two furtive hooded figures, preceded by Faust, enter, carrying what looks like a shrouded corpse—similar to the one already visible onstage lying on a slab. The men place the corpse on another slab. Faust gives them the coin purse and as they leave he conducts them to the door. He raises the candle and, staring at the corpse, says: *"Rien!"* (Nothing!). He castigates himself: *"J'ai langui, triste et solitaire."* (I languish, alone and unhappy) and moves between the two slabs to the stove. On the line *"Je ne vois rien!"* (I see no truth!) he picks up a scalpel from the stove and continues back to the slabs, mumbling as he goes, *"Je ne sais rien! rien! rien!"* (I know nothing, nothing, nothing!) During the next interlude Faust picks up the arm of a corpse and is about to start his dissection but, realizing the futility of his endeavors, throws the scalpel to the floor and, overcome with despair, moves quickly to the priedieu, burying his head in his arms.

A bit of light penetrates the gloom. Faust disconsolately rises from his kneeling position. He sighs and, anticipating another day of torture, looks up longingly at the cross above the priedieu and asks for death. Receiving no sign, he decides to take matters into his own hands and shouts at the Christ—*"Pourquoi n'irais-e pas vers elle?"* (Why don't I meet it halfway?). Relieved by his decision, his body sags against the priedieu. He rises slowly, *"Salut! ô mon dernier matin!"* (I greet you! my last day on earth!) and he moves with alacrity toward the stove. He does not begin to pour the poison into his cup until just before the villagers' chorus is heard offstage. Faust's action is a counterpoint to their song. It is customary to have Faust affected by their words, but he is long accustomed to them. Only the phrase *"Toute la nature ..."* (Nature is awakening to the call of love) arrests his attention. He leaves the cup on the stove and circles the stove. As he repeats *"Passez"* (Away) he shuts the window with a long pole. The room becomes darker. He moves back to the stove and seizes the poisoned cup as the chorus, now farther away, begins its second round. Faust steadies himself and starts to bring the cup to his lips. The words *"Le temps est beau!"* (The weather is beautiful!) give him pause, and as the chorus continues, he weakens and starts to tremble with weeping. He puts the cup back on the stove and crumples to the floor. *"Dieu!"* (God!), he pleads—three times—stretching his arms out to the crucifix. Again, no comfort. And now, seething with rage, he harangues

God—excoriates Him with his curses. At *"maudites la science"* (I curse all science) he knocks down several large books and moves toward the crucifix, defiantly shouting, *"À moi, Satan"* (Satan, come to me!). A voice is heard in the void: *"Me voici!"* (I am here!)—and during the brief orchestral passage following these words a corpse rises slowly. The figure is completely shrouded, seated on the slab as it says, *"D'où vient ta surprise?"* (You're surprised to see me like this?). Faust is rooted to the spot. The figure suddenly removes the shroud in three deft strokes, revealing the trim and jaunty figure of Mephisto; kicking away the winding sheet, he addresses Faust:*"Eh bien! docteur."* (What can I do for you, sir?). Faust has not moved from his position at the stove. He answers with feigned cockiness, "I'm not afraid of you. Go away." Mephisto hops back onto the slab and lounges playfully: *"Fi! c'est là ta reconnaissance?"* (Shame! Is this how you treat me?). Now convinced he has really summoned the dread spirit, Faust plucks up his courage and wants to know what Mephisto can do for him. Finding none of Mephisto's plans to his liking, Faust finally confesses, *"Je veux la jeunesse!"* (I want youth!). Mephisto smiles knowingly, hopping up and down on his slab like a delighted monkey. Faust moves down to a trunk near his desk and falls on his knees behind it, fantasizing, *"À moi les plaisirs"*(I want to experience youth's pleasures), but he cannot sustain his dream. His head sinks exhaustedly onto the trunk. Mephisto moves down from his slab and, standing behind Faust, places a hand on his shoulder:*"Fort bien!"* (I see I came just in time!). Faust cringes at the touch: "What must I do in return?" Mephisto moves away casually: "Practically nothing. Here on earth I'll be your servant"—and he bows to the ground—"but below you will be mine." Suddenly removing a piece of parchment from his belt, he shoves it at Faust, "Here— sign." Faust tentatively reaches for it, but instead staggers into the chair at the desk. Whirling about, Mephisto exhorts, *"La jeunesse t'appelle"*(Look, youth calls). He gestures and through the scrim wall a vision of Marguerite is seen, holding and touching a small bouquet of flowers. She is bathed in a warm glow of light. Faust turns and after *"Ô merveille!"* he moves slowly toward the vision. Faust's back is to the audience as Mephisto, at the side of the stove, dangles the parchment under Faust's nose, and Faust seizes it. Mephisto merely turns to the stove, picks up the cup left by Faust and, touching it, creates a puff of smoke."*Où fume en bouillonnant*" he cries and, holding it in mock sacerdotal style, slowly crosses to the desk singing "*Non plus la mort*" (No longer poison but an elixir of life). He places it in Faust's hand. Faust rises and as if in a trance returns to raise the cup forward toward the vision. Mephisto meanwhile takes up the signed parchment and lifts it to the Deity—smiling apologetically. Then he places the contract in his belt and moves between the slabs to stand near Faust, who drinks the potion. After "*Adorable charmant*" (Adorable vision), Faust suddenly collapses. Mephisto hovers over him. Faust remains fetuslike, kneeling in front of his demon progenitor. Mephisto divests Faust of the garments and trappings of old age. This ritual is re-enacted in the glow of the fire burning in the stove during the four-bar woodwind coda. The lights brighten as Mephisto moves forward, "*Viens!*" (Come!). Faust slowly rises. He is transformed—he now wears a doublet and hose—but he still has his glasses on. He comes toward Mephisto, who is posed waggishly on the trunk. At the conclusion of the duet Mephisto calls out "*Faust*" and, removing a silver tray from the desk, he holds it up as a mirror. Faust removes his glasses and throws them to the ground as Mephisto starts to laugh triumphantly. Faust joins in the merriment.

ACT I

(*The Kermesse: a town square*)

The curtain rises on the first chord. The scene is one of tumultuous gaiety and excitement. On the platform of a wagon a Gypsy fire-eater is demonstrating his skills, blowing huge billows of flame from his mouth over the frightened but delighted crowd. The wagon is surrounded by women and several children who scoot away quickly from the fiery display. Several well-to-do burghers and their wives enter. One man carries a boy on his shoulder. Simultaneously, a group of middle-aged burghers (also carrying children on their shoulders and accompanied by their wives) enters down a ramp near a Christ figure. Two beggars are seated at the base of the statue—one blind, one lame. In a booth nearby a vendor is selling fruits, candies, and other tidbits. Another booth represents a wine shop set up for the occasion. A man aided by a young boy serves the surrounding crowd, which consists mostly of soldiers and students involved in watching the youth Siebel throw dice. A small table operated by an itinerant gambler has been placed before the wine booth. The applause for the fire-eater's display has just ended as a shout rises from the gambling-table side. Wagner, a soldier who is second in command, steps in to take the dice from the flustered Siebel, to show the lad how things are really done, which leads directly into the chorus *"Vin ou bière"* (Wine or beer). Wagner orders a round of drinks for his companions before displaying his skill as a dice player. Mischievously, five or six curious ladies climb onto the fire-eater's platform and look down his throat. They peer cautiously, horrified and delighted. A juggler appears on another platform. The crowd of burghers, talking and milling about near the statue of Christ, moves closer to the juggler. A young boy and girl enter and look at several religious medallions at a small booth managed by an old friar. At the final *"Toujours"* of the male chorus the trumpet sounds its call and Wagner, shaking the dice in his hands and muttering imprecations, tosses them and wins. The soldiers shout and toast his success. As they sing *"Celui qui sait s'y prendre"* (As far as women are concerned), the juggler begins his act, and the crowd's applause rises counterpoint to the chorus. The juggler will continue until the tumblers arrive. He will juggle pins and spin a ball on the top of a wooden tube held in his mouth. Tossing the ball to one or two of the crowd gathered before him, he will encourage them to throw it back to him. He catches it on the edge of the tube each time and whirls it about, always to applause. This applause should be spontaneous and will not adhere to any musical cue. Two nuns enter and look about excitedly. They temporarily watch the fire-eater, now pressing sticks of flame against his bare chest. The young couple at the friar's booth leaves and moves to watch the juggler. At the second trumpet call in the orchestra following the line *"En payant rançon"* (They must pay a ransom), Wagner,

having finished his beer, cockily tosses his dice a second time—
and loses. The men groan and, looking at the dismayed Siebel,
shrug and order more beer.

Two nuns move to the friar's booth and chat with him. A
group of young male students, who have been partially lounging and greeting the entrance of each new girl with suggestive
looks and remarks, is joined by another group of students, nois-
ily pushing their separate ways through the burghers watching
the juggler. The students stand ogling the girls, who are still
rapt with the fire-eater's final trick. They sing sardonically *"Aux
jours de dimanche"* (There's nothing I like to do better on Sunday). The fire-eater concludes his performance while the tenors
sing *"Et je vois passer les bateaux"* (We like to watch the sail-
boats drifting by). As the fire-eater goes back into the wagon,
the girls timidly move up and try to look at him through the
closed curtain, while three or four students comment on this
action. They applaud the girls as they sneak a last look at the
departing fire-eater. The startled ladies look around at them and
move hastily down off the wagon platform. The two nuns, having purchased a medallion, receive the old friar's blessing and
leave. The young students start to choose partners among the
ladies. *"Voyez ces mines gaillardes"* (They are looking at us
wantonly). There is a good deal of coy by-play: some girls pre-
tend to be involved with the religious medals, some (too old for
hanky-panky) simply look on with pleasure. Several burghers
watching the juggler have become aware of the flirtation among
the young people and have surreptitiously moved to watch the
outcome. Three of the girls toss them suggestive glances, causing the burghers to blush, while hoping for more. The burghers'
wives suddenly become aware of their husbands' new preoccupation and castigate them, at the same time vilifying the girls.
"Voyez après ces donzelles" (Look at those shameless young
girls). The husbands disregard their wives and keep ogling the
girls, who are now enjoying the contest. The six-part chorus begins. The older women try to pull their husbands away and are
still at it when a monk appears between the wagon and the
statue. He is followed by two other monks carrying religious
banners. A group of five tumblers follows during the first choral
break. They enter as a pyramid supported by an acrobat dressed

as the Devil—tail, horns, and pitchfork. The other clowns are variously dressed as Death, an archangel, and other heavenly hosts. They are part of the religious aspect of the fair, and as it is All Fools' Day, they are allowed to mock the sacred mysteries. The Devil threatens the crowd and is caught by the angels, who twirl him about. The smallest angel delivers a telling stroke and the poor Devil faints. While the heavenly hosts are congratulating themselves and receiving the plaudits of the crowd, the Devil recovers and makes a dash to escape. He attempts to slide off on his belly, but his efforts to do so elicit a scream from one of the young girls watching the antics. This calls the attention of the heavenly acrobats to the Devil's attempted departure, and as they pursue him, the Devil tumbles across the length of the stage and is met by Siebel, holding out a beer mug for him. The Devil takes the mug, salutes the angels, drinks, and runs off with the angels in acrobatic pursuit. So on to the next town square—and another adventure in the perils of Satan.

The crowd rushes out after them, and the six-part chorus comes to an end. The shouts of the chorus are heard as they pursue the tumblers offstage. Marguerite and Valentin enter and greet a group of three girls and two students who have remained behind. As Marguerite sees the religious vendor's booth, the chorale theme is heard. Marguerite picks up a medallion from the counter and shows it to Valentin for his approval. He responds, "*O sainte médaille*" (O blessed medal). Marguerite wishes to purchase a memento for him prior to his leaving for the wars. They are both in good humor, but a gently melancholy air permeates the scene. In the background the two beggars start up the ramp and make their way laboriously: the halt leading the blind. Several other young couples saunter about, while two sit at the base of the Christ statue where the beggars had been. Wagner, who had left with his men to follow the acrobats, reappears through the curtained partition of the wine seller's shop. He sees Valentin and calls behind to his companions, "*Ah! Voici Valentin*" (Here's Valentin). "*Un dernier coup, messieurs*" (One more cup, my friends), Valentin urges, shaking Wagner's hand. During their exchange, Siebel moves down to Marguerite, still at the booth deciding which medal to purchase

for her brother. They exchange greetings, and Marguerite consults Siebel about the medals. While she is concluding her purchase, Siebel moves to Valentin and remarks, *"Plus d'un ami
fidèle"* (You have more than one friend), while the soldiers
compliment Siebel on his loyalty. Marguerite turns to Valentin,
holding out the purchased medal. Valentin, taking the amulet,
begins his aria, *"Avant de quitter ces lieux"* (Before I leave my
native land). As he asks God's protection for his sister, they both
kneel. The friar rises stiffly and lowers his head in prayer. He
blesses them and they rise before Valentin's *"Délivré d'une
triste pensée"* (I will banish all thoughts of sadness). Valentin
moves dashingly toward his comrades, cutting a fine figure for
his sister's admiration. Slowly the old friar closes his booth. Valentin ventures, *"Et si, vers lui, Dieu me rappelle"* (If God
should decide to call me). He looks directly at his sister, whose
face darkens with fear. He approaches her, *"Ô Marguerite"* as if
to belie that fear. Holding her close to him, he concludes his
aria. He kisses her tenderly and, waving to Wagner, moves off
with Marguerite. In most, if not all, productions of *Faust*, Va-
entin sings his aria alone. The most important reason for including his sister in this scene is to establish their tender regard for
each other. It is a lovely relationship, albeit jealously guarded
on Valentin's part. Actually, they rarely meet in the opera, although they affect each other's lives considerably. Granted both
characters think of and often refer to each other, these "offstage" references are dramatically ineffective and do little to
create the bone and sinew of their relationship. (How much
more affecting it is to remember this isolated, lovely day when,
in the final act, sickened with grief, Valentin rips the memento
of her love from round his throat and hurls it to the ground as he
prepares to die.)

Wagner comes forward, quite drunk, and, raising his cup,
launches into a drinking song that begins *"Un rat"* (A rat).
Groups of soldiers and students sit on the ground as Wagner
moves among them. During his recitation, he gestures *"Un
chat"* (a cat), and Mephisto appears suddenly from the wagon.
"Pardon!" he interrupts Wagner. Mephisto is now in resplen-
dent Gypsy costume—earring, red cap, and all. The scene
darkens for a moment as he continues, *"Je ferai de mon mieux"*

(I'll do my best to entertain you). Producing a violin from inside the wagon, he plays the opening measure of the "Song of the Golden Calf." He plucks the pizzicati effects on his violin and, as the chorus sings, he conducts them with his violin bow. He tosses the bow into the air and descends from the platform. The crowd is excited but slightly chilled by his jocular yet definitely sinister manner. He concludes the aria back on the platform of the wagon.

Valentin, returning at the conclusion of the first chorus, addresses his remark *"Singulier personnage"* (Singular character) to Wagner who, smiling drunkenly, moves toward Mephisto on the platform: "Would you care to join us in a drink?" he asks. Mephisto grabs his wrist and begins to tell his fortune. Put out by the forecast predicted, Wagner moves back to Valentin as Siebel takes Wagner's place on the platform steps. "Are you a fortuneteller?" Siebel asks, holding out his hand. Mephisto takes it caressingly. "No more flowers for Marguerite." "He mentioned my sister," Valentin interjects, and Mephisto descends the platform, moving toward Valentin. Looking directly at him, Mephisto warns of impending danger. A boy has stepped forward from the wine shop, carrying a single cup on a tray. Before Valentin can recover, Mephisto snatches the cup and raises it in salute, *"A votre santé."* He tastes it, then tosses the contents of the cup to the ground in disgust and, seeing the fruit vendor's booth, moves quickly to it. He picks up a large bunch of dark grapes. *"Permettez-moi de vous en offrir de ma cave"* (Allow me to offer you a cup of my vintage). He suddenly jumps up to the statue of Christ and crowns the figure with the grapes. *"Holà, seigneur Bacchus, à boire!"* (Ho there, my friend Bacchus, how about some wine!). Then he pulls the shaft out of Christ's wound—a gush of red blood flows from it. Everyone is startled and steps back. Placing his cup under the stream of blood, Mephisto fills it and raises it to the throng, then drinks in the name of Marguerite. Valentin approaches and threatens Mephisto, but the latter mocks, *"Pourquoi trembler?"* (Why are you trembling?). Valentin has drawn his sword and is poised for action. Mephisto, his back toward Valentin, suddenly turns at the completion of his phrase and Valentin's sword blade breaks in half. As the chorale begins, Mephisto turns and offers the cup to several groups nearby. They rush away. Turning, Mephisto confronts a phalanx of men threatening him. He laughs and, raising his toast to all and sundry, drinks of the body and blood of Christ. Valentin and Siebel move to the platform of the wagon. Valentin exhorts, *"Mais puisque tu brises le fer, regarde!"* (You who can shatter a sword, look!) and, turning his sword upside down, converts it into a crucifix; the other men follow suit. Mephisto, for once, feels the impact of their collective effort. His body trembles, and he attempts to move nonchalantly toward the wine shop. As Valentin closes in on him, leading a veritable charge of crucifixes toward the demon, Mephisto's anger is aroused. He slowly raises his cup toward heaven in a mock salute, but the effort it costs to maintain his attitude is apparent. As Valentin and his men approach Mephisto, the latter slowly pours the remainder of the wine onto the ground. He tosses the cup away and, raising his left arm, shoves aside the holy symbol in Valentin's hand. Valentin, shaken to the core, staggers, and Wagner supports him. Mephisto turns on the others and moves toward them. Their ranks scatter and they flee in panic. He attacks a few undecided men; then, in a fit of triumphal glee, flings himself across the platform of the wine vendor's shop, laughing hysterically. He is still laughing as the postlude ends.

Faust enters. He is now elegantly dressed as befits his new role in life; two young village girls are at his heels. They have been following him for some time, and he is a little annoyed at their commonplace attentions. Faust, seeing Mephisto still sprawled out, asks, *"Qu'as tu donc?"* (What's wrong?). Mephisto rises, *"Rien!"* (Nothing!), and puts his arm around Faust's shoulder. The two girls notice the palm-reading sign on the Gypsy wagon. As Faust rather peevishly demands to know where Marguerite is to be found, Mephisto moves toward the girls and encourages them to go into the wagon. As the girls go up the steps, Mephisto turns and says to Faust, *"Non pas! mais contre nous sa vertu la protége"* (Remember, her virtue is her shield). As Faust importunes Mephisto, the latter ushers the ladies into the wagon. At the curtain he beckons Faust to climb the platform and wait: *"Attendons!"* (Listen, she'll be here soon—just have patience). Faust remains unconvinced yet hopeful as Mephisto withdraws after the ladies into the wagon.

As he does so, several dancers with animal masks leap into view. Other dancers follow them. The chorus is the last to enter. These young dancers have been hired for the entertainment. The chorus surrounds them as the male dancers pursue the female in an effort to arrest their flight. Faust remains looking through the crowd for signs of Marguerite. The women's chorus dominates the front row, and they sway their skirts in time to the waltz. At the conclusion of the first chorus, the female dancers, who had been performing a peasant dance with their partners, suddenly push them to the ground and escape with the men in pursuit. The chorus looks off in the direction the dancers took. The chorus is visible, however, during the following exchange. Mephisto, Harlequin-like, sticks his head through the curtain and prods the still impatient Faust, *"Vois ces filles gentilles!"* (There are lots of pretty girls here!). Faust replies boyishly that his only concern is for the lady in the vision. Mephisto shrugs and disappears inside the wagon again.

Conventionally, this entire scene has the chorus remaining onstage through the waltz, on through Marguerite's entrance and the finale. The chorus consists of the same men who had attacked Mephisto earlier. Unless a double or new set of choristers is involved, Mephisto's presence among them at this point should chill their bones. In standard productions Mephisto often forces the crowd to freeze positions in order to facilitate any of the "intimate" moments during the scene. In keeping the action moving on and off, it is possible to frame the intimate scenes easily and preserve the logic of the entire act. Therefore Mephisto, once past the "Chorale of the Swords," is never again seen by any of the men.

Siebel enters through the curtains on the wine vendor's shop. *"C'est par ici"* (I'll wait for Marguerite here), he says, and sits on the steps. Six girls near the Christ figure, who have been watching the offstage dancers, catch sight of Siebel and move to him. Rejected by the youth, they retire and gossip among themselves. As the chorus continues the second part of the waltz, Siebel starts pacing and moves toward the dancers. Faust leaves the platform, deep in thought. Both pull themselves up short and circle around each other, continuing toward their intended destinations. As Siebel disappears offstage, two ladies appear from the wagon in a state of ecstasy at what has transpired inside. They descend and turn back to Mephisto, who has struck a Don Juan-like pose at the curtain. Breathing a deep sigh, the two ladies leave, obviously well satisfied with the palm reading. Faust looks at Mephisto, who shrugs, *"chacun à son goût."* Faust turns away contemptuously and, looking off, shouts *"La voici!"* (There she is!). Mephisto rushes to his side. Siebel enters quickly and calls *"Marguerite!"* Faust, at the sound of her name, turns about to do battle with the competitor, but Mephisto allays his anger and begins to tease the anxious Siebel. The six girls who had remained are watching. Siebel, embarrassed by their presence and Mephisto's efforts to embrace him, dashes off. The girls laugh among themselves. Faust turns abruptly to intercept Marguerite, but meets Marthe Schwerlein, who has entered hastily—a portly older woman, hardly what he anticipated. Faust draws back to allow her passage. Marthe disdainfully continues on, prayer book in hand. Faust sees Marguerite following Marthe at a slower pace, lost in thought. He is completely rattled and turns to Mephisto, who indicates that he bow. Faust complies, falling to his knees before Marguerite, who pauses with alarm. *"Ne permettrez-vous pas,"* Faust urges (Permit me, dear lady). Marthe sees this bit of effrontery and rushes to Marguerite, who appears confused. As Faust continues his homilies, Marthe questions Marguerite, but the latter shakes her head. She obviously does not know who the gentleman is. Properly coached by Marthe, who stands guardianlike beside her, Marguerite composes her thoughts and answers, *"Non, monsieur! je ne suis demoiselle ni belle"* (No sir! I'm neither a lady nor beautiful). Marthe nods her assent and, taking the girl's arm, pushes her past Faust. Marguerite looks back at him, intrigued by this sudden encounter; but Marthe shoos her off. Faust sinks onto the Gypsy wagon platform, completely enraptured. Siebel runs in, *"Elle est partie!"* (She's gone!). Mephisto hops down and mockingly repeats Siebel's words, while frightening the lad away a second time. Mephisto then moves to charm the small group of girls who have avidly watched the proceedings. They all want to know who the young gentleman is. Mephisto winks mysteriously and approaches his student prince, *"Eh! bien?"* (Well, how goes it?). Still idiotically en-

thralled with the meeting, Faust smilingly admits he was rejected—but it was worth it. Mephisto puts his arms around
Faust and in a fatherly and instructive tone leads him off to the
next phase of their adventure. Two of the six girls remaining
wave to several other girls approaching. They all meet to hear
the news concerning Marguerite's rejection of a most eligible
suitor. The dancers, again pursuing one another, re-enter and
the chorus follows in their wake. At the coda of the waltz the
juggler and tumblers appear and begin their antics all over
again as the curtain falls.

ACT II

*(Marguerite's bedroom and gardens. In the garden, a, statue of
the Madonna, a bench, a well. The grounds, which extend offstage to the barn, are surrounded by a stone wall with a gateway.)*

The curtain rises on the bar before the clarinet solo during
the introduction. It is dusk. Siebel is discovered in the roadway
outside the house, pacing back and forth. As the solo reaches its
climax, Siebel gives up the long wait for Marguerite and leans
against the gateway, a picture of dejection. Hope springs eternal, however, and as the orchestra begins the Allegro agitato,
Siebel decides to leave a memento before he departs. He opens
the gate and comes into the garden. Kneeling by the well, he
begins prayerfully, *"Faites-lui mes aveux"* (Do me a favor,
lovely flowers). He picks up a bloom and realizes it has withered suddenly at his touch. Throwing the wilted bud away, he
sits on the ledge of the well, now more despondent than ever.
He starts to walk away, kicking the discarded flower. He becomes aware of a statue of the Madonna and thinks, "What if I
bless myself with holy water?" He moves toward the niche and
contemplates it a moment: *"C'est là que chaque soir vient prier
Marguerite!"* (Marguerite prays here every evening!). He
places his fingers in the holy-water font and crosses himself
hastily. He picks another long-stemmed bloom from the shrubs
around the bench, but cannot bear to look at it immediately. But

look he must. *"Elles se fanent?"* (Has it withered?) No! And,
brandishing it as a sword, plunges it into the invisible fiend:
"Satan, je ris de toi!" (Satan, I laugh at you!). He begins gathering a few more blooms, then sits on the bench and, with a sudden onrush of love, sings *"C'est en vous que j'ai foi"* (Flowers,
speak for me). He remains on the bench, a picture of contentment, until *"Un baiser, un doux baiser"* (A lovely kiss), where-
upon he rises to emphasize his sentiment and, concluding, runs
off into another part of the garden.

Mephisto and Faust, dressed almost exactly alike as a pair of
Don Juans, enter like two shadows. Faust pauses at the gate:
"C'est ici?" (Is it here?). Mephisto prevents Faust from making
a rash move toward Siebel in the garden, and both hide behind
Marguerite's bedroom as Siebel re-enters carrying a small bouquet. Now he sits on the bench and surveys the scene before
him as if he were master of it. While Mephisto comments *"Sé-
ducteur"* (You seducer, you), Siebel places the flowers by the
holy-water font and disappears. Mephisto and Faust move from
their hiding place into the garden. Mephisto is full of high spirits, as if Marguerite were indeed *his* quarry. Faust seems hesitant and unsure. Mephisto dances round, touching him like a
partridge mother hen. *"Laisse-moi!"* (Leave me alone!), Faust
demands. Making his obeisances, Mephisto moves toward the
gate. Faust starts to follow, but Mephisto stops him. With a firm
hand he indicates Faust is to remain and wait for his return.
There is a pause. Faust hesitates. Then, on the spur of the moment, he starts to leave the garden. As he does so, the opening
of the cavatina is heard. Faust returns to the scene, as if compelled by an irresistible force. At the gate he sighs, *"Quel trouble inconnu me pénètre?"* (What's happening to me?). He
comes through the gate and realizes the nature of his malady:
"O Marguerite, I'm yours." During the introduction to the aria,
Faust approaches the house and looks through the open window into Marguerite's bedroom, pressing each detail in his
mind. Leaning against the window frame, he sings *"Salut! demeure"* (I salute you, modest dwelling). He comes forward after
the Larghetto section and picks a flower from the shrub before
him. Sitting on the house steps, he regards the night: *"Ô nature,
c'est là"* (O nature, it is here). Slowly, during the ensuing *"Cést*

là's," he turns to regard the front of the house. His back is to the audience as he resumes *"Salut! demeure";* he continues in this position until just before his isolated *"Salut!"*. Then, moving toward the well, he concludes the aria. During the postlude he drops the single flower into the well.

Mephisto appears carrying a small box. He moves swiftly to the gate and enters the garden to warn Faust of Marguerite's approach. Faust rises and seems determined not to go ahead with the plan. He moves toward the gate. Mephisto holds him back, looking about hastily. "Should I put this jewel box on her doorstep? *Voici,*" he thinks, looking at the statue of the Madonna. As he pushes the stumbling Faust off, he places the box of jewels on the bench (during the closing bars) and, looking at the Madonna as sweetly as he can, indicates that he hopes she doesn't mind. He exits.

The stage remains empty for seven bars. Marthe is the first to enter. She moves briskly and turns toward Marguerite, but the girl is behind her, lost in thought.

Marthe kisses Marguerite on the cheek and leaves. Marguerite enters the garden. *"Je voudrois bien savoir,"* (I'd love to know who he was), she wonders. She utters a sigh and enters the house as the prelude to the "King of Thule" aria is heard. Marguerite moves behind a screen and returns singing *"Il était un Roi du Thulé."* She carries a candle in her hand and, crossing to a bureau, places it on top. She begins her preparations for bed. (Young ladies went early to their slumbers in days gone by. What else was there to do?) She will retire, read her Bible a bit, and then nod off. As she undresses, she sings this little folk song, as is her wont, to allay her loneliness, and leans back on the bed: *"Cher Valentin!"* (Dear Valentin!). But the thought of her brother cannot calm her restlessness. She goes into the garden, *"Me voilà toute seule!"* (I'm all by myself!). As she comes near the Madonna she sees the bouquet. It is evident that as much as she likes the lad Siebel, he is a bit of a nuisance. She places her fingers in the font and, crossing herself, starts to kneel. As she does so, she notices the small casket on the bench. Discovering the key and admonishing herself for her trembling fingers, she opens the box. She starts to rush to Marthe's house to tell her of this fantastic discovery but hesi-

tates and sits on the ledge of the well instead, placing the box
beside her. She sings *"Si j'osais seulement"* (If I could only see
myself once with these jewels on), while busily putting on ear-
rings and a tiara. Picking up the mirror at the bottom of the
casket, she looks at herself, *"Ah!"* and turns away in wonderment. *"Non! non!"* (It isn't you! It's the daughter of a king), she
says. Then, musing on the young man she met earlier, she wonders what he would think of her now if he could see her. She
rises impulsively and dashes into the house during the interlude. She closes the shutters and, placing the jewel box on the
chest, she kneels before it, gleefully preparing her secret metamorphosis. She places bracelets on her arms and discovers the
coiled necklace. She places it round her neck ceremoniously.
"Ah!" she trills again. There are no prying eyes; she is safe
within the privacy of her room. Like a delighted child, she goes
slightly giddy from it all. Laughing aloud, she rises, waltzes
about, chatting gaily, *"Est-ce toi?"* (Could it be you? Imagine
how jealous the other girls would be!). And the young man—
she is almost brazen in her desire to be seen by him bedecked
in this manner. *"Marguerite, ce n'est plus toi."* She is in a
frenzy of joy. She waltzes again between the bedposts and, suddenly climbing onto the bed, stands framed between its posts as
she avows *"C'est la fille d'un roi"* (You're the daughter of a
king). She poses magnificently, takes another look at herself in
the hand mirror, and collapses in a fit of laughter, thus concluding the "Jewel Song."

At this point Marthe appears and dashes toward the gate. As
she enters the garden, the Allegretto vivo begins. Marthe is
carrying a small tray with a bed-time snack for Marguerite. Marguerite, hearing someone approach, rushes to hide the jewel
box still on the chest. Marthe surprises her in the act and almost
drops the tray at the sight and cries, *"Seigneur Dieu!"* Marguerite lets out a sigh of relief and sits on the bed with the jewels.
Marthe places her tray on a small table by the screen and sits
down next to Marguerite, who starts to put a few of the trinkets
on the preening and overwhelmed matron. They are having a
jolly time of it as Mephisto and Faust enter from around the
back of the house. They stand near the entrance as Mephisto
calls, *"Dame Marthe Schwerlein, s'il vous plaît?"* Both ladies
are suddenly alarmed and, as Mephisto continues his preamble,

Marthe instructs Marguerite to take the jewels into the back room and leave her to handle the situation—salutations or not, they may be thieves. As Marguerite quickly hides behind the screen, Marthe kneels beside the chest. In courtly fashion Mephisto steps into the small bedroom, again calling Marthe's name. Marthe rises and answers, *"Me voici!"* (Here I am!). But she has taken out a rather large pistol, left by Valentin for Marguerite's protection, and now brandishes it in front of her, pointing directly at the unexpected visitor. Mephisto swallows in amusement and, feigning terror, steps back. When he tells Marthe her husband is dead and asked to be remembered, the poor lady collapses onto the chest. Marguerite, with a long shawl over her nightclothes and still holding the jewel box, enters and cries, *"Qu'est-ce donc?"* (What's happened?). Mephisto replies soothingly, *"Rien!"* (Nothing!) and goes to the bereaved Marthe, thus revealing Faust to Marguerite's eyes. Faust, in the doorway, looks at her with confusion and yearning. Marguerite is alarmed by his presence as the quartet begins. Marthe's recovery is instantaneous. Discovering that her husband has left her penniless, she rises, places the gun back in the chest, and rushes out into the garden in vexation and anger. Mephisto follows her, indicating brusquely for Faust to make his move. Marthe sits near the well and Mephisto, continuing his blandishments, sits next to her. Marguerite, embarrassed to find herself half clad in the presence of the very man she had been thinking about, surreptitiously begins to remove her jewels. *"Pourquoi donc quitter ces bijoux?"* (Why are you taking off your jewels?), Faust asks. Marguerite protests, *"Ces bijoux ne sont pas à moi"* (These jewels do not belong to me). Faust, not sure of the next step, glances over at Mephisto, who is heavily engaged winning Marthe's confidence. Faust moves toward the gate, a lost and insecure young man. During the interplay between Mephisto and Marthe at the well, Marguerite sees Faust at the gate through her open door and suddenly realizes that the jewel box must have been left by him. She places the casket into the chest and, making a few adjustments, decides to at least be polite. Pulling her shawl tightly about her, she exits from the bedroom and goes near the Madonna. Mephisto rises during the Moderato assai interlude as Marthe coyly awaits his next move. Seeing the downcast Faust not properly occupied, Mephisto pushes Faust toward the awaiting Marguerite, and both men move into the next phase of their mission: the seduction proper.

Faust offers Marguerite his arm but she refuses, sitting instead on the bench. Mephisto extends his arm to Marthe. She runs her fingers along his shoulder down to his hands, squealing, *"Il est charmant!"* (He is charming!). Faust moves around the Madonna and sits on the bench next to Marguerite. The quartet begins. At its conclusion Faust gingerly takes Marguerite's hand, and Marthe and Mephisto turn toward each other, lust evident in her eyes and something else like it in his. The sight is too much for the rapacious widow, and she dashes girlishly around the well in a flirtatious game of cat and mouse. She notices Faust and Marguerite together. Somewhere her sense of responsibility is tapped by the sight—after all, a young virgin and a cavalier holding her hand—what next? *"Ainsi, vous voyagez toujours?"* (So you travel a lot?), she ventures to Mephisto, always watching the young couple. Mephisto, anticipating her next move, takes her arm. *"Toujours!"* (Always!), and he steers her reluctantly back to the well, where they sit. Pleading his own sad cause, Mephisto restores the amorous game to its previously spiralling course. Marthe, now making no pretense about her intentions, rises again and swings her hips before the startled demon, who had not expected quite this quick a conversion. *"Avant que l'heure"* (Let's not waste any time) she implies, and beckons suggestively to Mephisto. She slowly backs up toward the house, he follows, and they both wander off to an offstage barn to continue their lecherous play.

Marguerite, finding herself alone with a man, rises in mid-conversation and starts to walk away, with Faust at her heels. *"Eh quoi, toujours seule?"* (You mean you live all alone?). As Marguerite explains, she moves out farther into the garden. Remembering her dead sister, she sighs, *"Pauvre ange!"* (That poor angel!), and sits at the well. Faust remains standing beside her and offers his finest compliment, *"Si le ciel . . ."* (If she was anything like you, she must have been an angel indeed). Mephisto re-enters, followed by Marthe, whose hair now hangs loosely about her. Both of them are covered by strands of straw from the barn. The reluctant demon had been practically raped by the inflamed Marthe, and he beats a hasty retreat to the comparative safety of the house. Inside, he sits on the chest; Marthe, beside herself with frustration, is on the bed. As the quartet continues, Mephisto fastidiously picks the bits of hay off his person and drops them. As Marthe entreats *"Pourquois vous hâter"* (Why must you go away), she moves up to Mephisto, who systematically continues his straw picking—only now Marthe is the object of his endeavors. Her hair particularly is filled with strands. Every move of her body rubbing against the demonic flanks speaks volumes. As the·quartet concludes, Mephisto realizes he has left his sword in the barn. Marthe, supposing this is a ruse to get back to the barn, rushes out, promising to fetch it for him. Mephisto, relieved of her presence, sighs profoundly and sits on the chest again. Marguerite rises to leave Faust, for it is now long past her bedtime. Faust grabs her arm. In a sudden unexpected burst of coquetry, she dashes to the part of the garden behind the house. Faust follows. Hearing Marthe approaching, Mephisto says, *"L'entretien devient trop tendre"* (She's getting a bit too familiar) and hides behind the screen. Marthe reappears holding the missing sword aloft and, mumbling to herself, enters the room. Finding Mephisto gone, she runs out to and beyond the gate, calling, *"Seigneur!"*. His muffled response from the house, and the voice of Faust heard offstage, only confuse the poor lady. Looking this way and that, still holding up the sword like a prized flag, she goes off in the wrong direction in search of Mephisto.

The latter, having watched these shenanigans through a chink in the shutters, comes into the garden the moment Marthe leaves. He stands there, solemnly regarding his surroundings, *"Il était temps!"* (It's now time!). Seeing the young couple cavorting happily, he pauses before the statue of the Madonna. He looks up at her and sighs amorously, *"Gardons nous de troubler"* (Let's not interfere in any way in allowing love its proper course). He smiles wickedly at the statue, then starts his invocation to the night. As he exhorts, he moves backward slowly, and at his final *"Marguerite!"* he turns and disappears behind the house. Darkness has descended.

Marguerite enters. She is carrying Siebel's bouquet in her hand. She has held onto it from the time Faust first sat beside her, an almost protective gesture. She bids Faust good night again, but this time he finds it infinitely easier to detain her. As he asks, *"Laisse-moi contempler ton visage"* (Let me look at your face again in the moonlight), she sits on the steps and he kneels before her. She averts her face from his gaze, but he forces her to turn to him. Stilled by this first avowal of love, Marguerite leans against his chest and admits her own feelings: *"Ô silence . . . Ô bonheur!"* (This blessed silence, this perfect hour!). She rises girlishly, *"Laissez un peu"* (Let me be a moment) and begins to pull the petals off the bouquet: "He loves me, he loves me not." Faust's importunate move toward her sends her scuttling around the well. She drops the petals in his direction. "He loves me," the last petal declares, and she stands by the well, deeply contented by this omen. Faust, behind her, pours out the full dimension of his love. She can only stare at him, profoundly moved. Face to face, and without touching, they breathe as one, *"éternelle!"* (forever!). They kiss lightly and again repeat "forever." Faust kisses her hand and sinks to his knees in the brief pause following. Marguerite sits by the well, and Faust, sitting on the ground, leans his head against her. *"Ô nuit d'amour"* (Oh night of love), he rhapsodizes. Marguerite leans over and tenderly strokes his hair, *"Je veux t'aimer"* (I want your love). As she professes she would die for him, Faust draws her gently down to the ground. Unable to resist any longer, he kisses her passionately. Frightened by this sudden change in his manner, Marguerite rises and runs toward the house. Faust pursues and stops her.

"Ah! partez, partez," (Please go now), she protests, but Faust continues to kiss her neck, holding her from behind in a tight embrace. As their brief duet terminates, he spins her round and kisses her mouth with great fervor. At the clarinet solo she begins to cry; slowly she sinks to the ground, her back to the audience. Mephisto has quietly entered, leaning against the gate post, playing with a long-stemmed white rose. Faust kneels beside the prostrate girl and assures her, *"Divine pureté, j'obéis"* (Divine girl, I'll obey you), and raising her up, elicits a promise that he may return tomorrow. Marguerite, momentarily happy to be free, evasively agrees. She enters her room, unable to look at Faust. He remains on her doorsill, beseeching, *"Tu m'aimes?"* (Do you love me?). During the interlude Marguerite

slowly turns to him and, answering with a nod of her head, immediately exclaims, *"Adieu!"* She collapses on her bed. The exultant Faust leaves by the gate and is startled to see Mephisto. *"Laisse-moi!"* (Leave me alone!), he angrily fires at him. But Mephisto obsequiously asks indulgence so they may overhear Marguerite's confession. He gestures with the rose and Marguerite rises from her bed. She opens the shutters and looks out into the starry heavens: *"Il m'aime,"* (He loves me). As she reveals her deepest longings, abandoning all pride and pretense, Faust slowly re-enters the garden. Marguerite, standing by the bedpost, calls, *"Viens!"* (Come to me!). Faust calls her name and rushes into her open arms. He tosses aside her shawl and they embrace. Slowly she sits on the bed, with Faust beside her, tenderly caressing her.

Mephisto steps into the garden and, seeing the Madonna, hails her mockingly. As he leans down over the edge of the well, Marguerite leans back on her pillow. Faust starts to kiss her hungrily. The light in the room fades. Only the Madonna and Mephisto are visible in the garden. In a sudden gesture, Mephisto tears the rose from its stem and, holding it above him, drops the white petals over his lasciviously squirming body. He emits a frightening peal of laughter, an obscene desecration of love.

The curtain falls.

ACT III—SCENE 1

(A church)

The curtain rises during the four bars prior to the organ solo. Two ladies are kneeling in prayer in the front row of pews. Marguerite appears in the center aisle. She walks slowly, lost in thought. One of the two praying ladies notices her and pokes her companion. Marguerite, visibly pregnant, becomes suddenly aware of their whispering and draws her cloak around her swollen body. She moves down to a priedieu and kneels. The two women, anxious to spread gossip, rise and move quickly up the center aisle, turning to get a last view of Marguerite. They

then genuflect and leave as the last bars of the organ solo conclude. Marguerite crosses herself: *"Seigneur, daignez per-
mettre"* (My lord, permit your humble servant to kneel before
you). Mephisto's voice is heard out of the darkness. Marguerite
looks up slowly, but as the sepulchral sound stops, she bows
her head and tries to resume her prayer. She is startled by the
offstage chorus and looks up. Mephisto's voice is heard again:
"Souviens-toi du passé" (Think of the past). Three cowled
monks move slowly down the aisle. Could it be one of them
addressing her? Marguerite wonders. She watches their approach with apprehension. Two more monks appear and move
solemnly across the rear of the church. At the same time a single monk bustles in, carrying a large and impressively orna-
mented book. Marguerite rises and goes to him, but the figure
avoids her and ascends the pulpit stairs. All this time the pun-
ishing voice continues. The monk places the book on a lectern,
opens to a section, and flicks a small red marker into place. He
then descends the stairs, followed by Marguerite's frightened
gaze, and disappears up one of the side aisles. Marguerite begins *"Dieu! quelle est cette voix?"* (God! what is that voice?).
As the first bars of the chorus of priests and boys are heard,
Marguerite frantically rushes up the nave and stands looking off
in the direction of the offstage voices. During the next two choral responses, two groups of monks come in and leave by several
side exits. Marguerite whirls in their direction, now completely
panicked. She tries to calm herself, *"Hélas! hélas!"* (Oh God, is
there no end to this!). She sits on a chair just as Mephisto's
voice resumes his harangue, this time seeming to come from
another direction. *"Non! pour toi Dieu n'a plus de pardon!"*
(No. There is no forgiveness for you ever!). Marguerite puts her
hands over her face in anguish. A double procession of monks,
carrying long burning tapers, appears. They march up the sides
of the church aisles and move off during the three choral sections. Marguerite seems rooted to her chair. She tries to get up
but can't: *"Ah! ce chant m'étouffe"* (Oh, that chant, I can't
breathe). Mephisto's voice thunders *"Adieu les nuits d'amour"*
(Farewell, nights of love), and Marguerite, uttering a cry of despair, rises and leans against the pulpit, breathing spasmodi-
cally. The voice surrounds her. It seems to come from every-

where yet nowhere. As Marguerite begs, *"Seigneur! accueillez la prière"* (God, I beg you to hear me), she stumbles back to the priedieu and sinks to her knees imploringly. At her words, *"Descende sur eux!"* (Help someone who needs you!), the candlelit procession reappears on either side of the nave. A single monk leads one of the group. As the chorus warns, *"Marguerite, sois maudite!"* (Marguerite, you are cursed!), she approaches the monk. In supplication she kisses the hem of his robe. The monk suddenly sings *"À toi l'enfer!"* (Your soul is damned!) and, removing his cowl, reveals the face of Mephisto wearing a red tonsure that intensifies the bestiality of his expression. Marguerite screams and crawls away. Mephisto advances on her, covering his head as he does. Marguerite, sounding like a frightened animal, remains on the ground, stupefied by what she is witnessing. The two processions move toward her from either side. She is completely enveloped by them as the lone monk makes his way up the steps to the pulpit. Once there, he raises his arms, a signal for the other monks to kneel. And as he makes the Black Mass sign of the cross, Marguerite, uttering a piercing scream, rises and runs up the center aisle away from this hellish sight.

The curtain falls.

ACT III—SCENE 2

(The house and front yard of Marguerite and Valentin, and the street adjacent)

As the flute and oboe join the clarinet in a reprise of the Soldiers' Chorus, the curtain rises. Marthe Schwerlein is sitting in a chair in the yard, peeling apples, holding a wooden bowl in her lap. A small group of young people run quickly up the street toward the festivities offstage. A second group of older people appears shortly thereafter and follows suit. As a third group of girls and urchins enter, Siebel appears in their midst. He stops at the gateway and beckons to Marthe to join the fun. The victorious army has come back to town. Marthe complies with alacrity and joins Siebel. An old scholar, weighed down by a large and heavy book, moves along the path. A bustling crowd surges past him and he is buffeted aside. Crablike, he continues his journey, reminding one of the Faust of the prologue. Marguerite appears, coming down the street against the tide of the villagers who pay no attention. As she enters the yard the old scholar passes her. Marguerite, just back from experiencing the nightmare in the cathedral, is dazed and frightened. She still wears her cape and, as she walks, is completely oblivious of her surroundings. She starts to go inside the house when she notices the bowl of apples left by Marthe. The first bars of the Soldiers Chorus are heard from offstage: *"Déposons les armes"* (Let us put down our arms). This chorus and the ensuing march are conventionally sung onstage, but in this version they are meant both to help create the sense of an approaching army and serve as an ironic counterpoint to the human drama about to unfold.

Siebel has made his way through the crowd to alert Marguerite of her brother's return. As he arrives at the gate, he is arrested by a chilling sight. Marguerite has picked up the knife from the bowl of apples and is looking at it strangely. She slowly extends her hand; Siebel, to forestall a disaster, rushes forward and wrests the knife from her grasp, forcing it to fall to the ground. Marguerite, suddenly an ocean of tears, allows herself to be led into the house by Siebel, who takes the knife with him. As they leave, the offstage chorus concludes its opening measures.

After a slight pause, a flock of villagers is seen rushing onstage. They find places in the street, allowing a passageway for the returning soldiers. The crowd cheers and the martial theme is heard. A group of soldiers enters briskly. One soldier, carrying the colors of his division, precedes the others through the gate into the yard, where they stand at attention. A second platoon follows on their heels. The rest of the regiment takes its place in the streetway as Valentin moves into the yard. The army is ragged, tattered, and, in many instances, seriously maimed and injured, but they are glad to have survived. At Valentin's appearance the two platoons kneel in tribute, as do the two flag-bearers. *"Gloire immortelle de nos aïeux"* (Glory to the heroes of the past). As the men sing *"Pour toi, mère patrie"* (For you, our motherland), the mayor of the town and his assistant move forward toward Valentin. The mayor embraces Valen-

tin and signals to the assistant who, having unrolled a parchment, reads Valentin his salutation. At *"Le fer à la main"* (With
our swords in our hands), the two soldiers bearing the regimental colors rise and, crossing behind Valentin and the mayor, turn
smartly to face them. As the chorus repeats its opening theme,
pianissimo, one of the regimental flags is lowered and the
mayor, taking the ribbon proffered him by his assistant, ties it to
the top of the mast. He repeats the same ceremony with the
other flag. Two old cowled monks step toward the flags and Valentin kneels as the prelates bless him and his colors. The mayor
and his assistant join Valentin as Siebel enters from the house.
He stands on the platform, uncertain as to the next move. Valentin, seeing the lad, opens his arms and Siebel comes into his
embrace. Valentin introduces Siebel to the mayor. Realizing the
ceremony is at its end, Valentin steps forward, removes his
sword from its scabbard, and raises it in salute as the chorus
concludes, *"en flamme nos coeurs!"* (inflame our hearts!). The
villagers cheer mightily as the two platoons, followed by the
rest of the regiment, take their leave. The mayor and assistant
remain chatting with Valentin while Siebel retires to the steps
of the house. A group of three women come forward to greet
Valentin and congratulate him. The villagers have followed the
soldiers off, and as the last strains of the martial music come to
an end, the mayor and assistant bid Valentin farewell and depart.

"Allons, Siebel," Valentin says with relief, and starts to go
into his house. Siebel rises, warning him not to go inside. When
Valentin questions him, Siebel looks away. Valentin, deeply
upset, demands an explanation. Siebel remains evasive and
grabs Valentin's shoulder. *"Laisse-moi,"* Valentin commands
and, breaking away, rushes into the house. Siebel sinks to his
knees, crosses himself, and makes a hasty retreat through the
gate.

Raucous laughter is heard offstage and a motley assemblage
makes its drunken way down the street. Faust and Mephisto,
dressed as soldiers, enter with three female camp-followers.
They pass a long-stemmed bottle of wine between them. Faust
seems dour and uncomfortable. He is the first to appear. Stop-
ping at the gate with a lady slung over one shoulder, he hangs

his head. *"Qu'attendez vous encore?"* (What are you hesitating for? Go in!), Mephisto chides. Faust does so and stands looking at the house. Following him, Mephisto bids him make a hasty farewell to his lady-love, as the revelries of Walpurgis Night beckon. Faust bleats an anguished *"Marguerite!"*, which amuses everyone. The others enter the yard. One of the harlots plunks Faust down in a chair and stands behind him while the other two sit on the doorstep. Mephisto, seeing the Madonna's statue, greets her effusively and begins his serenade by her side: *"Vous qui faites l'endormie"* (Don't tell me you are sleeping). [Note: There is no guitar, nor is any attempt made to pantomime one.] Faust cannot bear this blatant mockery and starts to leave with one of the ladies, thus provoking Mephisto's first burst of laughter. The oldest harlot sits in the chair vacated by Faust, and Mephisto quickly darts behind her *"Catherine, que j'adore."* (I adore you, Catherine. Let me kiss you), and he kisses one of her bare shoulders. He then picks up an apple from the bowl and tosses it into the air. Which of the two Eves is to receive the gift?—obviously the younger. As he says *"Et ton coeur l'en croit"* (And you know it in your heart), he sticks the apple into the mouth of the young girl. Mephisto laughs as the girl struggles with the apple. He then hops onto the steps and continues his serenade, staring up at the windows. Faust sits on the wall close to the gate. His companion is plying him with wine from her bottle. He wants to go, yet wants to stay— his unfortunate predicament in life. Halfway through the final stanzas, the girl eating the apple looks up and sees that the top window has been opened. At *"Ne donne un baiser, ma mie"* (Give me a kiss, won't you), Valentin appears, looking down at the scene. The girl calls Mephisto's attention to Valentin's presence, causing Mephisto's final outburst of laughter.

Valentin enters the yard three bars later and stands there scowling. The young harlot eating the apple on the steps puts her arm around Valentin's leg; he shrugs her off, demanding, "What do you all want?" Faust has come to the gate at Valentin's entrance. Mephisto bows, *"Pardon! mon camarade."* Faust, hearing Valentin mention his sister, comes into the yard with the girl in tow. Mephisto is standing with the two other ladies draped over his shoulders. Valentin demands his satisfaction for the apparent insult to his sister reflected in Mephisto's serenade. Mephisto, spurred to action, commands the ladies to wait outside. They hover in the background, three beldames intent on enjoying a bit of bloodshed. Valentin removes a gauntlet and flings it to the ground between himself and the other two men. Naturally, Mephisto cajoles Faust into picking it up, but Faust hesitates and the trio begins. As it concludes, Faust reluctantly picks up the gauntlet. Mephisto and Faust join the three harlots by the wall. Valentin removes his breastplate and places it on the ground. He is now aware of his sister's physical state and, seeing the medal around his neck, he begins *"Et toi qui préservas mes jours"* (And you that have been with me through all these days of tribulation . . . you, my sister's gift, I don't want you any more). He breaks the chain and throws it away. Mephisto runs to pick it up. Twirling it in his hand, *"Tu t'en repentiras"* (You'll regret this, my friend), he tosses it to the ladies. During the repeat of the trio, the ladies fight for posses- sion of the medallion as Valentin kneels before the statue of the Madonna. By the end of the trio, two of the ladies have rushed off in pursuit of the third, who has managed to hold onto the prize. Mephisto jumps up on the wall as Valentin, unsheathing his sword, cries *"En garde!"* As Faust turns to Mephisto for his last instructions, Valentin, his sword scabbard held to his lips, salutes the Madonna and the duel begins. On the second feint, Marguerite suddenly appears at the doorway. On the third en- counter Valentin bests Faust, who falls to the ground. Valentin is about to stab him when Marguerite dashes down to him, screaming, "Valentin! Valentin!" As Valentin hesitates, to ward off his sister, Mephisto rushes to Faust and takes his hand. While Valentin is struggling with Marguerite, Mephisto pushes Faust forward and, supporting his sword hand, thrusts the blade into Valentin's back. Faust turns and looks at Mephisto in dis- may. Valentin whirls about; raising his two locked hands above his head, he deals Faust a blow on the head, causing him to fall to the ground. Valentin moves back to regain his sword but can- not manage the move. He dizzily sinks against Marguerite's shoulder. Several people have been strolling in the street out- side from both directions. Seeing the men locked in combat, they have rushed off to alert the other villagers. As Faust lies there, Mephisto says, *"Voici notre héros entendu sur le sable!"* (Look at our hero sprawled out on the ground!). This is usually meant to refer to Valentin. But, our Faust being what he is, Mephisto's statement is ironic and serves to emphasize our non-hero's non-heroism. "Get up," Mephisto urges, "Let's go!" He himself is already outside the gate as he again commands the rising Faust to make haste. Faust's and Marguerite's eyes meet. The two mean to move toward each other, but Valentin, sufficiently recovered, begins to turn back to the fray. Faust dashes out, with Valentin in stumbling pursuit. As the unholy pair disappears a crowd of the villagers enters, impeding Valentin's progress. He finally falls in the street. Siebel is seen returning with members of Valentin's regiment, who pick him up. As he rises, he imagines he is still in pursuit, but the sight of his gate sobers him. Looking about at the concerned villagers and friends, he repeats *"Merci! merci!"* (Save your tears, there's no reason for them. I've faced death on a battlefield). Marguerite has been watching her brother carefully, unsure of his condition. As Valentin concludes *"pour en avoir peur"* (there's nothing to fear), he touches the wound and regards his bloody hand. *"Valentin! Valentin!"* Marguerite, her worst fears confirmed, cries *"Ô Dieu."* Valentin, seeing his sister, tells her to go inside, but she turns away. Marthe slips by Valentin at the gate and goes to comfort the girl. Valentin, finally aware of the gravity of his state, says, *"Je meurs par elle"* (I'm dying because of her). All pretense, all honor gone, he starts toward the house. Two soldiers come forward from the crowd in support as the villagers echo Valentin's accusation. Valentin manages the steps, then suddenly pushes his two aides aside and turns to Marguerite: *"Ecoute-moi bien, Marguerite"* (Listen carefully, Marguerite). He shamelessly curses her and, stumbling down the steps toward her, rips off her cloak, screaming *"Va!"* (Go!), thus revealing Marguerite's swollen body to the throng. The two soldiers come to Valentin. Marguerite in shame tries to hide from the villagers' staring eyes. Valentin shouts at her, *"Meurs!"* (Die!) and flings her to the ground. The two soldiers try to hold him back, but as he repeats *"Sois maudite"* (I curse you), he pushes one soldier onto the prostrate Marguerite and forces the other to do likewise, thus emphasizing his sister's harlotry. He lurches backward, regarding the now supplicant chorus with distaste. Marthe and Siebel have pushed aside the two soldiers hovering over Marguerite and try to comfort her. The soldiers follow Valentin as the villagers plead for his sister's forgiveness. They have climbed over the wall and come into the garden. Valentin reaches for his discarded armor and starts to put it on. As the two soldiers go to help him, he pushes them off. In a moment of weakness Valentin falls to his knees before the Madonna. As the chorus ends its entreaty he rises, now completely dazed through loss of blood. He starts for the house again, calling *"Marguerite"* in a small boyish voice. He has to grab the steps for support, but he sees her, still crouching on the ground. Unrepentant and summoning his last burst of energy, he curses her once more. He steadies himself and is in the process of putting on his breastplate when his right knee buckles and the stubborn tiger goes down. (Valentin, in most productions, lies prone from the time he is wounded until his death. This created a static tableau reminiscent of a Victorian oleograph. In fact none of the action indicated here is in the printed score.)

As the villagers ask for God's mercy on Valentin's soul, the two attendants slowly kneel and remove their helmets in silent tribute. Marguerite rises during the postlude and, coming to Valentin, spreads her fallen cloak over his body. Placing his head in her lap, she strokes his forehead, looking far off, a thin, sickly smile on her face.

The curtain falls.

ACT III—SCENE 3

(The prison. Just before dawn)

The curtain rises with the beginning of the clarinet solo in the prelude. Marguerite is on the ground. On the floor beside her a bundle of rags and hay simulates a child in swaddling clothes. She stares vacantly ahead in a catatonic state, much as we left her in the previous scene. The same sickly smile plays across her lips. Her clothes are now threadbare, and her disheveled hair hangs in strands. She remains still for a long time. As the flute joins the clarinet, she slowly comes to life. She picks up her imaginary child and fondles it tenderly. She raises herself up to her knees and begins to pantomime water (a running brook in front of her). She dabs her face and hair and lifts the child to see the stream. She begins to wash the child's face with the edge of her dress. That strange smile returns and she looks about to see if anyone is near. She raises the bundle of rags and slowly lowers it toward the water during the final descending scale of the clarinet solo. At the fortissimo she places her hands over the bundle and presses downward, as if to drown the child. She repeats this action three times, then raises the bundle and looks at it. She shakes it, slaps it. Reassured that the baby is still alive, she crawls away to sleep on a pile of hay beside a post. Silence. The Allegro begins. As the woodwinds join the strings, Mephisto, carrying a lantern and dressed in a dark suit and long black cape, appears. He watches the sleeping girl, then rushes up the stairway to open the door, permitting Faust to enter. Faust steps into the prison. He is also in black. Both are two shadows moving about. Mephisto warns Faust to make haste, as it will soon be dawn. Handing Faust the key, he exits through the door, shutting it behind him. Faust, unused to the gloom, remains at the top of the stairway. During his recitative he makes his way cautiously down the steps and reaches the ground on *"Son pauvre enfant tué, tué par elle!"* (Her poor child was killed by her own hand!). He turns and, seeing Marguerite, descends into the dungeon, calling her name. He kneels behind her and she awakens as from a fondly remembered dream. The girl realizes the dream has come true: *"Oui, c'est toi. Je t'aime"* (Yes, you've come. I love you). She leans against him. He faces her, his eyes filled with tears, then rises and bids her follow him. He starts to climb the stairs. Marguerite, picking up her imaginary infant, moves toward him. Suddenly she turns: *"Attends!"* (Listen!). She seems to be seeing her old haunts again. Faust does not understand this hesitation and moves to guide her up with him, but she slips away, waltzing with the bundle in her arm to distantly remembered strains. She kneels. *"Ne permettrez vous pas?"* (Will you permit me, mademoiselle?). She speaks to the child as she recalls the past, converting the memory into a lullaby. Faust suddenly realizes the full import of the scene before him. He sinks onto the bench and stares at the pitiful sight. Finally he goes forward and gently insists, *"Oui, mon coeur"* (Yes, my love, but let us go. It's getting late). Marguerite persists, *"Et voici le jardin charmant"* (Here is the lovely garden). She places the infant in Faust's arms; he kneels beside her in an agony of guilt and remorse. Refusing to leave, she leans against him again. Faust hands the infant back to Marguerite. Mephisto reappears at the door and warns Faust to move quickly. Marguerite looks up and cries, *"Le démon . . . le dé-mon! Le vois tu?"* (It's the devil, don't you see?). Mephisto starts down the stairs to Faust, and Marguerite, crawling on the ground, tries to hide behind the bench. Faust moves to her as Mephisto races back up the steps to watch at the door. "Come," Faust cajoles Marguerite, "there's still time." The girl is terrorized and cries *"Anges purs, anges radieux"* (Help me, you angels of God). As she continues lost in prayer, Faust rushes and meets Mephisto halfway up the stairs. They argue briefly and again Faust returns to the demented girl: "Come, you must," but she is deaf to his plea. Faust turns to Mephisto, who gesticulates from the doorway to carry her away by force. As Faust moves to do so, Marguerite crawls forward and the trio starts. Faust moves to Marguerite, and Mephisto slowly descends the stairs. He is on the bottom step for the climactic page of music. A drum roll sounds; Mephisto wheels about and looks up the stairway. Faust again tries to move Marguerite, but she pushes him away in a fit of violence: *"Tu me fais horreur!"* (I'm sick of the sight of you!), she screams. Faust sinks to the ground as Mephisto stands above Marguerite and proclaims *"Jugée!"* (Damned!). He gestures downward over her prostrate form as the offstage voices contradict him, *"Sauvée!"* (Saved!). Mephisto, seeing the approach of several nuns and priests, picks up Faust and together they hide. A group of nuns and priests enters. The nuns kneel by the stairway, the priests near Marguerite. One priest descends the stairs and approaches the girl. At first sight she mistakes him for the demon, again trying to torment her in clerical guise, but is reassured as the Father Confessor reaches out to her. He blesses her and gives her holy communion and the sign of absolution, then lifts her up and guides her toward the stairs. She moves to pick up her infant, left on the bench, and hastily she climbs onto the staircase. As she does so, the figure of the executioner appears at the top of the stairs, hooded and in black. Marguerite sees him and turns back to the father, who nods in confirmation. Her life seems to pass before her in a flash. She looks down at the infant in her arms and realizes it is only a bundle of rags and hay. The dazed look goes out of her eyes and a sad kind of acceptance comes over her. She lets the bundle break apart, allowing the straw child to fall to the ground. Her smile now is one of understanding. She turns and, looking up at the executioner, starts toward him, moving slowly, surely, even confidently. The executioner disappears into the darkness as the chorus concludes. The monks and nuns bow their heads in prayer. Faust rushes from his hiding place and starts to run up the stairs to join Marguerite, but the door shuts in his face. In a gesture of despair he leans over the banister and encounters the figure of Mephisto holding the contract aloft—a bargain is a bargain! Faust slowly descends the stairs and picks up the remnants of straw and rags. He kneels and holds the imagined child to his bosom.

The curtain falls.

N.B. As indicated in Chapter 7, this finale is purely my invention—a reinterpretation of Marguerite's salvation. As marked in the score, the finale is a tableau of heavenly intervention, replete with thundering organ introducing whatever hordes of angelic hosts can be managed within the local impresario's budget.

Stage Plans

(Courtesy of New York City Opera)

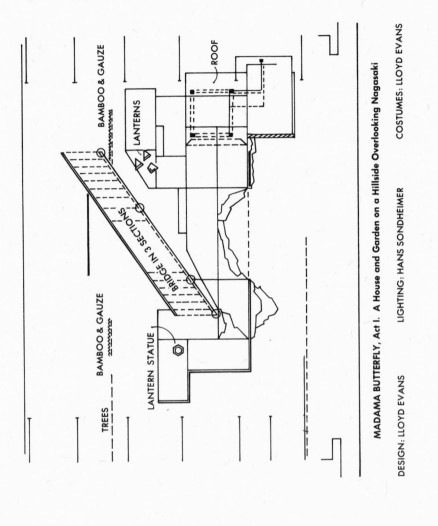

BAMBOO & GAUZE

LANTERNS

ROOF

BAMBOO & GAUZE

TREES

LANTERN STATUE

BRIDGE IN 3 SECTIONS

MADAMA BUTTERFLY, Act I. A House and Garden on a Hillside Overlooking Nagasaki

DESIGN: LLOYD EVANS   LIGHTING: HANS SONDHEIMER   COSTUMES: LLOYD EVANS

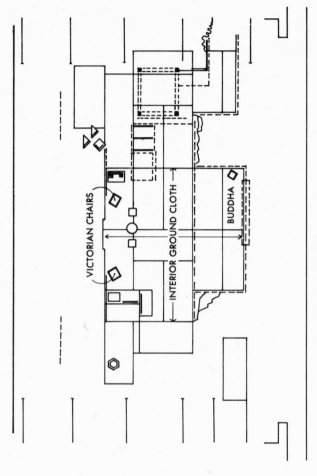

MADAMA BUTTERFLY, Acts II and III.

Inside Cio-Cio-San's House

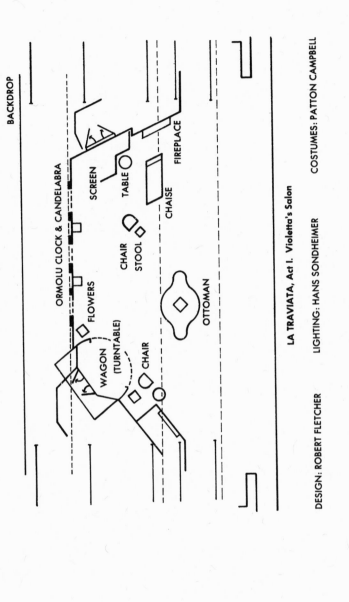

BACKDROP

ORMOLU CLOCK & CANDELABRA

SCREEN

TABLE

CHAISE

FIREPLACE

CHAIR

STOOL

FLOWERS

OTTOMAN

WAGON
(TURNTABLE)

CHAIR

LA TRAVIATA, Act I. Violetta's Salon

DESIGN: ROBERT FLETCHER

LIGHTING: HANS SONDHEIMER

COSTUMES: PATTON CAMPBELL

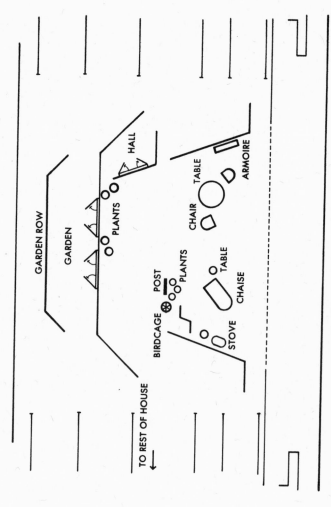

LA TRAVIATA, Act. II. Salon of Country House

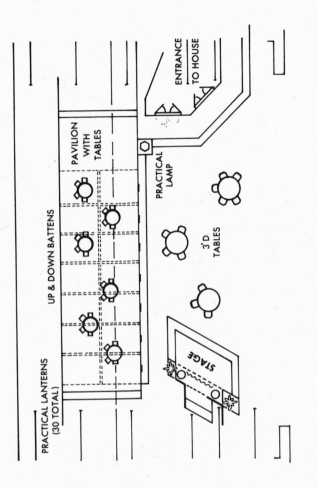

LA TRAVIATA, Act. III. Flora's Garden

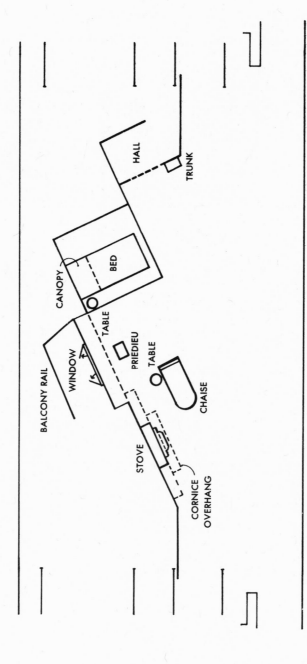

LA TRAVIATA, Act IV. Violetta's Bedroom

FAUST, Act I, Scene 1. Faust's Laboratory

DESIGN: MING CHO LEE

LIGHTING: HANS SONDHEIMER

COSTUMES: JOSE VARONA

Labels within diagram: PLATFORM, CHEST, WIRE FIGURE, WINDOW, TABLE, TABLE, OVEN, PRIEDIEU, DESK, CHAIR

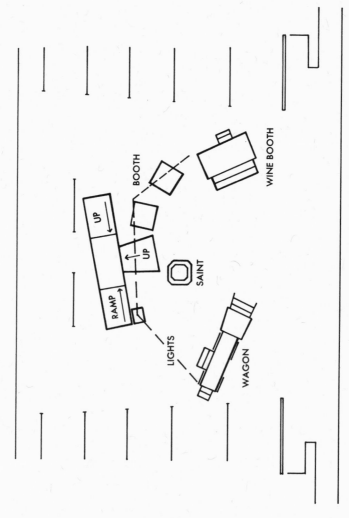

FAUST, Act I, Scene 2. Town Square

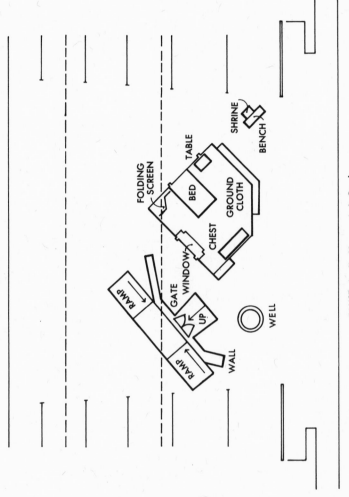

FAUST, Act II. Marguerite's Garden

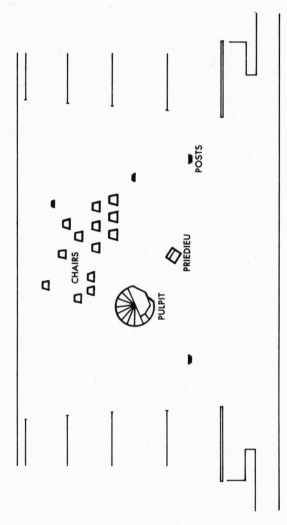

POSTS

CHAIRS

PRIEDIEU

PULPIT

FAUST, Act III, Scene 1. A Church

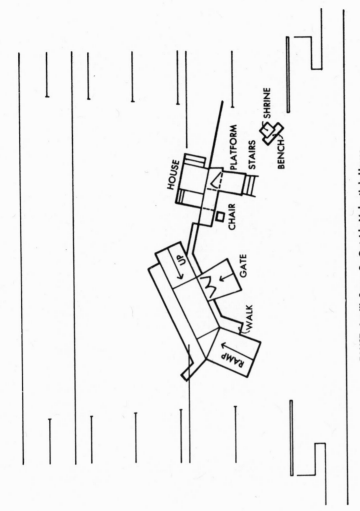

HOUSE

PLATFORM

STAIRS

SHRINE

BENCH

CHAIR

UP

GATE

WALK

RAMP

FAUST, Act III, Scene 2. Outside Valentin's House

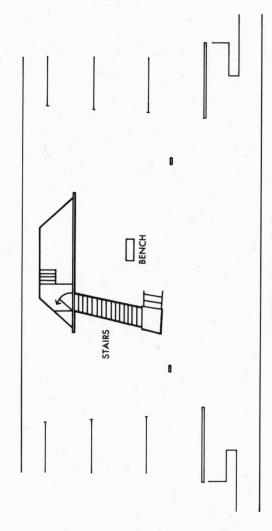

STAIRS

BENCH

FAUST, Act III, Scene 3. Prison

Index

Index